Also by Dan Cohn-Sherbok

ISSUES IN CONTEMPORARY JUDAISM
ISLAM IN A WORLD OF DIVERSE FAITHS (*editor*)
RELIGION AND PUBLIC LIFE (*editor*)
JUDAISM AND OTHER FAITHS

Beyond Death

Theological and Philosophical Reflections on Life after Death

Edited by

DAN COHN-SHERBOK

and

CHRISTOPHER LEWIS

Introduced by Lionel Blue

St. Martin's Press   New York

Selection and editorial matter © Dan Cohn-Sherbok and
Christopher Lewis 1995
Introductory Reflections © Lionel Blue 1995
Text © Macmillan Press Ltd 1995

All rights reserved. For information, write:
Scholarly and Reference Division,
St. Martin's Press, Inc., 175 Fifth Avenue,
New York, N.Y. 10010

First published in the United States of America in 1995

Printed in Great Britain

ISBN 0-312-12482-1 (cloth)
ISBN 0-312-12483-X (paper)

Library of Congress Cataloging-in-Publication Data
Beyond death : theological and philosophical reflections on life after death / edited by Dan Cohn-Sherbok and Christopher Lewis.
p. cm.
Includes bibliographical references and index.
ISBN 0-312-12482-1. — ISBN 0-312-12483-X (pbk.)
1. Future life.   2. Near-death experiences.   I. Cohn-Sherbok, Dan.   II. Lewis, Christopher, 1944–
BL535.B44   1995
291.2'3—dc20   94-34880
                                                                           CIP

For John Hick

Contents

Preface	ix
Notes on the Contributors	xi
Introductory Reflections: Life beyond Life **Lionel Blue**	1

PART I THE AFTERLIFE IN THE WORLD'S RELIGIONS 11

1 A Christian Approach to Eternal Life **Peter Vardy**	13
2 'Go Joyfully': The Mystery of Death and Resurrection **Kallistos Ware**	27
3 The Christian Heaven **David Brown**	42
4 The Jewish Doctrine of Hell **Dan Cohn-Sherbok**	54
5 Life and Beyond in the Qur'an **Muhammad Abdel Haleem**	66
6 The Indestructible Soul – Indian and Asian Beliefs **Geoffrey Parrinder**	80
7 Death's Rituals **Victor de Waal**	95
8 Mourning: The Song is Over but the Memory Lingers On **Martin Israel**	104

PART II NEW PERSPECTIVES   117

9   Death and Immortality: Towards a Global Synthesis
    Paul Badham   119

10 Beyond Death: The Case of New Religions
    Peter Clarke   127

11 Death and the Afterlife: New Approaches to an Old Question
    Arthur Berger   137

12 Are Near-Death Experiences Really Suggestive of Life after Death?
    Christopher Cherry   145

13 The Near-Death Experience: A Glimpse of Heaven and Hell?
    David Lorimer   164

14 Human Survival of Death: Evidence and Prospects
    Arthur Ellison   173

15 Life After Death: A Fate worse than Death
    A. N. Wilson   183

16 Beyond the Crematorium – Popular Belief
    Christopher Lewis   199

Suggestions for Further Reading
    Paul Badham   207

Index   209

Preface

Throughout history human beings have been preoccupied with personal survival after death. As a consequence, most of the world religions proclaim that life continues beyond the grave, and in different ways they have depicted the Hereafter in a variety of forms. These various conceptions constitute answers to the most perplexing spiritual questions: Will we remember our former lives in the Hereafter? Will we have bodies? Can bodiless souls recognise each other? Will we continue to have personal identity? Will we be punished or rewarded, or absorbed into the Godhead? These issues serve as the basis of this collection of essays. The volume begins with an introduction by Lionel Blue in which he reflects on the nature of the 'beyond life' which intersects with earthly existence; although reluctant to speculate about the nature of the Afterlife, he is convinced that in our daily lives we can perceive intimations of another spiritual dimension.

Part I, 'The Afterlife in the World's Religions', commences with Peter Vardy's discussion of the nature of the Hereafter in Christian theology. Here he provides an historical outline of the doctrine of the Beatific Vision as it developed through the centuries. This is followed by Kallistos Ware's exploration of death and resurrection; death, he insists, is not the end but rather the beginning of life. In the next chapter David Brown offers a defence of the Christian understanding of Heaven in the face of modern criticisms. Paralleling this treatment, Dan Cohn-Sherbok describes the doctrine of Hell as it evolved in Jewish sources. Such a belief, he emphasises, has been a central feature of Judaism for centuries despite the fact that today many Jews find it difficult to accept such an idea. As Abdel Haleem explains in the next chapter, Islam too holds that human existence must be understood in relation to a final judgement in which the righteous will be rewarded and the wicked punished. Turning to the religions of the East, Geoffrey Parrinder provides a detailed description of central features of belief in an Afterlife in Hinduism, Buddhism and Jainism. For these faiths belief in life beyond death serves as the basis of their understanding of human existence. In the next two chapters

Victor de Waal and Martin Israel describe traditional religious rituals connected with death and mourning – these practices, they argue, serve to give meaning to the process of dying and the life beyond.

Part II is devoted to a consideration of new approaches to the issue of life after death. In the first chapter Paul Badham explores the possibility of the formulation and global conception of the Hereafter, drawing on the major world religions. In his view, the world's faiths point toward an ultimate destiny of humanity in the life beyond. The next chapter by Peter Clarke focuses on the insights about life, death and the Hereafter provided by the New Religions. Another new direction in approaching the issue of life after death is provided by scientific research into evidence for a Hereafter. In his chapter, Arthur Berger outlines various new ways of exploring paranormal phenomena as well as out-of-the-body experiences. This is followed by Christopher Cherry's critical investigation of near-death experiences and David Lorimer's consideration of whether near-death experiences give a glimpse of Heaven and Hell. In the next chapter Arthur Ellison provides an overview of such evidence and surveys a wide variety of empirical and paranormal experience related to belief in an Afterlife. According to Ellison, such data do not prove that human beings survive death, yet they do provide important support for this belief. In the following chapter A. N. Wilson, departing company from mainstream religious belief, advocates non-existence after death as preferable to eternal life. Life, he asserts, has seemed much pleasanter since he gave up believing in what he now considers to be a fantasy. In the final chapter, Christopher Lewis offers an interpretation of what people actually do believe about life after death. As he illustrates, the common conception among many is that all will be well.

These essays thus provide a framework for understanding traditional conceptions of the Hereafter as well as new perspectives.

DAN COHN-SHERBOK

CHRISTOPHER LEWIS

Notes on the Contributors

Paul Badham is Professor of Theology and Religious Studies at the University of Wales, Lampeter, and Director of its MA programme on 'Death and Immortality'.

Arthur Berger is Director of the International Institute for the Study of Death, USA, and President of the Survival Research Foundation.

Lionel Blue is a rabbi who lectures on spirituality at Leo Baeck College, London, and is a broadcaster and writer.

David Brown is Van Mildert Professor of Divinity at the University of Durham, England, and a Canon of Durham Cathedral.

Christopher Cherry is Reader in Moral Philosophy at the University of Kent at Canterbury, and Master of Eliot College.

Peter Clarke is Senior Lecturer in the history and sociology of religion at King's College, University of London, and Director of the Centre for New Religions.

Dan Cohn-Sherbok is a rabbi, University Lecturer in Theology at the University of Kent at Canterbury, and Visiting Professor at Middlesex University.

Victor de Waal is Chaplain of the Society of the Sacred Cross, Tymawr, and an Honorary Fellow of the Institute of Advanced Research in the Humanities in the University of Birmingham, England.

Arthur Ellison is an Emeritus Professor of Electrical Engineering. He has twice been President of the Society for Psychical Research.

Muhammad Abdel Haleem is Senior Lecturer in Arabic at the School of Oriental and African Studies, University of London, and a member of the Advisory Panel for the Centre for the Study of Islam and Christian–Muslim Relations, Selly Oak Colleges, Birmingham.

Martin Israel is Priest in Charge of Holy Trinity with All Saints, South Kensington, London, and President of the Churches Fellowship for Psychical and Spiritual Studies.

Christopher Lewis is the Dean of St Albans, England.

David Lorimer is Director of the Scientific and Medical Network and Chairman of the International Association for Near-Death Studies in the United Kingdom.

Geoffrey Parrinder is Emeritus Professor of the Comparative Study of Religions at the University of London, a Fellow of King's College, London, and a Methodist minister.

Peter Vardy is Lecturer in the Philosophy of Religion at Heythrop College, University of London.

Kallistos Ware is Assistant Bishop in the Greek Orthodox Archdiocese of Thyateira and Great Britain, and Lecturer in Eastern Orthodox Studies at the University of Oxford.

A. N. Wilson is an author and journalist in London. He is also Literary Editor of the *Evening Standard*, London.

Introductory Reflections: Life beyond Life

LIONEL BLUE

I cannot very well speak about the after-life, not because I do not believe in it, but because it is a contradiction. When I die both time and space will die with me so there can be no after (nor a before for that matter). And there is another problem, too: all one can ever know is life, whether this life, another sort of life or eternal life. So death can never be experienced. But although you cannot speak of an after-life, you *can* talk about a beyond-life. And that is something which I, and lots of people, have come to, not through dogma or official teaching, but by experience. It is probably a good way to approach religious matters. After all, it is 'taste and see that the Lord is good' in the Hebrew Scriptures, and 'by their fruits ye shall know them' in the Gospels. So the proof of the pudding really is in the eating. One should not puff one's goods in religion. One should remember that honest descriptions apply to religious metaphysics as much as they do to any other goods in the supermarket. Our experiences do not prove what you might call a 'beyond-life' but they do point to it. And if you are prepared to base your life on it, then it does not let you down. Now, what are these experiences? Well, there are a number of very general experiences which I have and lots of other people have too.

The first thing is that a lot of people have out-of-the-body experiences of some type or other. For me it usually occurs not in churches or synagogues but at cocktail parties. I am holding a piece of asparagus in one hand and a glass in the other, yackety-yacketing away, and while I am doing all this a part of me steps outside of me and from somewhere near the ceiling looks down on the whole caboodle, with pity and compassion, both for myself and everybody else. Lots of other people recognise this too.

There is another experience which many people share and that is the feeling or the intuition (or whatever you like to call it) that although the world is not a bad place, and one can enjoy it to an extent, at the same time it is not home. It comes up to me in this situation: I am dark-looking and when I went on one of my package holidays I was in the luggage checkout at Palma Airport, and some German tourists rushed up to me, thinking that I was Spanish, and started to speak to me in bad Spanish. I replied in equally bad German and I had to tell them, 'Entschuldigen, aber...' ('Excuse me but I'm only a visitor here'). And it suddenly occurred to me as I said it that this does not just apply to that situation – it applies to lots of other situations in life. I *do not* feel that this is home. In some sense I am a stranger here and lots of human beings feel that. Yes, it is an interesting place – yes, you strike up friendships in the departure lounge – but sooner or later your flight is called and off you go. You are a bit apprehensive about where you are going to, but at the same time this is not really the place where you belong and if you try to feel too permanent here, it always lets you down. It is not that sort of place. So that is another experience which I think that people have. That 'I'm only a visitor here', 'I'm *also* a stranger here', is recognisable.

Another experience is that when people go into a silent synagogue/church/place of worship they often feel that they have stepped into a different dimension. In the stillness, they are not quite sure what is up, but they feel that they have stepped into another world. It can also be triggered by great art or music, or sometimes by love. Then you may find something interesting: that you can make that beyond-world happen. You do not just have to *wait* for it to happen; you can *make* it happen. Sometimes if you give yourself to it, and you can try this yourself, then the feeling comes back. You do something which is a bit dotty and a bit altruistic (you could kick yourself) but at the same time you get a kind of glow and you feel as if you have experienced the *gravity* of some unseen beyond-world.

Let me give you another example: I am in a train, reading a book on religion, which I am thoroughly enjoying, and I really am getting a great deal of benefit from it. But there is this lady standing up (a foolish virgin who has not reserved a seat). I try to ignore her but my book keeps on telling me 'you jolly well stand up for her'. So finally, in a very grumpy fashion, I do, because I know that if I do *not* then I cannot carry on reading the book and getting the nice sensations from it. So I stand up though part of me says 'you are a bloody fool', but another part of me feels that I have made that world happen. And I think lots of people also feel as if they are pulled by a kind of gravity from some unseen world, which pulls their lives out of their normal trajectory and makes them do silly things, altruistic things, all sorts of odd things. But when they do them, once again that feeling returns.

You provide your own evidence and I think the real evidence for the beyond-life is not even in these experiences I have mentioned. I think the only evidence for it, convincing evidence, is the evidence you provide yourself. In other words, you have to *become* your evidence. You can talk glibly about the beyond-life, for and against, until the cows come home, but only when you invoke it and allow it to work on you and you see what it makes of you, only then is it convincing. It is only when, as it were, things turn inside out, that you find yourself not using it, but *it* using *you*.

At the beginning this beyond-life is fun. It gives you little shivers down your spine, it gives colour to a rather drab life, it makes you have little chats with the cosmos, it makes you feel quite somebody. And you can play about with it quite a lot. But then there comes a point when it starts answering back, when it starts making demands on *you*. Then you find you are in a quandary because you either have to say 'get out of my life' or you have to say 'well, it was nothing really in the first place', in which case you have lost it and there is a real sense of grieving and bereavement if you do (I personally could not do that). Or else you have to go along with it, at least in part, and when you do that, you realise that something which started off as a nice idea packs a very powerful punch. And that is when you start sitting back and respecting it.

I think many people find that if you invoke that beyond-life, that other dimension, it has a great power. For example, alcoholics, who are not officially religious, say 'we rely upon a power greater than ourselves to help us out of our addiction'. They have found by experience that without it they cannot do anything. They do not call it God, they just say 'a power greater than ourselves'. Well, it affects anybody who really invokes it, and does not just play around with it – anybody who cries that most basic prayer, 'help' (because you are out of your depth), and you do find that something happens.

My parents wanted me to be a doctor but I could not because I cannot stand the sight of blood and so I faint. Whenever I have tried to give blood, I have always fainted and they have told me to go away because my blood is not worth the trouble it takes to get it. That is one reason why I became a rabbi, I suppose, because souls are much less messy and gory than bodies. But life has a habit of turning back and biting you and I found myself a chaplain to hospitals and that is becoming an increasing part of my work. Now when I start to go into hospital I am not quite sure what is going to happen (am I going to faint because there is a lot of gore about?) – that is when I invoke that beyond-life. It gets me through my hospital visit. I can have my attack of nausea after I come out of the hospital (I can also have a brandy when I come out!) but it helps me over the stile while I am there. I think lots of people have found that.

I have found that beyond-life has also been important in my own personal life. I was living with someone for years – and then it finished. It was on the Continent. I knew it was ending. I remember going into a church and thinking 'what the hell do I do now?' I remember that, as if in a conversation, something was saying to me that all the loves I had in this life were reflections of the real thing and *one* day, but not in this life, (perhaps at the *end* of it) I would meet the real thing. At least, that is how it came to me. I pushed the thought aside; it seemed too sentimental to bother about. But I remember that we were trying to work out who owned what and we got to the business of 'I said', 'you said', 'he said', 'she said' (you know all the quarrels which go on with this sort of thing) and we were just about to have a real ding-dong of a row, of the kind that happen when couples break up, when I suddenly felt as if the face I was looking at was a kind of mask and beyond it was this beyond-life. One moment the beyond-life was there, and the next it was not, as if a light was being turned on and off inside my friend's face. It was a funny sensation – I burst into laughter and said 'Look, we can't carry on like this: let's go to the pub'. As a result, we ended things pleasantly and we still see each other. So, that beyond-life has also affected my personal relationships.

Sometimes this dimension has a personal face and sometimes it has no face. At different times in one's life one adds more imagination or less imagination to it. People are aware that beyond the world of things there is another reality. You cannot deal properly with the world of things without relying upon that *other* reality.

I think the difficulty about the beyond-life is very simple – it is just not visible. But even people who just concern themselves with the world of visible things know very well that you cannot deal with the world of visible things justly or fairly or even constructively, without recourse to that *invisible* world. My thinking came to a head when I got my dog. I had a big, black mongrel (a cross between an Alsatian and a Labrador) who was the love of my life. Whenever I went out of the house, she used to stand on the stairs and look at me tragically. And then, when I came back *into* the house, she gave a startled look, once again from the stairs, bounded down, threw me over, stood on my chest and licked my face and went into paroxysms of delight. Now this happened whether I went away for two weeks to the Continent or whether I went away for two or three minutes to get a newspaper. Finally, I went to a vet and said 'look, doesn't that pooch ever learn? I mean . . .'. And he said to me 'Well, you have to remember, she's only an animal and, like all animals, what's *real* to her are the things that she sees, smells and touches and when you go *out* of the world of the senses and she can't see you, touch you or smell you, then as far as she's concerned, you cease to exist. Then when you come in through the door again, suddenly you come *into* the world of her senses again and so you come alive for her.' And then I began to understand, because if I saw the death and resurrection of my best friend, two or three times a day, I would also have a rather rocky emotional life.

That text suddenly occurred to me: 'for God created man a little higher than the animals and a little lower than the angels'. We are animals and, like all animals, anything which we can sense, which we can touch, see, smell (as with my dog) exists as real. When something goes *out* of the world of our senses, it is not sensed and by very easy transition becomes *nonsense*. Yet, we are also a little lower than the angels – we are the first animals in the evolutionary life who can give reality to things which are outside our senses. Our hold on that reality is very, very slight. We may get to know things like God, conscience and the beyond-life but it is very easy for us to think 'oh, it's just an idea – it isn't real like the freezer, the washing-up machine, the car and the mortgage'. It is a great fight, on our part, to be able to take that step and, as it were, improve on our animal heritage. We are, I think, the first of the animals who ever got that far, so it is not easy.

Why do people bother to invoke this other world at all, or try to become acquainted with it, become friends with it? I think it is because sooner or later the world of sensed things lets you down. It must do. Because everything that we are ever given in life sooner or later has to be given up or given away, which you can either do gracefully or with groans, grunts and passing the buck. But sooner or later the world of things *does* let us down, through illness, through somebody snitching somebody we love, through someone repossessing our home. And even if none of these things has happened, one day we are going to die.

Then, when that world of things lets us down, we try to get new strength and we suddenly invoke that world which is *not* sense. If it *is* invoked, as I have said before, something happens. Sometimes the world of things lets one down, either dramatically and catastrophically as in a concentration camp or, sometimes, it is only saying goodbye to everybody, and dying quietly and gently and pleasantly. But it comes to the same thing. Then one has to put one's faith in that other dimension. Now, you can give that beyond-life a human face or not. Some of the greatest Christian saints, like Teresa of Avila or John of the Cross, sometimes thought of that dimension as having a human face: the face of Christ. At the same time they also felt that sometimes it did *not* have that face; it was beyond that face. And I think that is a matter of temperament, environment and imagination: the clothes that you dress it in. But the reality of it is well-attested. It even works on a very practical level: you are wanting to go on holiday and you are looking at the holiday brochure and you check up – balcony? yes; sea view? yes; bath facilities? three course meals twice a day? And that is fine. But then you know very well you can have all these things and it still does not add up to what you want. I, for example, have had holidays in first class hotels and in grotty boarding houses. I have been both happy and unhappy in first class hotels and also in grotty boarding houses. (I have to admit I would far prefer to be unhappy in a first class hotel than a grotty boarding house.)

You see, the world of things deals with the comfort problem, but the happiness problem is something else, and that is something which comes from that beyond-life. It means peace with oneself, and coming to terms with one's anger. Comfort and happiness are not the same. And for happiness you have to deal with that beyond-life. Even agnostics and atheists have learned this. Marcus Aurelius, who was no friend to Christians, says that if god exists, then you might follow him; but if he doesn't, be like a god yourself. He says that we should, as it were, construct a temple inside ourselves and go into that. That is fair enough. Whether you contemplate the absolute, have a love affair with Jesus, listen to the voice in the burning bush, it is the same kind of thing. People know, just from the business of going on holiday, that the problems of this world cannot be solved in its own terms. You have to invoke another dimension, for even this world to work. Otherwise you end up very disappointed and very annoyed.

Also, in practice, it's not easy defining where you end and other people begin, or where the living end and the dead begin. If you wish, you can make room inside your mind for someone whom you want to continue living in it. All sorts of people can inhabit your mind if you are prepared to give them houseroom. I find that, when I think of my own personality, it is not just tricks of speech that have been adopted from other people (odd expressions) but occasionally when I come to a situation, I know 'I can't do this.' Why? because, say, a girl I knew who has died but says 'Lionel, how can you *possibly*?' and I know I cannot. I think also that religious people incarnate what they worship. So you can see Jesus or the Risen Christ, as it were, in the Christians who are devoted to him. That is, I think, the way that most people perceive somebody else's god. This sharp division as to where one person ends and somebody else begins is not quite there.

Lately, this business of the 'near-death experiences' has come up. I do not know what to make of them – these circles of light and meeting people one knew. But one would also have to remember that one would have to meet the people one did not like, as well as the ones that one did. It might all be because of the lack of oxygen to the brain. Who can say?

Most people I have met, who have died, died puzzled because life is such an unfinished business and most people seem to die with the questions 'Why me? why now?' At the same time, I have also noticed that when people accept that they are dying, a change happens. The problem comes in letting go. But once you have let go, people often give up their sleeping tablets and pain killers. Any nurse or doctor can tell you that. Once you look at where you are going to rather than where you have come from, then it is as if something in you relaxes and loosens up. Quite often you find, for example, at a deathbed that the dying person is really having to cope with and, in an odd sort of way, comfort the people around him or her, not vice versa.

A rabbinic story has helped me: there is a strange text which says 'the day of one's death is better than the day of one's birth'. The rabbis asked 'how could this be?' And they said: 'at a birth, as the baby is born, everybody there thinks it is a wonderful thing, a matter of rejoicing. Everybody except one: the baby. The baby, which comes from the security of its mother's womb, to the cold world outside, has not experienced it as a birth. It has experienced it as a death. When we come to our death, it is the same situation but in reverse. The mourners see the world that the dead person is leaving and see it as a death, but the person who is dying may well be seeing the world he or she is going into and may experience it as a birth. Once again, the difference is your point of view.'

I used to go to dying people in hospitals, in cancer wards, or in AIDS wards, thinking 'I must do it but it is going to be dreadful'. The strange thing is that it is not dreadful. It is rather the opposite. I am not the only person who has felt this, because I have discussed it with other chaplains. Many of us feel that it is in these wards that we get our spirituality, that people seem to rise to the occasion of their death. It is as if part of them has already joined that beyond-life and a kind of peace comes from them. Also, the fact of death and dying, in a ward, does not bring on the horrors. On the contrary, it usually brings out a great deal of affection and love, and kindness. It was after coming from an AIDS ward that I suddenly realised that *heaven* is a place where people love each other, and hell is a place where they do not. This AIDS ward was the closest to heaven I had ever known. There was a great deal of hugging and cuddling; they really were helping each other and I came away feeling elated.

I find that I need my own input of spiritual experience. If

you are a professionally religious person, earning your living by it, you cannot just keep on giving. You need to get something. Where do you get it from? I get it from people in trouble. I get it from alcoholics, from dying people and from AIDS sufferers. These are the people who give me my spirituality. When I do retreats with them, their retreats start off where other kinds of retreats end, and we deal with the nitty gritty straight away. For them the beyond-life is not an idea, is not something they can debate. The whole of the material world is no longer substantial enough to lean on, therefore every resource has to come from that beyond-life, from that world which is not sense. Therefore the most unlikely people are forced to invoke it, or come to terms with it. When they do, an enormous flowering takes place and although I am supposed to *take* the retreats, in fact I get more out of them than I give. That is not banality or politeness, it is the truth. Many other people who do this work have experienced exactly the same sort of thing. When you are out of your depth and the ground seems to go away from under you, that is the time when you cry 'help'. You cannot get a sure footing on *this* life any more, so you call on that beyond-life in desperation, to help you, and the fact is that if you really do it with all your being, it supports you.

This is why, although I cannot talk about the after-life, I can talk about the beyond-life. I cannot prove it and it is not even good to, because all of us are secret materialists, who would love the things of the spirit to become material. This is why we would like holy statues to wink or to dance, and would like extraordinary miracles to take place. We would like to materialise the spirit, because we are materialistic. I cannot say I believe in the beyond-life. What I *would* say is that if you base your life on the beyond-life and its existence and invoke it, it just does not let you down.

Part I

The Afterlife in the World's Religions

1
A Christian Approach to Eternal Life
PETER VARDY

1 INTRODUCTION

Christian ideas of eternal life vary dramatically. Recently an increasing minority of Christian theologians and philosophers have rejected the idea that eternal life should be seen as involving personal survival of death. Instead they see eternal life as a different quality of life here and now. To 'live in the eternal' is to live life in a different way, to turn one's back on self-interest and materialism and to live a life of self-giving love for others. By living this sort of life one may overcome death, not by surviving it but by refusing to let death trivialise the meaning of life. If someone 'walks with God' by living the holy life, then whatever adversity may affect such an individual, nothing can really harm him or her as nothing can take away the individual's inner orientation. Eternal life, on this view, is not something to be sought after death but a different way of approaching life and living in this world. The words of absolution in the Anglican Alternative Services Book (ASB), when compared with the wording in the Book of Common Prayer, can be seen to leave room for this approach. The Book of Common Prayer said:

> Almighty God, our heavenly Father . . . have mercy upon you; pardon and deliver you from all your sins; confirm and strengthen you in all goodness; and bring you to everlasting life.

while the ASB altered this to:

> Almighty God who forgives all who truly repent have mercy

upon you . . . confirm and strengthen you in all goodness and keep you in life eternal.

The difference can be seen as significant. Whereas the Prayer Book saw everlasting life as something which individuals come to after death, the ASB recognises it as something that starts in this world and which the Christian should already enjoy.

However persuasive and philosophically attractive the view that eternal life is confined to this world may be (and I do not, of course, maintain that this was the intention of the authors of the ASB), I believe it to be mistaken. Christianity is built upon the claim that Jesus rose from the dead on Easter Sunday as an individual. If this claim is false, then although Christianity may have some advice to offer on how life should be lived, it is essentially false. St Paul recognised this when he said: 'If for this life only we have hoped in Christ, we are of all people most to be pitied.' (1 Corinthians 15:19).

For the purpose of this chapter, therefore, I am going to assume that Christianity, as it has traditionally done, still maintains that human beings survive death. Eternal life may indeed begin in this life, but the claim is that it also continues after death and how this is to be understood is the issue I seek to address in this chapter.

There are two possible approaches to this problem. The first is to consider what it is that survives death and the second to consider what life after death may be like. I believe the latter to be more productive but will first outline the issues that arise in discussion of the former.

2 THE NATURE OF PERSONHOOD

There is no unanimity among Christians as to what it means to be a person, yet this issue is at the heart of any understanding of life after death. There are three main possibilities. Firstly the dualist view of Plato and later Descartes which maintained that a human being is made up of soul and body which are united in this life. At death, however, the soul which is the true self, the real I, separates and goes elsewhere.

The dualist approach suffers from significant identity problems – in what sense could a disembodied soul be me? Peter Vardy is embodied and it is far from clear what a disembodied Peter Vardy would be or whether, indeed, it is not a contradiction in terms. There are also grave difficulties in understanding how soul and body interact or the separation between the brain (which is clearly a physical organ which can be affected by disease and drugs) and a disembodied soul. The dualist approach also tends to devalue the physical and Christians have traditionally maintained that in the incarnation Christ took human flesh and the old sacred/secular distinction was abolished.

The second alternative was put forward by Aquinas who was strongly influenced by Aristotle. For Aquinas, the soul was the form of the whole body – the soul is almost, expressing the point simply, the blueprint of the body. Aquinas maintained that the soul separates from the body at death but is incomplete without the body. The soul is an immaterial substance and can exist temporarily without the body but needs the body to express itself. After death, the soul goes to purgatory or hell. Souls in purgatory endure tremendous pain but this is partly assuaged by the knowledge that all these souls eventually attain the Beatific Vision of God (which I will return to later). At the last judgement, an individual's soul is given a new and glorified body.

There are difficulties in this account. Aquinas said that 'My soul is not I'. He was no dualist, but nevertheless claimed that it is a person's soul which is in purgatory. However, either the soul is in purgatory and the soul is me or else I am not in purgatory. Aquinas attempts to circumvent this problem by claiming that the soul is not fully the person, but this is problematic. Either I will or I will not go to purgatory and this must mean that either I am or am not my soul. It is difficult to make sense of the idea that I will only partly go to purgatory because my soul is not fully me.

The third view of personhood maintains that a human being is a psycho-physical unity. On this view, if a person dies then the person can only rise from the dead as an embodied individual. This has considerable attractions – not least that if a person dies and an embodied individual rises, there seem to be far fewer identity problems. However, this is only apparently true – the first difficulty is to know whether, if a person dies, it is the same person who rises or an identical copy. The after death person is not even likely to be identical to the before death one. After all, a ninety year old lady who dies may not be keen to have the same body as on her deathbed and if she has a different body, would it be the same person? In this life it is spatio-temporal continuity or the persistence of a body through time which determines identity and this is broken on death. There are formidable philosophical problems in determining whether identity has been preserved once the old body ceases to exist and a new one is created.

Secondly, if an individual survives death as an embodied person, then this raises questions as to the location in which life after death is lived, what kind of life this would be and what its purpose would be. Would bodily resurrected persons breathe, eat and drink? Would they have sexual natures? Because if I am to rise bodily I would presumably rise as a man. There are no simple answers to these problems.

The biblical account of Jesus' resurrection appears to support the third of the above options, but the position is not clear. Although Jesus is clearly recorded as having a body (he could walk with his disciples, take breakfast with them and even allow Thomas to feel his hands and side), it was a rather special body. He specifically told Mary not to touch him and he could appear in a locked room.

Whichever of the three models is adopted, the identity problems involved in claiming that individuals survive death are grave and there is no straightforward way of showing that what survives death is the same as the person who died. However, the philosophic difficulties in this area are no more serious than the problems that arise for the philosopher in trying to decide whether he or she is the same person he or she was yesterday, and we seem to be able to live with these latter difficulties without undue stress! Perhaps, therefore, another way needs to be found to understand life after death and it is to this alternative approach I now want to turn.

3 THE NATURE OF LIFE AFTER DEATH

(a) The Greek Background

Philosophers and theologians of the ancient and medieval world recognised in God the *Summum Bonnum*. Augustine maintained that Plato was the first to recognise this. In the final passage of the banquet described by Plato there is a hymn to beauty retold by Socrates (*Plato's Symposium*, p. 93 of the Penguin edition):

> Beauty is first of all eternal; it neither comes into being nor passes away, neither waxes or wanes ... it is absolute, existing alone with itself, unique, eternal, and all other beautiful things partake of it, yet in such a manner that, while they come into being and pass, it neither undergoes any diminution or suffers any change.... What may we suppose the felicity of the man who sees absolute beauty in its essence, pure and unalloyed, who ... is able to apprehend divine beauty where it exists apart and alone.

Plato's theory of the Forms, his story of the Cave and many other sections of his writings point to the superiority of truth and beauty and goodness. Plotinus follows closely in the Platonic tradition as follows:

> There are three kinds of men, there are those who satisfy themselves with things of sense, for whom the goods of sense is the *summum bonnum*, who see in suffering an evil, in pleasure happiness, and who employ their wits to secure one and avoid the other; heavy birds, weighed down for having imbibed too much from earth, who cannot fly though nature gave them wings. There are others, rising up a little, attracted to a higher beauty by that which is best in them; but impotent to look on high, of virtue having but the name, descending to baser actions that first they had assayed to shun. But there is a third kind, a race divine, endowed with superior power and penetrating glance. Their eyes have seen the splendour from on high, they have raised themselves up ... and despise the things of earth, and enjoy this region where truly they are at home, as after a long voyage the wanderer truly returns to his native country.

Plotinus identified Plato's Forms with God and sees the end of man as lying in the vision of God:

> The soul enjoys the contemplation of God because it is with Him, it is unity because it is one with Him; it is less a vision than a union, two flames in one and the same brightness. (Quoted in R. Arnou, 'The Desire of God in the Philosophy of Plato', p. 244)

The Christian writer Boethius followed in the same tradition arguing that God is beatitude and that beatitude is divinity itself. It is by acquiring divinity that one must acquire beauty – so in the vision of absolute beauty man becomes God-like.

Aquinas had the legacy of two traditions – that stemming from Plato outlined above, and the Aristotelian. Aristotle also saw supreme happiness lying in contemplation – the action of man's noblest ability in contact with his noblest object – but he regarded such activity as that of God, and man must be satisfied with human happiness.

(b) Aquinas' Views

Aquinas has been the seminal influence in the Roman Catholic tradition in outlining life after death. In Chapters 27–34 of the *Summa Contra Gentiles* (SCG), Aquinas first rejects the idea that man's happiness can lie in any finite pleasures. In Chapter 37 he argues that man's ultimate happiness will come from contemplating God. This brings Aquinas to the view that man's ultimate happiness can only come once a state of immortality has been reached. He quotes Aristotle (*Ethics* 10: vii) saying that man's ultimate happiness in this life consists in speculation and as we never reach the end of speculation, we cannot achieve happiness here. Finally in Chapter 51, Aquinas effectively opts for the Platonic option outlined above. Thus:

> The immediate vision of God is promised to us in Holy writ (1 Cor. 12:12) ... it is according to this vision that we become most like unto God and participators in his bliss; since God understands his substance by his essence and this is His bliss. Wherefore it is said (1 John 3:2) 'When He shall appear we shall be like to Him; because we shall see Him as He

A Christian Approach to Eternal Life

is'.... Accordingly (this) ... is to enjoy the same bliss as that which makes God happy and to see God as he sees himself.

He goes on to say that it is only through God's grace that we can see God – it is beyond our natural powers to do so. Therefore:

> It is said (Romans 6:23) 'The Grace of God is life everlasting'. For we have proved (Ch. 1) that man's happiness consists in seeing God which is called life everlasting (Ch. 52).

It is important to recognise the strong Greek philosophic influence on Aquinas' thought and on subsequent Catholic theology. For Catholic theologians, God (and Jesus as the second person of the Trinity) is literally timeless, utterly immutable, bodiless, spaceless and without parts. The final end for human beings is the contemplation of God in a Beatific Vision which is itself literally timeless. Aquinas considers, therefore, that the eventual end for human beings is for them to become timeless and to enjoy the timeless Beatific Vision of God which may vary between individuals but which will be wholly satisfying.

In the Beatific Vision, the individual will get as much knowledge as God, except that no human being will have knowledge of God's motives and intentions. Aquinas seems to consider that there are three possible levels of knowledge:

Level 1: This is the highest level that can be attained by the created intellect. It is sufficient to give knowledge of God, but not the Beatific Vision. This is the level that Aristotle considered that man must be content with.

Level 2: This is only possible by Divine Grace and involves participation by man in God's vision. This is the Beatific Vision. Once granted, this vision cannot be lost as the individual becomes timeless and no change is possible.

Level 3: This is God's perfect knowledge which exceeds Level 2 as it includes God's motives and intentions.

Between Levels 1 and 2 lies the transition from the finite to the infinite, from time to timelessness. No transition is possible between Level 2 and Level 3 and nor can an individual who has been granted a certain level of understanding in the vision based on his intellect at the time of death progress to a higher level of understanding.

In the Beatific Vision, all desires and goals will be fulfilled and so man will achieve his ultimate happiness. The only way of fulfilling these goals is in the vision of God's glory and the knowledge that this brings (SCG, Ch. 63). God is the object of all human striving and desire even though humanity may not be aware of this. Boethius says this happiness is 'A state of life made perfect by the accumulation of all goods' and Aquinas quotes this with approval.

The following is my brief summary of the idea of the Beatific Vision as put forward by Aquinas:

(1) Absolute goodness, truth, beauty and wisdom are synonyms for or proceed from God who is infinite.

(2) God, the three persons of the Trinity, is literally timeless, spaceless, bodiless and wholly immutable.

(3) The ultimate happiness of each human being lies only in the contemplation of (not the search for) absolute truth, beauty and wisdom and this is found in the Beatific Vision.

(4) Man is a finite, temporal creature and cannot achieve this vision by himself.

(5) The contemplation of God does not make man equal to God as there will still be things he does not know.

(6) The contemplation is instantaneous, comprehensive and all embracing. The individual becomes timeless and therefore no time passes.

(7) Anyone can share in the Beatific Vision no matter what his intellectual capacity provided only that God's grace is given to him (or, presumably, her!). The content of the vision may vary between individuals depending on their capacities at the time of death.

It is easy to see why this idea should have appeared so attractive to the Church. It enables the believer to see that his only end lies in God, yet a God identified with the supreme Platonic values. However, the ideas Aquinas puts forward seem to suffer from real difficulties. Almost all the issues are arguable – for instance, the claim that man's ultimate happiness rests on the contemplation of God seems to be an assumption that could be challenged. Also, to say that God is absolute goodness raises real questions about the nature of the Universe as well as opening up Plato's Euthyphro dilemma (in which Plato has Socrates ask whether the only standard of goodness is what the gods want or whether there is some independent standard against which the wishes of the gods can be measured). However, the key problems seem to be as follows:

(1) The literal timelessness of God which is the cornerstone of traditional Catholic theology can be questioned. Most Christians think of Jesus as in some sense an individual who survived death, yet on Aquinas' approach, Jesus is the timeless second person of the Trinity who is bodiless, spaceless and totally immutable.

(2) The ultimate end for human beings consists in their becoming timeless and enjoying the Beatific Vision. However, it is a legitimate question as to whether a human being could be a person at all and still less the same individual if he or she is timeless. Everything that makes a human being involves time and it could be maintained that temporality is a necessary feature of human identity. Also, Aquinas considers that at the second judgement persons will be given a new and glorified body (to go with the soul which temporarily separated on death) but it is not clear how a person can have a body and yet be timeless.

Once humans achieve the vision, they are said to be alive, immortal and eternal – yet the lack of time contradicts this. Further development is ruled out and understanding cannot increase. As Hume has his character Cleanthes say in the *'Dialogues'*:

> A mind whose acts and sentiments and ideas are not distinct and successive, one that is wholly simple and totally immutable, is a mind which has no thought, no reason, no will, no sentiment, no love, no hatred; or in a word is no mind at all. It is an abuse of terms to give it that appelation.

(3) Central to the biblical idea of heaven appears to be a community with an active social life focused on Christ and on continual praise of God. The whole idea of the heavenly Jerusalem is of a social community and this does not fit at all easily with the idea of a timeless vision.

As we have seen, Aquinas distinguishes a two-fold beatitude for man that I have described as Level 1 and Level 2. The first of these man is capable of realising by his own natural efforts and the second is the free gift of God. Aquinas frequently says:

(1) the Beatific Vision is beyond the powers of man, and

(2) it is naturally desired by all rational creatures.

Without God, the human mind is only capable of a finite, relative end and yearns to go beyond this to an end which is infinite and absolute. I am going to try to build on this idea and to put forward a more cogent view but before doing so must express doubts about the basic concept of Level 1 knowledge. The idea of this originated from Aristotle and is really dependent on his philosophy. It seems to express a too hopeful view of man's abilities – certainly to regard this level as 'natural' to man seems questionable. Few individuals (I would be tempted to say none) on this earth attain this sort of knowledge. The most that might be said is that Level 1 is the limit of knowledge to which an individual could aspire by his own efforts given infinite time in which to achieve this. The fact that no-one has such a period of time on this earth means that no-one actually manages it.

4 A REVISED ACCOUNT OF THE BEATIFIC VISION

In *De Malo* X:xvi, Article 3 Aquinas puts forward an interesting view of the position of fallen angels in relation to the Beatific Vision. He says that they wanted to obtain this vision, but wished to do so by their own unaided powers. They wished to obtain Level 2 knowledge but rebelled against God as they wished to obtain this by themselves. Intelligence may conceive of what perfect beauty consists yet it cannot be found outside God (*De Malo* Q:xvi, Art. 2). The Demons, therefore, are trying to achieve this beatitude by their own efforts. Certainly there is a long tradition in Satanism of ascent by initiation into continually higher levels of knowledge.

This can open the way for an altered view of the Beatific Vision. Human beings are free and must employ their intelligence to decide where the true object of their individual destiny may be found. They have a wide choice in this life – they can study beauty, whether in art or literature; wisdom, either in scientific research or philosophy: or truth in some other form. They can study horology, campanology, lepidoptery, forestry or football – dancing, sex, power, the pursuit of pleasure or, on the other hand, the acquisition of kindness, gentleness and compassion. Throughout the lives of human beings they are free to make their own choices as to what they consider to be important and as to what sort of person they want to become.

There are, thus, many options available to the individual in this life, no one of which is completely right or wrong. However, the priorities the individual decides upon will be crucial for what happens hereafter. The deciding test would be whether the prime motivation was love of God and love of fellow human beings. To put it in Kierkegaard's terms, whether the relationship with God was the one thing willed. Thus two people may study philosophy – one in humble obedience to what he or she considers God's will and the other with a view to worldly power and advantage. One Canon of Canterbury Cathedral may be there because he is genuinely trying to serve God, another may be after a bishopric! In any walk of life, it is not so much the job that is done but the way it is done and the motivations that are brought to it that will be important.

The Beatific Vision could then be granted after death to those who have spent their lives in an appropriate manner. Since the 'test' was whether an individual put his or her relationship with God first, it would be appropriate that after death the individual should be given the Vision which stemmed directly from this relationship. However, it would not be the vision suggested by Aquinas, but rather an insight, born of understanding, into God's purposes arising out of love of and obedience to God. This would place the individual's life in a wider context and help him or her to make sense of what had previously been incomprehensible.

This insight would not confer total knowledge but would leave room for further development within the heavenly kingdom. On this view, the Beatific Vision would include knowledge of or greater insight into God and the greater insight thus enjoyed would be one of the chief features of the heavenly kingdom. Instead, therefore, of the timeless beatific vision, I would argue that Christianity has traditionally maintained that we will survive death as individuals and we will then be judged on the decisions we have made in our lives. To a large extent we will judge ourselves – we will have decided, by the choices we make, whether we want to be in fellowship with God or whether, by our pride and self interest, we have exiled ourselves from Him. We make ourselves into the sort of persons we are at death and most of us will not want to be with God as our selfishness and self concern would simply make us out of place. Christianity maintains that our conduct in this life is decisive. We decide our own fate after death. The possibility is open to us of a life lived in fellowship with God in a heavenly society where the Christian idea of agape or mutual love prevails. We can strive for this or ignore the possibility and instead concentrate on the pleasures of this life – the choice is ours.

The timeless beatific vision does not do justice to the centrality of the idea of individuals surviving death. Jesus rose from the dead as an individual and most Christians believe that he lives after his death as an individual. To maintain, as Catholic theology has traditionally done, that Jesus no longer exists as an individual but only as the timeless, immutable, bodiless, spaceless second person of the Trinity is attractive philosophically but does not do justice to the resurrection. It introduces a radical discontinuity between the risen Jesus who appeared to the disciples and the unknowable, timeless, ineffable substance that God is held to be.

The Beatific Vision should not be seen as a final static purpose but a dynamic joy which comes to the individual out of God's grace, based on the sort of life he or she has lived and the sort of person he or she has become. The final end for human beings would be a social one – living in the Heavenly Kingdom with progress in this kingdom still a possibility. The purpose of this would lie in itself, just as the purpose of love lies in itself. Those who, in this life, pursued knowledge or pleasure or power as ends in themselves would find themselves in a similar position to the Demons in Aquinas' *De Malo* – they would have exiled themselves from God as they could not bring themselves to accept their dependence and to acquire the humility to accept that trust and faith were required. The 'great gulf' referred to in the story of Dives and Lazarus would be that between those who had become creatures of compassion, love, gentleness and concern for others and who lived their lives under the willing acceptance of the governance of God and, on the other hand, the individual's assertion of his or her own supremacy and the primacy of self-interest.

The revised view I am suggesting seems to fit in well with many of St Paul's ideas. The famous Chapter 13 of Paul's first letter to the Corinthians could almost have been written with this formulation in mind:

> For now we see in a mirror dimly, but then we will see face to face. Now I know only in part; then I will know fully, even as I have been fully known. (13:12)

Christians maintain that in a new, heavenly society the 'lion and lamb shall lie down together and a little child shall lead them' (Isaiah 11:6). This is expressing the essentially social element of the kingdom as well as its spirit – a spirit of individuals who have put self into second place and have devoted their lives to love of others and of God. They have become, literally, transformed by love.

The idea that everyone will go to heaven and that all that is required is to live a normal life and not to do anything exceptionally bad is not borne out by the Gospels which suggest that the path will be a narrow, stony and arduous one and that only those who are willing to take up their personal cross by following in Christ's footsteps and attempting, however unsuccessfully, to become Christ-like will be eligible. The transformation of the enormous demand and cost of following Christ into a simple matter of social convention may be one of the greatest delusions of our time.

SUMMARY

Christianity maintains that we each, as individuals, will survive death and what happens after death will be determined by the lives we have lived and the choices we have made. I have tried to argue that the heavenly kingdom should be seen as a social one and that Aquinas' idea of a timeless beatific vision is too limited. There is no easy answer as to what form we shall be as individuals after we survive death. The dualist approach is, I suggest, mistaken not least because it denies the resurrection of the body and also carries implications that 'matter' and our bodies are in some way secondary or of limited importance. Christ became incarnate as a human being and the division between the spiritual and the physical was done away with. The resurrection of some form of body seems to be necessarily required for survival of death to be maintained, but what form this body might take is not easy to determine. One necessary condition, however, would be for the existence of memory. If spatio-temporal continuity is broken (as it is when we die and our human bodies decay) then some identity criteria are essential. Memory must be one essential component of this. Our lives may contain painful memories, but in the absence of these memories or of the spatio-temporal continuity of our bodies, we could not claim to be the same person. Memories are essential – even though we may see the painful memories in a new light.

The Christian claims may, of course, be mistaken. Perhaps Jesus did not rise from the dead – in this case although he may have been an admirable person, Christianity is based on a mistake. If, however, it is true, then we as individuals will survive our deaths and we must be the same individuals as we were before death – even though our new existence will be richer and fuller than we can possibly imagine.

2
'Go Joyfully': The Mystery of Death and Resurrection
KALLISTOS WARE

> *The end is where we start from.*
> T. S. Eliot

'I KNEW YOU WOULD COME...'

In the worship of the Russian Orthodox Church, while the prayers of preparation are being said before the start of the Eucharist, the doors in the centre of the icon screen remain closed. Then comes the time for the Divine Liturgy itself to begin: the doors are opened, the sanctuary stands revealed, and the celebrant sings the initial blessings. It was precisely this moment that the religious philosopher Prince Evgeny Trubetskoy recalled as he lay dying. These were his last words: 'The royal doors are opening! The Great Liturgy is about to begin.'[1] For him death was not the closing but the opening of a door, not an end but a beginning. Like the early Christians, he saw his death-day as his birthday.

Let us think of our human existence as a book. Most people regard this present life as the actual text, the main story, and they see the future life – if, indeed, they believe that there *is* any future life – as no more than an appendix. But the genuinely Christian attitude is the exact reverse of this. Our present life is in reality no more than the preface, the introduction, while it is the future life that constitutes the main story. The moment of death signifies not the conclusion of the book but the start of Chapter One.

Two things, so obvious that they are easily overlooked, need to be said about this end-point which is in fact the starting-point.

Death is an unavoidable and certain fact; death is a mystery. This means that we are to view our coming death with contrasting feelings – with sober realism on the one side, and at the same time with awe and wonder.

DEATH IS AN UNAVOIDABLE AND CERTAIN FACT

In this life there is only one thing of which we can be sure: that we are all going to die (unless perchance the second coming of Christ should occur first). Death is the one fixed, inevitable event to which every human must look forward. And if I try to forget about this fixed event and to hide its inevitability from myself, then it is I myself who am the loser. True humanism and the awareness of death are dependent variables, for it is only by facing and accepting the reality of my coming death that I can become authentically alive. As D. H. Lawrence observed, 'Without the song of death, the song of life becomes pointless and silly.' By ignoring the dimension of death, we deprive life of its true grandeur.

This is a point that has been powerfully expressed by Metropolitan Anthony of Sourozh:

> Death is the touchstone of our attitude to life. People who are afraid of death are afraid of life. It is impossible not to be afraid of life with all its complexity and dangers if one is afraid of death. . . . If we are afraid of death we will never be prepared to take ultimate risks; we will spend our life in a cowardly, careful and timid manner. It is only if we can face death, make sense of it, determine its place and our place in regard to it, that we will be able to live in a fearless way and to the fullness of our ability.[2]

Our realism, however, and our determination to 'make sense' of death should not lead us to diminish the second truth: **Death is a mystery.** Despite all that we are told by our different religious traditions, we understand almost nothing about

> The undiscover'd country from whose bourn
> No traveller returns. . . .

The Mystery of Death and Resurrection

Truly, as Hamlet remarks, the dread of it 'puzzles the will'. We must resist the temptation to try and say too much. We are not to trivialise death. It is an unavoidable and certain fact, but it is also the great unknown.

The attitude of sober realism with which we are to confront the fact of death is well expressed by a Syrian writer of the seventh century, St Isaac of Nineveh:

> Prepare your heart for your departure. If you are wise, you will expect it every hour. Each day say to yourself: 'See, the messenger who comes to fetch me is already at the door. Why am I sitting idle? I must depart for ever. I cannot come back again.' Go to sleep with these thoughts every night, and reflect on them throughout the day. And when the time of departure comes, go joyfully to meet it, saying: 'Come in peace. I knew you would come, and I have not neglected anything that could help me on the journey.'[3]

DEATHS GREAT AND LITTLE

In determining death's place and our place in regard to it, there are three aspects to be kept constantly in view:

Death is closer to us than we imagine.

Death is deeply *un*natural, contrary to the divine plan, and yet it is God's gift.

Death is a separation that is no separation.

Death is far closer to us than we imagine – not just a distant event at the conclusion of our earthly existence, but a present reality that is going on continually around us and within us.[4] 'I die daily', said St Paul (1 Cor 15:31); in T.S. Eliot's words, 'The time of death is every moment.' All living is a kind of dying: we are dying all the time. But in this daily experience of dying, each death is followed by a new birth: all dying is also a kind of living. Life and death are not opposites, mutually exclusive, but they are intertwined. The whole of our human existence is a mixture of mortality and resurrection: 'dying, and behold we live' (2 Cor

6:9). Our earthly journey is an unceasing passover, a constant crossing over through death into new life. Between our initial birth and our eventual death, the whole course of our existence is made up of a series of lesser deaths and births.

Every time we fall asleep at night, it is a foretaste of death; every time we wake up again next morning, it is as if we had risen from the dead. There is a Hebrew benediction which says. 'Blessed art thou, O Lord our God, King of the universe, who createst thy world every morning afresh.'[5] So it is also with ourselves: each morning, as we awake, we are as it were newly created. Perhaps our final death will be in the same way a re-creation – a falling asleep followed by an awakening. We are not afraid to drop off to sleep each night, because we expect to wake up once more next morning. Can we not feel the same kind of confidence about our final falling-asleep in death? May we not expect to wake up again re-created in eternity?

The death–life pattern is also apparent, in a somewhat different way, in the process of growing up. Repeatedly, something in us has to die so that we may pass on to the next stage of living. The transition from the baby to the child, from the child to adolescent, from the adolescent to the mature adult, involves at each juncture an inner death in order that something new may come alive. And these transitions, particularly in the case of the child becoming a teenager, can often be crisis-ridden and even acutely painful. Yet if at any point we decline to accept the need for a dying, we cannot develop into real persons. As George MacDonald says in his fantasy-novel *Lilith*, 'You will be dead so long as you refuse to die.' It is precisely the death of the old that makes possible the emergence of fresh growth within ourselves, and without the death there would be no new life.

If growing up is a form of death, then so is parting, the separation from a place or person that we have come to love: *partir, c'est mourir un peu*. Yet such separations are a necessary element in our continuing growth into maturity. Unless we have sometimes the courage to leave our familiar surroundings, to part with our existing friends and to forge new links, we shall never realise our true potentiality. By hanging on too long to the old, we are refusing the invitation to discover what is new. In the words of Cecil Day Lewis:

Selfhood begins with a walking away.
And love is proved in the letting go.

Another kind of death that all of us have to face at some point is the experience of being rejected: rejection, perhaps, when we apply for a job–how often does every school-leaver or university graduate today have to live through that particular form of dying!–or else rejection in love. Something does indeed die within us when we find that our love is not returned, and that someone else is preferred in our place. And yet even this death can be a source of new life. For many young people such rejection in love is precisely the moment when they really begin to grow up, their initiation into adult life. Bereavement, the loss of a loved one, involves equally a death in the heart of the one who remains alive. We feel that a part of ourselves is no longer there, that a limb has been amputated. Yet bereavement, when faced and inwardly accepted, makes each of us more authentically alive than we were before.

Almost as traumatic as the death of a friend or partner can be, for many believers, the death of faith – the loss of our root certainties (or seeming certainties) about God and the meaning of existence. But this too is a death-like experience through which we have to pass if our faith is to become mature. True faith is a constant dialogue with doubt, God is incomparably greater than all our preconceptions about him; our mental concepts are idols that need to be shattered. So as to be fully alive, our faith needs continually to die.

In all these cases, then, death turns out to be not destructive but creative. Out of dying comes resurrection. Something dies – something comes alive. May not the death that ensues at the end of our earthly life fit into this same pattern? It is to be seen as the last and greatest in the long series of deaths and resurrections that we have been experiencing ever since the day that we were born. It is not something totally unrelated to all that has been happening to us previously throughout our life, but it is a larger, more comprehensive expression of what we have been undergoing all the time. If the little deaths through which we have had to pass have each led us beyond death to resurrection, may this not be true of the great moment of death that we await when it is finally time to depart from this world?

Nor is this all. For Christians, the constantly repeated pattern of death–resurrection within our own lives is given fuller meaning by the life, death and resurrection of our Saviour Jesus Christ. Our own story is to be understood in the light of his story – that story which we celebrate annually during Holy Week, and also each Sunday at the Eucharist. Our little deaths and resurrections are joined across history to his definitive death and resurrection, our little passovers are taken up and reaffirmed in his great passover. Christ's dying, in the words of the Liturgy of St Basil, is a 'life-creating death'. With his example as our assurance, we believe that our own death can also be 'life-creating'. He is our forerunner and our firstfruits. As we Orthodox affirm at the Paschal midnight service, in words attributed to St John Chrysostom:

> Let none fear death, for the death of the Saviour has set us free.
> He has destroyed death by undergoing death....
> Christ is risen, and life reigns in freedom.
> Christ is risen, and there is none left dead in the tomb.[6]

BOTH TRAGEDY AND BLESSING

Death, then, is present with us throughout our life, as a constant, ever-recurring daily experience. Yet, familiar though it may be, at the same time it is deeply *un*natural. Death is not part of God's primary purpose for his creation. He created us, not in order that we should die, but in order that we should live. What is more, he created us as an undivided unity. On the Jewish and Christian view, the human person is to be seen in thoroughly holistic terms: we are each of us, not a soul temporarily imprisoned in a body and longing to escape, but an integrated totality that embraces soul and body together. C. G. Jung was right to insist on what he terms the 'mysterious truth': 'Spirit is the living body seen from within, and the body the outer manifestation of the living spirit – the two being really one.'[7] As the separation of body and soul, death is therefore a violent affront against the wholeness of our human nature. Death may be something that awaits us all, but it is at the same time profoundly abnormal. It is monstrous and tragic. Confronted by the death of those close to us and by our own death, despite all our realism we are justified in feeling also a sense of desolation, of horror and even indignation:

> Do not go gentle into that good night.
> Rage, rage against the dying of the light.[8]

The Mystery of Death and Resurrection

Jesus himself wept beside the grave of his friend Lazarus (John 11:35), and in Gethsemane he was filled with anguish at the prospect of his own coming death (Matt 26:38). St Paul regards death as an 'enemy to be destroyed' (1 Cor 15:26), and he links it closely with sinfulness: 'The sting of death is sin' (1 Corinthians 15:56). The fact that we are all going to die is a reflection of the fact that we are all living in a fallen world – in a world that is distorted and out of joint, crazy, *écrasé*.

Yet, even though death is tragic, it is at the same time a blessing. Although not part of God's original plan, it is none the less his gift, an expression of his mercy and compassion. For us humans to live unendingly in this fallen world, caught for ever in the vicious circle of boredom and sin, would have been a fate too terrible for us to endure; and so God has supplied us with a way of escape. He dissolves the union of soul and body, so that he may afterwards shape them anew, uniting them again at the bodily resurrection on the Last Day and so re-creating them to fullness of life. He is like the potter whom Jeremiah watched: 'So I went down to the potter's house, and there he was working at his wheel. The vessel he was making of clay was spoiled in the potter's hand, and he reworked it into another vessel, as seemed good to him' (18:4-5). The divine Potter lays his hand on the vessel of our humanity, marred by sin, and he breaks it in pieces, so as to mould it again on his wheel and refashion it according to its first glory. Death serves in this way as the means of our restoration. In the words of the Orthodox funeral service:

> Of old thou hast created me from nothing
> And honoured me with thy divine image.
> But when I disobeyed thy commandment,
> Thou hast returned me to the earth whence I was taken.
> Lead me back again to thy likeness.
> Refashioning my ancient beauty.[9]

As Benjamin Franklin stated in the epitaph that he composed for himself, death is the way in which we are 'corrected and amended':

> The body of
> Benjamin Franklin, printer,
> (Like the cover of an old book,

> Its contents worn out,
> And stript of its lettering and gilding)
> Lies here; food for worms!
> Yet the work itself will not be lost,
> For it will, as he believed, appear once more
> In a new
> And more beautiful edition,
> Corrected and amended
> By its Author!

There is, then, a dialectic in our attitude to death, but the two ways of approach are not in the final analysis contradictory. We see death as *un*natural, abnormal, as contrary to the original plan of the Creator, and so we recoil from it with grief and despair. But we see it also as part of the divine will, as a blessing, not a punishment. It is an escape from the *impasse,* a means of grace, the doorway to our re-creation. It is our way of return: to quote the Orthodox funeral service once more, 'I am the lost sheep: call me back and save me, O Saviour.'[10] We therefore draw near to death with eagerness and hope, saying with St Francis of Assisi, 'Praised be my Lord for our Sister, bodily death', for through this bodily death the Saviour is calling home the child of God. We look beyond the separation of body and soul at death to their future reintegration at the final resurrection.

This dialectic is clearly apparent at an Orthodox funeral. No attempt is made to hide the painful and shocking reality of the fact of death. The coffin is left open, and it can often be a harrowing moment when the relatives and friends approach one by one to give the last kiss to the departed. Yet at the same time it is customary in many places to wear not black but white vestments, as in the resurrection service at Paschal midnight; for Christ, risen from the dead, is summoning the departed Christian to share in his own resurrection. We are not forbidden to mourn at a funeral; and this is surely wise, for tears can have a healing effect, and when grief is suppressed the wound goes deeper. But we are not to grieve 'as others do who have no hope' (1 Thess 4:13). Our grief, however heart-rending, is not a hopeless grief; for, as we confess in the Creed, 'we are expecting the resurrection of the dead and the life of the age to come'.

CONTINUING COMMUNION

Death is, in the third place, a separation that is no separation. This is a point to which Orthodox tradition attaches the utmost importance. The living and the departed belong to a single family. The chasm of death is not impassable, for we can all meet around the alter of God. In the words of the Russian writer Iuliá de Beausobre (1893–1977), 'The Church... is a meeting-place of persons dead, alive and yet to be born, who, loving one another, come together round the rock of the Altar to proclaim their love of God.'[11] The point is well developed by another Russian author, the missionary priest Makary Glukharev (1792–1847) in a letter to one recently bereaved:

> In Christ we live and move and have our being. Whether alive or dead, we are all in him. It would be more true to say: We are all alive in him, for in him there is no death. Our God is not a God of the dead but of the living. He is your God, he is the God of her who has died. There is only one God, and in that one God you are both united. Only you cannot see each other for the time being. But this means that your future meeting will be all the more joyful; and then no one will take your joy from you. Yet even now you live together; all that has happened is that she has gone into another room and closed the door.... Spiritual love is not conscious of visible separation.[12]

How is this continuing communion maintained? There is, first, a false turning which some have found attractive, but which the Orthodox tradition utterly rejects. Communion between the living and the dead is *not* to be maintained through spiritualism and necromancy. There can be no place within true Christianity for any techniques seeking to communicate with the dead through mediums, ouija boards and the like. Indeed, such practices are highly dangerous, often exposing those who indulge in them to invasion by demonic forces. Spiritualism is also the expression of an illegitimate curiosity, much in the manner of one trying to look through the key-hole of a closed door ('What the butler saw...'). As Fr Alexander Elchaninov (1881–1934) puts it, 'We must humbly admit the existence of a Mystery, and not try to slip round by the backstairs to eavesdrop.'[13]

As we learn from the lives of the saints, there are certainly occasions when the dead communicate directly with the living, either in dreams or in waking visions. But we on our side are not to attempt to force such contacts. Any contrivance aimed at manipulating the dead is surely abhorrent to the Christian conscience. The fellowship between us and them is not on the psychic but on the spiritual level, and the place of our meeting is not the *séance*-parlour but the eucharistic table. The only legitimate foundation for our fellowship with the dead is communion in prayer, above all at the celebration of the Divine Liturgy. We pray for them, and at the same time we are confident they are praying for us: and it is through this mutual intercession that we and they are joined, across the boundary of death, in a firm and unbroken bond of unity.

Prayer for the dead is not seen by Orthodox Christians as an optional extra, but it is an accepted and unvarying feature in all our daily worship. Here are some of the prayers that we say:

> O thou who with wisdom profound orderest all things in thy love for mankind, who bestowest on all, O only Creator, that which is best for each: give rest, O Lord, to the souls of thy servants, for they have set their hope in thee, our Maker and Creator and our God.

> Give rest, O Lord, to the souls of thy servants, where there is no pain, no sorrow, no sighing, but life without end.

> May Christ give you rest in the land of the living, and open for you the gates of paradise; may he receive you as a citizen of the Kingdom, and grant you forgiveness of your sins: for you were his friend.

Yet some of the prayers strike a more sombre note, reminding us of the possibility of an eternal separation from God:

> From the ever-burning fire, from the darkness without light, from the gnashing of teeth and the worm that torments without ceasing, from every punishment, deliver, O our Saviour, all who have died in faith.

To this intercession for the dead no rigid bounds can be set. For whom do we pray? Strictly interpreted, the Orthodox rules allow prayers by name, in public liturgical worship, only for those who have died in the visible communion of the Church. But there are occasions when our prayers are far more wide-ranging. At Vespers on the Sunday of Pentecost, prayers are said even for those in hell:

> On this final and saving festival thou art pleased to accept intercessory propitiation for those imprisoned in hell, affording us great hopes that thou wilt send down relaxation and refreshment to all held fast in bondage....[14]

What, is the doctrinal basis for this constantly repeated prayer for the dead? How can it be theologically justified? To this the answer is extremely straightforward. The basis is our solidarity in mutual love. We pray for the dead because we love them. Archbishop William Temple calls such prayer the 'ministry of love', and he states in words that any Orthodox Christian would be happy to make his own: 'We do not pray for them because God will otherwise neglect them. We pray for them because we know that He loves and cares for them, and we claim the privilege of uniting our love for them with God's.'[15] To refuse to pray for them is, Dr. Pusey says, so cold a thought, so contrary to love, that it must needs, on that ground alone, be false.[16]

No further explanation or defence of prayer for the departed is necessary or, indeed, possible. Such prayer is simply the spontaneous expression of our love for each other. Here on earth we pray for others; should we not continue to pray for them after their death? Have they ceased to exist, that we should cease to make intercession for them? Whether alive or dead, we are all members of the same family; and so, whether alive or dead, we intercede for each other. In the risen Christ there is no separation between the dead and the living; in Fr Makary's words, 'We are all alive in him, for in him there is no death.' Physical death cannot sever the bonds of mutual love and mutual prayer that unite us all to one another in a single Body.

Of course we do not understand exactly *how* such prayer benefits the departed. Yet equally, when we intercede for people still alive, we cannot explain how this intercession assists them. We know from our personal experience that prayer for others *is* effective, and so we continue to practise it. But, whether offered for the living or for the dead, such prayer works in a way that remains mysterious. We are unable to fathom the precise interaction between the act of prayer, the free will of the other person, and God's grace and foreknowledge. When we pray for the departed, it is enough for us to know that they are still growing in their love for God, and so need our support. Let us leave the rest to God.

If we truly believe that we enjoy an unbroken and continuing communion with the dead, then we shall take care to speak of them so far as possible in the present tense, not the past. We shall not say, 'We loved each other', 'She was so very dear to me', 'We were so happy together,' We shall say, 'We *still* love each other – now more than before', 'She *is* as dear to me as ever', 'We *are* so happy together.' There is a Russian lady in the Orthodox community at Oxford who strongly objects to being called a widow. Although her husband died many years ago, she insists: 'I am his wife, not his widow.' She is right.

If we learn to speak of the dead in this way, using the present tense and not the past, this can help with a particular problem that sometimes causes people anguish. All too easily it can happen that we postpone seeking a reconciliation with someone whom we have alienated, and death intervenes before we have forgiven each other. In bitter remorse we are tempted to say to ourselves: 'Too late, too late, the chance has gone for ever; there is nothing more to be done.' But we are altogether mistaken, for it is *not* too late. On the contrary, we can go home this very day, and in our evening prayers we can speak directly to the dead friend from whom we were estranged. Using the same words that we would employ if they were still alive and we were meeting them face to face, we can ask their forgiveness and reaffirm our love. And from that very moment our mutual relationship will be changed. Although we do not see their face or hear their response, although we have not the slightest idea how our words reach them, yet we know in our hearts that we and they have together made a fresh start. It is never too late to begin again.

A HUNDRED TIMES FINER AND MORE SUBTIL...

There remains a question that in our present state of knowledge is unanswerable, and yet it is often asked. We have said that the human person was originally created by God as an undivided unity of body and soul and that we look, beyond the separation of the two at bodily death, to their ultimate reunification on the Last Day. A holistic anthropology commits us to believing, not merely in the immortality of the soul, but in the resurrection of the body. Since the body is an integral part of the total human person, any immortality that is to be fully personal must needs involve body as well as soul. What, in that case, is the relationship between our present body and our resurrection body in the age to come? At the resurrection, shall we have the same body as we do now, or will it be a new body?

Perhaps the best response is to say: It will be the same body, and yet not the same. Christians sometimes understand the bodily resurrection in a crude and narrow sense. They imagine that the material elements constituting each body, which have been dissolved and scattered at death, will be somehow gathered together once more at the Last Day, so that the reconstituted body contains exactly the same minute fragments of matter as it had before. But those who affirm a continuity between our present body and our body on the Last Day are not necessarily committed to such a literal-minded view as this. St Gregory of Nyssa, for example, in his works *On the Creation of the Human Person* and *On the Soul and Resurrection*, suggests a more discriminating and imaginative approach. The soul, he maintains, imparts to the body a distinctive *eidos* or form, marking the body with its own special imprint or seal, although in this instance the seal is imposed not from the outside but from within. It is by virtue of this imprint that the body of each person expresses that person's character or inner spiritual state. During the course of our earthly life, the physical constituents making up our body change many times over; yet because the form or seal imprinted by the soul possesses an unbroken continuity throughout all these physical changes, our body may truly be said to remain the same. There is a genuine bodily continuity, because there is a continuity in the form imparted by the soul. As C. S. Lewis puts it, 'My form remains one, though the matter in it changes continually. I am, in that respect, like a curve in a waterfall.'[17]

At the final resurrection, Gregory continues, what will happen is that the soul will imprint upon our risen body the same seal or form as it possessed previously during this present life. There is no need for the identical fragments to be reassembled. It is sufficient that there should be the same seal, and this will be enough to ensure that it is the same body. Between our present and our resurrection body there will indeed be a true continuity, yet there is no need to interpret this continuity in naïvely materialistic fashion.

Nevertheless, although it will in this way be the same body as previously, it will also be different. In St Paul's words, 'It is sown a physical [or natural (*psychikon*)] body, it is raised a spiritual body' (1 Cor 15:44). 'Spiritual' here is not to be taken to signify 'non-material'. The resurrection body will still be a material body, but it will at the same time be transformed by the power and glory of the Spirit, and so released from all the limitations of materiality such as we know it at this present moment. As things now are, we experience the material world and our own material bodies solely in a fallen state, and it lies largely beyond the power of our imagination to conceive the characteristics that matter will possess in an unfallen world.

We can only guess dimly at the transparence and vivacity, at the lightness and sensitivity, with which our resurrection body, at once material and yet spiritual, will be endued in the age to come. In the words of St Ephrem the Syrian (d. 373):

> Consider the man in whom there dwelt a legion of all kinds of devils [Mark 5:9]: they were there though they were not recognized, for their army is of stuff finer and more subtil than the soul itself. That whole army dwelt in a single body.
>
> A hundred times finer and more subtil is the body of the just when they are risen, at the resurrection: it resembles a thought that is able, if it wills, to stretch out and expand, or, should it wish, to contract and shrink: if it shrinks, it is somewhere; if it expands, it is everywhere.
>
> The spiritual beings [in paradise] . . . are so refined in substance that even thoughts cannot touch them![18]

That is perhaps as good a description of the resurrection glory as we can expect to find. Let us leave the rest to silence. 'What we will be has not yet been revealed' (1 John 3:2).

YOU ARE THE MUSIC...

Two weeks before his death, Ralph Vaughan Williams was asked what the future life meant to him. 'Music,' he said, 'music. But in the next world I shan't be doing music, with all the striving and disappointments. I shall be being it.'[19]

'You are the music while the music lasts', says T. S. Eliot. And in heaven the music lasts for ever.

Notes

1. Nicholas Arseniev, *Russian Piety* (London, 1964) p. 90
2. 'On Death', *Sobornost* 1:2 (1979) p. 8
3. *Mystic Treatises by Isaac of Nineveh*, tr. A. J. Wensinck (Amsterdam, 1923) p. 309; *The Ascetical Homilies of Saint Isaac the Syrian*, tr. Dana Miller (Holy Transfiguration Monastery, Boston, 1984) p. 315 (translation modified).
4. In what follows, I am indebted to the talk of Fr John Dalrymple, 'Dying before death', given in Edinburgh to the Fellowship of St Andres: see *The Experience of Death*, ed. Donald Reid (Edinburgh, 1985) pp. 1–8.
5. Barbara Green and Victor Gollancz, *God of a Hundred Names* (London, 1962) p. 19.
6. For the full text, see Vladimir Lossky, *The Mystical Theology of the Eastern Church* (London, 1957) pp. 247–9.
7. *Modern Man in Search of a Soul* (Ark Paperbacks, London, 1984) p. 253.
8. Dylan Thomas, *Collected Poems* (London 1952) p. 116.
9. *The Lenten Triodion*, tr. Mother Mary and Archimandrite Kallistos Ware (London, 1978) p. 128.
10. Ibid.
11. *Creative Suffering* (London, 1940) p. 44.
12. In S. Tyszkiewicz and T. Belpaire, *Ecrits d'Escètes Russes* (Namur, 1957) p. 104.
13. *The Diary of a Russian Priest* (London, 1967) p. 43.
14. *The Service of the Blessing of the Waters on the Epiphany; The Service of Kneeling for Whitsunday* (Williams & Norgate: London, 1917) p. 79 (translation modified).
15. Quoted in *Prayer and the Departed: A Report of the Archbishop's Commission on Christian Doctrine* (London, 1971) p. 90.
16. Op. cit., p. 85.
17. *Miracles: A Preliminary Study* (London, 1947) p. 180
18. Sebastian Brock, *The Harp of the Spirit: Eighteen Poems of Saint Ephrem* (Studies Supplementary to *Sobornost* No. 4: 2nd edn, London, 1983) p. 23–4.
19. D. J. Enright, *The Oxford Book of Death* (Oxford, 1983) p. 332.

3

The Christian Heaven
DAVID BROWN

CONTEMPORARY DOUBTS

One recent survey of religious belief in Europe found that while three-quarters of the general population still believe in God less than half could subscribe to a belief in heaven. A similar pattern emerges among regular churchgoers. One poll discovered that in a typical Anglican congregation one would be lucky to scrape a bare majority who still believed in life after death, still fewer prepared to employ the credal affirmation of resurrection of the body. Is heaven then, as it were, going the same way as hell? If so, there is this interesting difference: whereas in the nineteenth century there was a strong rearguard action (e.g. the dismissal of F. D. Maurice in 1853 from his chair at King's College, London), in the late twentieth century heaven seems just sleepily to be passing from faith's horizon. Why, and is it right that it should do so? In what follows I shall seek to argue that something very like the traditional doctrine continues to remain defensible. But the only plausible form of defence is one which takes seriously the objections and doubts thrown up by the modern world, and so that is where we must begin.

Single cause explanations are seldom right, and this is no exception. An important factor within Christianity is undoubtedly embarrassment at the way in which the doctrine was used in the past to turn the believer away from this-worldly concerns, and thus from social or political involvement. Added to this has come the realisation of a very different pattern of hope within the New Testament itself, through the rediscovery of the eschatological character of so much of its teaching, that is to say, hope for a radical transformation of *this* world and the eventual emergence under God at the *eschaton* (the end) of a new heaven and a new earth. Whereas theologians of earlier generations such as Harnack or Bultmann responded to these eschatological elements either by denying their centrality (Harnack) or by insisting upon their demythologisation (Bultmann), much contemporary theology takes such this-worldly hopes as absolutely central to the Christian message. So we find today's most influential Protestant theologian, Jurgen Moltmann, asking: 'But is there any way of talking about the heaven of glory except in terms of a visionary future of a new earth?', and his answer is neatly encapsulated in the formula: 'We call the determined side of this system "earth", the undetermined side "heaven".'[1] In other words, for Moltmann heaven is the open future for this world that becomes possible through God's grace.

Contemporary theology may thus be seen as reinforcing popular retreat from an other-worldly hope. In some respects this must undoubtedly be seen as a benefit. Most religions (Christianity included) are concerned to address the whole person and so any attempt to use a doctrine to exclude key aspects of our existence can only be regarded as a distortion. Indeed one cannot but be encouraged by the transformation effected through such ideas by Liberation theology and the 'base ecclesial communities' that have sprung up all over Latin America in consequence, with the traditional message of compensation in the next life for passive acceptance of suffering in this replaced by a present consciousness of the individual's intrinsic worth and dignity and a real hope for transformation of their present lot.

None the less, has the corrective not gone too far? In so far as any notion of survival of death is retained, it now seems postponed to some distant eschatological prospect, when God will create a new heaven and a new earth. But is this new heaven not just as problematic as the traditional, other-worldly one? While it no longer constitutes a flight from this-worldly issues, the discontinuity remains just as troubling. For what reason has the present 'me' to take an interest in a very different 'me' in a radically different world, possibly millions of years distant, especially as in the interim either nothing of me survives or what does 'sleeps'? Faced with such difficulties it is perhaps not surprising that theologians have failed to substitute in the popular imagination for the traditional belief this vision of the resurrection of the body in some distant eschatologically renewed order. Instead, the Church seems to have lost out in both directions, with those in the pew believing in neither a distant future reality nor a contemporaneous one. What this suggests to me is that what is really required is not the abandoning of heaven as another, different world, but rather the establishment of some integral relation with our own, one in which legitimate social and political aspirations are brought to fruition and not denied.

A second key factor in heaven's demise has undoubtedly been a general decline in belief in the immaterial aspect of ourselves. It is one thing for a very different entity from ourselves like God to inhabit such a world, but what sense does it make when we think of physical beings like ourselves? Has modern science not made us all acutely conscious of the dependence of mind upon brain? That is indeed so, and the theory of evolution would seem to leave no place for a special creation of souls. Our human identity has emerged naturally out of the material order.

But, though commonly thought to require this, such an admission need not be synonymous with assuming there to be no other reality than this present material order. Admittedly, earlier this century, discussion still tended to solidify into two opposed camps, with one side being reductionist materialists and the other insistent upon two distinct substances or entities in human beings, a body and a soul. Now, however, while a few scientists (e.g. Sir John Eccles) and some philosophers of religion (e.g. H.D. Lewis, Richard Swinburne) continue to support the latter view, there is in fact emerging a general consensus among believer and non-believer alike, which advocates a mediating position. According to this, while the mind or soul is incapable of existence independent of the body, it is none the less not reducible to, or explicable purely in terms of, the material. One technical way of drawing this distinction commonly employed is to say that dual aspect (mental/physical) has replaced dualism (soul and body) as two distinct entities).

In this respect, modern thought has in fact moved much closer to the biblical picture which sees human beings as essentially psychosomatic unities, that is, integrated unities of body (*soma*) and soul (*psyche*). It is often wrongly assumed that the immortality of the soul is a fundamental element of Christian doctrine, but this is in fact a Greek rather than a biblical belief. The issue was for long debated and even within the Roman communion not formally required until the fifth Lateran Council in 1513. Without dualism the belief can no longer be defended (there is no entity which will naturally survive death), but that does nothing to undermine the biblical picture, which speaks rather of a resurrection of the body brought about by divine grace. Naturally, we disintegrate into dust and ashes, but God has the power to reconstitute us, if he so desires.

In the history of the Christian tradition this has often been understood very literally; hence opposition in the past to cremation. But Paul's image in 1 Corinthians, 15 of seed transformed into wheat suggests something rather different. Karl Rahner, the most influential Roman Catholic theologian this century, has made an impressive attempt to reconcile Catholic dogma with our present awareness of the soul's dependency upon the material. The traditional picture envisaged a period of the soul existing on its own before being reunited with its body. Instead, Rahner suggests that at death the soul immediately enters into a relation with the world as a whole ('it becomes open towards the "all"'), the world thus in some sense functioning as the soul's body.[2]

However, I find it hard to comprehend what could be meant by such a shared body, and so would prefer to think of individual bodies. But this emphatically does not mean that they therefore occupy the same space and time as ourselves. To say that we need matter to exist is not to say that we need the same matter or even the same type of matter. Admittedly this is a crude analogy, but it may help to think of our minds as somewhat like the non-physical aspect of computer programs: just as these are compatible with radically different kinds of computer hardware, so the software that is our mind will be able to operate within a very different piece of hardware in the next life. Indeed, might not current scientific speculation about parallel universes be used to suggest the possibility of heaven running alongside our own universe, with its own distinct matter and time?

But almost certainly for most people the strongest objection lies not in 'pie in the sky' nor in the inconceivability of immaterial existence, but in the difficulty of making any sense of the notion of a heavenly existence. The philosopher Bernard Williams refers us to Janáček's opera *The Makropoulos Case* which tells the story of a woman granted an elixir of life which allows her to remain the same age (42) for ever. Though free from all pain, life after a few centuries has become so unchallenging and boring that she decides to cease to take the elixir, and so dies.[3]

In a more popular form that same objection of boredom

reemerges with the idea of heaven being a continuous hymn of praise. For the Puritan seventeenth century divine, Richard Baxter, heaven was exactly that, but significantly Baxter loved hymn-singing! But for most of us heaven would need to comprise much more than that if the prospect of such a future existence is to engage our interest. That is no doubt why the Victorians went to such lengths in picturing its details, the famous Baptist preacher Spurgeon, for instance, advocating work as well as praise and the Anglican, Charles Kingsley, even including sexual love (though only in a private letter to his wife Fanny).

But those very details also have their dangers, as the 1868 bestseller *The Gates Ajar* (by E. S. Phelps) reveals all too clearly: heaven has become merely an extension of the Victorian home and its values. But simply projecting this world onto the next was by no means a temptation unique to the Victorians. While in the sixteenth century Luther and Calvin reflect the egalitarian desires of that age and make everyone equal in heaven, to the Middle Ages with their much less fluid society this seemed inconceivable, and so a rigid hierarchy is transposed to heaven. Thus Hildegaard of Bingen dresses her saints in silk and white shoes while astonishingly *Piers Plowman* makes the penitent thief eat his food off the floor.[4]

So clearly, in answering this difficulty, a delicate balance will be necessary. On the one hand, something must be said to make life in heaven conceivable, while on the other it must not become a mere projection of what our own society happens to value (but perhaps few others in the history of humankind). That said, we may now turn to some positive characterisation.

HEAVEN ABOVE US

A brief reminder of the way in which Christian teaching on the subject has developed would seem apposite. Within the New Testament itself, as we have already noted, resurrection is seen as a gift of God and not a right; even of Christ himself it is said that he was raised from the dead rather than that he rose of his own accord. In his case his new life clearly began long before the end of the age, and much the same seems to be implied for a number of others (those who come out of their tombs in Matthew's Gospel – Matt. 27:52–3; the penitent thief in Luke – 23:43; and perhaps Paul himself with his expression of longing to be immediately with his Lord – Phil. 1:23). But against that must be set the many passages which speak of a more distant eschatological hope with the dead 'sleeping' meantime (e.g. 1 Thess. 4:14, etc.). To us the two perspectives seem in marked opposition to one another, but for the Bible's early readers this would not have appeared so. For the early Church's belief in the imminence of the end of the world meant that the second option constituted only a short postponement, and so the difference cannot have been seen as particularly significant.

However, as such hopes receded, inevitably the Church had to wrestle with what had now become a much more significant choice, though a dogmatic definition was only finally given in Pope Benedict XII's Bull *Benedictus Deus* of 1336. According to this the fate of individuals (known as the particular judgment) is determined immediately upon death (heaven, hell, or purgatory), though they must await the creation of a new earth (the general judgment) before the great mass of them can be restored to bodily existence, there currently only being a few privileged exceptions such as Jesus and his Mother. Purgatory, though not a biblical doctrine, arose in response to the question of how sinners could be suitably prepared for the purity of God's presence in heaven. The doctrine thus had nothing to do with the notion of a second chance, but rather with purifying the individual from any evil that may still lie engrained within them. Such, at any rate, is Augustine's conception. But by the Middle Ages the notion had degenerated into a system of compensatory punishments, which was why the Reformers rejected the doctrine with such vehemence, as it seemed to detract from the unique and complete forgiveness offered by Christ through the Cross.[5]

In thinking how we might better approach the issue in today's world, it would seem to me that, paradoxically, the most effective guarantee for ensuring that heaven is restored to its proper place in the scheme of things is to begin by taking this life and its significance with the utmost seriousness. Indeed, so far from being regarded as an escape from this world, heaven should be seen as a viable possibility only when built upon the identity we have acquired in this life. Heaven would quickly become hell unless there is some match between the character we have formed in this life and the sort of life we might expect to lead in the next. Initially that might seem to argue for making our lives now conform to our vision of heaven but that really is to put the cart before the horse. The Christian revelation offers very few details about the character of heaven but a considerable quantity of advice regarding what is required of us in this life. So we may reasonably infer that it is by taking that message seriously that we prepare ourselves for heaven, a message concerned both with our personal transformation and that of society as a whole, in short, with every aspect of our existence.

Death is thus arguably more important for the believer than the non-believer, not less.[6] Thus, while for the latter it merely marks the end of an existence that may well have been lived without any sense of direction, for the believer death is what should shape life, not in the sense of fearing its approach but acknowledging a responsibility, that a finite span of years has been given us in which to shape our characters through God's grace after the pattern of Christ. That is why, for me at least, notions of purgatory as a second chance make little sense, robbing as they do the present life of its full significance. This is not to say that only Christians will be saved. Whether one thinks of Paul's appeal to conscience (Romans 2:15), the patristic notion of 'baptism by desire' or a contemporary version like Rahner's 'anonymous Christian', it has always been the case throughout Christian history that alternatives to an explicit response have been acknowledged and accepted.

But if the failure to take this life seriously is refuted, what of the related point, that what one is then offered subsequently is still 'pie in the sky', unmitigated and unrealistic optimism? And can this really be maintained in the face of a doctrine like purgatory, especially once it is divested once more of its medieval accretions? The essential point is not punishment but purgation, the purifying of ourselves for heaven, and it takes but a moment's reflection to realise what a painful process that must be. So much of our lives are lived in self-deception, a pretence of our own goodness and a reluctance to face the hurt and damage which we inflict on others. Yet clearly with all such lumber from the past we must properly come to terms, before we can enter the pure and holy presence of God. Little wonder then that T. S. Eliot sums up the Christian message in the famous but shivering phrase: 'We only live, only suspire / Consumed by either fire or fire'.[7]

Entry into heaven means that moral perfection has been achieved, but that should not be taken to imply the end of all exploration and development. Bernard Williams had a legitimate point in objecting that boredom would quickly set in for essentially temporal beings like ourselves, unless we had some aims still to be realised. In the past some theologians have tried to circumvent the problem by suggesting that we enter a new form of timeless existence, but is is hard to see what this could mean for creatures with bodies. For bodies seem to imply movement and change. But already in the fourth century an alternative solution has been found, with Gregory of Nyssa's suggestion that our understanding of God will never reach completion. There will always be fresh aspects to comprehend, fresh vistas to see, as finite beings try in vain to grasp infinity.

But such exploration will be by no means confined to the infinite riches of God. The Christian Bible closes with a vision of heaven as a city, of people in complex interrelations with one another. Jesus in his teaching had already pronounced against any preferential significance for family relations in heaven (Mark 12:25), and in this he is followed by the great weight of the Christian tradition, for instance Augustine, Aquinas, Luther and Calvin. It is only in modern times that heaven became thoroughly domesticated, and thereby lost its credibility. For surely we must see heaven as an enlargement, as a perfecting, of our love, not simply as a reinforcement of its present limited concerns. What was a necessity on earth ceases to be so in heaven, where the inevitable restrictions of time and opportunity no longer apply.

Such exploration may be extended even further. For heaven is traditionally supposed to contain many other non-human beings apart from God, namely the angels. Here contemporary disbelief is perhaps at its greatest, and it is interesting to speculate why. Certainly if one believes in God, there can be no serious difficulty in believing that other unembodied beings exist. My suspicion is that the decline in belief in angels is due to two principal causes, twentieth century arrogance and lack of imagination: arrogance because, contrary to what is commonly claimed, human beings are now placed more at the centre of our world than was ever the case in the Middle Ages and that despite their belief in the earth as the centre of the universe, since weighed against that was their conviction of a hierarchy of beings all superior to man;· lack of imagination because previous generations had an imaginative grasp of symbolic language which seems to have been lost by our own generation.

Certainly it seems odd that when nature teems with numerous forms of life inferior to our own we should none the less predicate an absolute blank between ourselves and God. Is Aquinas not much more impressive when he talks of God being 'at the head of an immense hierarchy of beings, like an abundant source which flows from the summit of a mountain, divided into many streams' (by convention nine levels of angelic being were distinguished)? But one suspects that the symbolic problem runs deeper. Religion is of course full of symbolism, but it would be interesting to discover how many, even among believers, mistake the image for the reality, and suppose, for instance, that in some sense angels have wings. Of course, if they are to make themselves known to human beings whether on earth or in heaven they would need to assume some temporary appearance, but that does not mean that that appearance in any sense constitutes their real being. In the Bible wings commonly indicate their character as divine messengers (*angelos* being the Greek for 'messenger'), but arguably the symbolism is even more basic than that. As Plato long ago remarked, a wing suggests something naturally light and so something naturally heavenly (what is light in weight rises). Moreover, as if to emphasise the unreality of the image, in Christian art, as the art critic Ruskin observed, the wing was attached at the shoulder, an anatomical impossibility. But, whatever the point of the symbolism, there can be no doubt about the key heavenly role given to them in the Bible. Over two hundred and eighty times God is described as 'Lord of hosts'. God thus emerges as a naturally social being. Heaven is already a city even before it comes to be populated by human beings.

Yet the symbolism runs still deeper than this. For heaven itself is of course a symbol. Were any readers deceived by my talk of 'heaven above'? If so, they need to be reminded of what the symbolism of heaven is all about, imagery so basic to religion that in many languages the word for 'God' is itself derived from heaven. The obvious connection is that the image of heaven suggests something enormously exalted above us (as high as the sky). The imagery of heaven is there to remind us of the exalted destiny to which God calls us, but of course that does not mean that this spiritual heaven is literally above us. As my earlier analogy with scientific talk of parallel universes was meant to imply, this heaven is directly alongside us. It is with the implications of that claim that I wish to conclude this discussion.

HEAVEN WITH US

One commonly made contrast between liturgies of the western and eastern Church is that, whereas the former focus on the crucifixion, the latter have the resurrection at their heart. The result has been that, whereas western eucharistic imagery has been of the crucified Christ coming down to 'tabernacle' with us once more, Orthodoxy has seen the liturgy as a foretaste of heaven, as a matter of the believer being caught up into its worship. Put that starkly, the contrast is certainly exaggerated. Western medieval liturgies for instance include the request: 'We beseech thee, Almighty God, that Thou wouldst command these offerings to be borne by the hands of thy holy angel unto thine altar on high' (retained in Eucharist Prayer I of the modern Roman Mass).

None the less, the contrast contains some truth, and one finds implicit acknowledgement of this in the modern Alternative Service Book of the Church of England, which is markedly less cross-centred than Cranmer's Prayer Book. But the change of emphasis is still a long way from the profound Orthodox consciousness of, as Dostoevsky puts it, 'touching other worlds' through the liturgy. The Orthodox theologian Alexander Schmemann expresses it thus: 'The early Christians realised that in order to become the temple of the Holy Spirit they must ascend to heaven where Christ has ascended. They realised also that this ascension was the very condition of their mission in the world . . . For there – in heaven – they were immersed in the new life of the Kingdom; and when after this "liturgy of ascension", they returned into the world, their faces reflected the light, the "joy and the peace" of that Kingdom.' Archimandrite Vasileios who has done so much to revitalise monastic life on Mount Athos makes a similar point: 'When the believer is within the Divine Liturgy, he has gone beyond the world of corruption. He lives and dances for joy, extended beyond the threat of time, outside the prison of space . . . When man comes down from the mountain of his experience of the Liturgy . . . he goes about his business in the created world in a different way. . . . He is a dynamic presence, like a grain of mustard seed: a witness to the Kingdom.'[8]

To think in this way would certainly give the believer an improved consciousness of the reality and importance of heaven. Even so, such up–down imagery has its limitations, suggesting as it does not only heaven's distance but also perhaps that heaven is only accessible through the Church's worship. That is why I prefer the analogy of parallel universes, of heaven not so much above us as alongside, all about us. Newman tried to recapture that sense in his account of angels: 'Every breath of air and ray of light and heat, every beautiful prospect, is, as it were, the skirts of their garments, the waving of the robes of those whose faces see God in heaven.'[9] From the context it is clear that he wants to make them agents in the world, additional to the natural causes detected by the scientist. But such a role is both superfluous and unnecessary. His beautiful image may be allowed to point us in a much more helpful direction.

Traditional Christian theology speaks not just of a Church 'militant here in earth' but also of the Church expectant and the Church triumphant. In speaking thus it denotes a community that knows no borders of death, all united in a common love: 'My God, I love thee; not because / I hope for heaven thereby / . . . . But as thyself hast loved me, / O ever-loving Lord.' Within such a community what could be more natural than mutual concern, and with that, the most obvious way in which Christian concern expresses itself, mutual prayer? The Christian on earth will thus naturally seek the prayers of the Church triumphant in heaven, just as it will be natural for the living to pray for the newly dead (the Church expectant) as they embark upon their slow and painful process of self-discovery.

That surely is a vision which could excite and inspire once more the human imagination, a vision of living and dead united in a common identity and purpose. But not just human society and higher levels of existence such as angels; for Christianity asserts that the lower levels too will be given some fresh significance in a transformed order. Scientists tell us that our present universe is running down (fortunately for us, very slowly). Whether the new heaven and new earth will naturally supervene when this finally happens or be brought about as a result of some cataclysmic event, it is idle to speculate. What we can say is that such future value for the created order provides us with additional reason to treat its present reality with proper respect.

But I have, I hope not unjustly, ignored that larger vision, because it seems to me that the ultimate plausibility of a doctrine of heaven stands or falls not with the final destiny of the world which may well be millions of years distant but with whether we can make sense of heaven as an already existing, present reality. By a happy accident (Cranmer translated the Latin by an ambiguous English term), whereas Roman and Orthodox Prefaces to the Sanctus ('Holy, holy, holy . . .) speak only of us joining the angelic host in its worship, Cranmer's gift to Anglican liturgies was that marvellous phrase: 'with angels, and archangels and the whole company of heaven'. Might we not then hear 'and with the whole company of heaven' with fresh ears? It really is the entire company of the redeemed, living and dead, worshipping together the God to whom we owe everything: living of course in a shared expectation of the completion of all things at the end of the world, but also supremely confident in the present reality of heaven with its angels and 'saints' all about us.

Notes

1. J. Moltmann, *God in Creation* (London: SCM, 1985) pp. 170 and 163.
2. K. Rahner, *On the Theology of Death* (New York: Herdes & Herdes, 1971) p. 31. An excellent, basic introduction to Rahner's ideas is to be found in M. Murphy, *New Images of the Last Things* (New York: Paulist Press, 1988).
3. B. Williams, 'The Makropoulos Case', in *Problems of the Self* (Cambridge: Cambridge University Press, 1971) pp. 82–100.
4. W. Langland, *Piers Plowman*, XII.202–5. C. McDannell and B. Lang provide a fascinating survey of the great range of images which have been used to depict heaven in *Heaven: A History* (New Haven, Conn.: Yale University Press, 1988).
5. The gradual development of notions of purgatory is traced in J. Le Goff, *The Birth of Purgatory* (London: Scolar Press, 1981).
6. S. Tugwell, *Human Immortality and the Redemption of Death* (London: DLT, 1990) is also concerned to assert the significance of death, though from a rather different angle.
7. T. S. Eliot, 'Little Gidding', IV, in *Four Quartets*.
8. A. Schmemann, *The World as Sacrament* (London: DLT, 1966) p. 32; Archimandrite Vasileios, *Hymn of Entry* (New York, 1984) p. 79.
9. J. H. Newman, *Parochial and Plain Sermons*, II.29.

4
The Jewish Doctrine of Hell
DAN COHN-SHERBOK

In a wide variety of introductions to the Jewish religion, Jewish apologists maintain that there is no explicit Jewish doctrine of the afterlife. Chaim Pearl and Reuben S. Brookes, for example, in *A Guide to Jewish Knowledge*, argue that in regard to life after death, 'Judaism adopted a stand of its own.... Having provided the belief in the deathlessness of the soul, the authoritative teaching of Judaism warns us against useless speculation about the details of the afterlife.' According to these writers, Judaism is concerned with earthly existence: 'The Jewish faith teaches us to concentrate all our efforts and energy in conducting ourselves as children of God in this world, here and now.'

Similarly, in his *Commentary to the Prayer Book*, the late Chief Rabbi Dr J. H. Hertz argues that 'our most authoritative religious guides ... proclaim that no eye hath seen, nor can mortal fathom, what awaiteth us in the Hereafter, but that even the tarnished souls wil not be forever denied spiritual bliss. Judaism rejects the doctrine of eternal damnation'.

More recently, Rabbi Abba Hillel Silver writes that 'eternal punishment for the wicked finds no official acceptance in Judaism'. Again, Rabbi David de Sola Pool asserts that 'not infrequently the Jew has thought and spoken of a physical heaven or hell awaiting one after death, but Classical Judaism more generally conceives of them not as places but as abstract states of existence'. In a similar vein, H. Wouk in *This is My God* writes that the idea of Hell in Judaism is 'a parable. We do not know where it is, or what it is like, or what precisely the parable implies'.

The purpose of this chapter is to dispose of this incorrect view of the Jewish attitude to the afterlife. Throughout the formative period of rabbinic Judaism, which laid the groundwork for mainstream Judaism, speculation about life after death engaged Jewish thinkers with the same force as questions concerning the minutiae of the Law, and their opinions are recorded in the Talmud and various Midrashim. It is there that an elaborate doctrine of eternal punishment is explicitly formulated.

THE BIBLICAL VIEW

Until long after the exile, the Jewish people shared the view of the entire ancient world that the dead continue to exist in a shadowy realm of the nether world where they live a dull, ghostly existence. According to K. Kohler, 'throughout the Biblical period no ethical idea yet permeated this conception, and no attempt was made to transform the nether world into a place of divine judgement, of recompense for the good and evil deeds accomplished on earth'. This was so because Biblical Judaism stressed the importance of attaining a complete and blissful life with God during earthly life; there was no need to transfer the purpose of existence to the hereafter. In the words of R. H. Charles, 'So long indeed as Yahweh's jurisdiction was conceived as limited to this life, a Yahwistic eschatology of the individual could not exist; but when at last Israel reached the great truth of monotheism, the way was prepared for the moralisation of the future no less than that of the present.' It was only then under social, economic and political oppression that pious Jews looked beyond their bitter disappointment with this world to a future beyond the grave when virtue would receive its due reward and vice its befitting punishment.

Thus, though there is no explicit reference to Hell in the Old Testament, a number of expressions are used to refer to the realm of the dead. In Psalms 28:1 and 88:5, *bor* refers to a pit. In Psalm 6:6 as well as in Job 28:22 and 30:23, *mavet* is used in a similar sense. In Psalm 22:16 the expression *afar mavet* refers to the dust of death; in Exodus 15:2 and Jonah 2:7 the earth (*eretz*) is described as swallowing up the dead, and in Ezekiel 31:14 the expression *eretz tachtit* refers to the nether parts of the earth where the dead dwell. Finally, the word *she'ol* is frequently used to refer to the dwelling of the dead in the netherworld.

In addition, the words *ge ben hinnom, ge hinnom* and *ge* are used to refer to a cursed valley associated with fire and death where, according to Jeremiah, children were sacrificed as burnt offerings to Moloch and Baal. In later rabbinic literature the word ordinarily used for 'Hell' (*Gehinnom*) is derived from these names.

Though these passages point to a Biblical conception of an afterlife, there is no indication of a clearly defined concept of Hell; it is only later in the Graeco-Roman world that such a concept began to take shape.

THE RABBINIC VIEW

When we turn to the writings of the rabbis, we find an extensive and detailed description of the name and creation of Hell, its nature and divisions, the punishments of its inhabitants, and deliverance from its torments.

1. The Name of Hell

In rabbinic sources the word ordinarily used for 'hell' is *Gehinnom*, originally the valley near Jerusalem where Moloch was worshipped, because of its biblical connection with the netherworld. This identification is reinforced by the rabbinic view that one of the three gates of Hell is located in Jerusalem.

2. The Creation of Hell

According to one rabbinic tradition God created Hell on the second day along with the firmament, fire, and the angels. For this reason, God could not say of this day as of the others that he 'saw that it was good'. In another rabbinic tradition, however, Hell is described as pre-existent, created two thousand years before heaven and earth.

3. The Purpose and Nature of Hell

When God resolved to create the world, the Torah (the Jewish tradition personified) was sceptical about the value of an earthly world because of the sinfulness of men. God, however, dispelled her doubts by assuring her that sinners would have the opportu-

The Jewish Doctrine of Hell

nity of mending their ways, and that Hell was created to punish those who would not repent.

The punishment of the wicked in Hell follows the Biblical principle of 'measure for measure' which is enunciated in the Mishnah: 'With that measure a man meets it shall be measured to him again. She bedecked herself for transgression – the Omnipresent brought her to shame; she began transgression with the thigh first and afterwards with the belly – therefore the thigh shall suffer first and afterwards the belly.' In general, fire was the punishment for sinners who committed incest, murder and idolatry or cursed their parents and teachers. Other sins which merit the punishments of hell are adultery, idolatry, pride, mockery, hypocrisy and anger as well as following the advice of one's wife, instructing an unworthy pupil and speaking in an unseemly fashion.

Through repentance one could escape the torments of Hell, but this was not the only way; the sages of the Talmud produced a list of exemptions which restricted the number of sinners condemned to punishment. Those, for example, who during their lives suffered from the harshness of grinding poverty, from painful and odious bowel diseases, from the persecution of the Romans or from a bad wife were excluded. In addition, giving charity to the poor, teaching Torah to the son of an ignoramus, visiting the sick, eating three meals on the Sabbath, and saying the *Shema* regularly and devoutly help protect one from the fires of Hell.

We know that Hell is exceedingly hot, because when God visited Abraham after he was circumcised, God bored a hole in Hell so that its heat might reach the earth, thereby preventing any wayfarer from venturing abroad on the highways and disturbing Abraham in his pain. In another midrash Isaac was alarmed by seeing Hell at the feet of Esau. Scarcely had he entered the house when its walls began to get hot because of the nearness of Hell which Esau brought with him. The rabbis also asserted that the springs of Tiberius are hot because its waters pass the gates of Hell.

Other sources portray the coldness of Hell. For example, the angels who guided Enoch through the realms of heaven told him that God had prepared a terrible place for sinners in the northern regions of the third heaven where there was fire as well as cold and ice on all sides.

According to one rabbinic source, fire is located in a southern chamber of Hell next to a cave of smoke. The wind blowing from this direction brings heat and sultriness; were it not for the winged angel which keeps the south wind back with his pinions, the world would be consumed. These fires of Hell are reflected in the evening twilight. According to the Babylonian Talmud, the sun passes paradise in the morning and Hell in the evening. Thus, just as dawn reflects the roses of paradise, so the evening twilight reflects the fires of Hell. In another passage God tells Elijah that the four phenomena (wind, earthquake, fire and a still small voice) represent the worlds through which man must pass; fire representing the tribunal in Hell. In another passage Hell is described, not as a place of light and fire, but dark with impenetrable gloom as thick as a coin.

According to the rabbis, the entry to Hell is through three gates (one in inhabited land, another in the wilderness, and a third at the bottom of the sea). The entrance is guarded over by a special angel, Dumah, who announces the arrival of newcomers to the netherworld. He takes the souls of the wicked and casts them down into the depths of Sheol. This is repeated every week at the close of the Sabbath, since during the day of rest the souls are released from their torment but must return as the Sabbath ends.

As to Hell itself, it is described as having seven divisions. In the Babylonian Talmud, R. Joshua b. Levi deduces them from Biblical quotations: *she'ol, abaddon, be'er shahat, bor sha'on, tit hayawen, zel mawet,* and *erez ha-tahtit*. This Talmudic concept of the seven-fold structure of Hell is greatly elaborated in midrashic literature. According to one source it requires 300 years to traverse the height or width or the depth of each division, and it would take 6300 years to go over a tract of land equal in extent to the seven divisions. Each of these seven divisions of Hell is in turn divided into seven subdivisions, and in each compartment there are seven rivers of fire, and seven of hail. The width of each is 1000 ells, its depth 1000, and its length 300; they flow from each other and are supervised by the Angels of Destruction. Besides, in each compartment there are 7000 caves, and in each cave there are 7000 crevices, and in every crevice there are 7000 scorpions. Every scorpion has 300 rings, and in every ring 7000 pouches of venom from which flow seven rivers of deadly poison. If a man handles it, he immediately bursts, every limb is torn from his body, his bowels are cleft, and he falls upon his face.

The fires of Hell are also described in detail. One devours and absorbs, another devours and does not absorb, the third absorbs and does not devour, the fourth neither devours nor absorbs, and the last devours fire itself. There are also coals in Hell which are as big as huge stones, the Dead Sea, hills and mountains, and there are rivers of pitch and sulphur flowing and seething like coals. According to later kabbalists, these seven compartments symbolise the seven-fold punishment referred to in Ezra 7:80–1.

In other passages, the divisions of Hell are mentioned in connection with their inhabitants. According to *Ma'aseh de Rabbi Joshua b. Levi*, Absolom is charged with the control of the ten heathen nations in the second division; in the fifth division, Ahab dwells under the supervision of the Angel Oriel; and in the sixth division Micah dwells under the guidance of the angel Hadriel and is the only one who is spared Hell's tortures.

4. The Tortures of Hell

Confinement to Hell is the result of disobeying God's Torah as is illustrated by the midrash concerning the evening visit of the soul to Hell before it is implanted in an individual. There it sees the Angels of Destruction smiting with fiery scourges; the sinners all the while crying out, but no mercy is shown to them. The angel guides the soul and then asks: 'Do you know who these are?' Unable to respond the soul listens as the angel continues: 'Those who are consumed with fire were created like you. When they were put into the world, they did not observe God's Torah and His commandments. Therefore they have come to this disgrace which you see them suffer. Know, your destiny is also to depart from the world. Be just, therefore, and not wicked, that you may gain the future world'.

The soul was not alone in being able to see Hell; a number of Biblical personages entered into its midst. Moses, for example, was guided through Hell by an angel, and his journey there gives us the most complete picture of its torments.

When Moses and the Angel of Hell entered Hell together, they saw men being tortured by the Angels of Destruction. Some sinners were suspended by their eyelids, some by their ears, some by their hands, and some by their tongues. In addition, women were suspended by their hair and their breasts by chains of fire. Such punishments were inflicted on the basis of the sins that were committed: those who hung by their eyes looked lustfully upon their neighbours' wives and possessions; those who hung by their ears listened to empty and vain speech and did not listen to the Torah; those who hung by their tongues spoke foolishly and slanderously; those who hung by their feet did not go to the synagogue; and those who hung by their hands robbed and murdered their neighbours. The women who hung by their hair and breasts uncovered them in the presence of young men in order to seduce them.

In another place called Alukah, Moses saw sinners suspended by their feet with their heads downward and their bodies covered with long black worms. These sinners were punished in this way because they swore falsely, profaned the Sabbath and the Holy Days, despised the sages, called their neighbours by unseemly nicknames, wronged the orphan and the widow, and bore false witness.

In another section Moses saw sinners prone on their faces with 2000 scorpions lashing, stinging, and tormenting them. Each of these scorpions had 70,000 heads, each head 70,000 mouths, each mouth 70,000 stings, and each sting 70,000 pouches of poison and venom. So great was the pain they inflicted that the eyes of the sinners melted in their sockets. These sinners were punished in this way because they caused other Jews to lose their money, were arrogant in the community, put their neighbours to shame in public, delivered their fellow Jews into the hands of the gentiles, denied the Torah, and maintained that God is not the creator of the world.

In another place called Ṭit ha-Yawen sinners stood in mud up to their navels while Angels of Destruction lashed them with fiery chains, and broke their teeth with fiery stones. These sinners were punished in this way because they ate forbidden food, lent their money at usury, wrote the name of God on amulets for Gentiles, used false weights, stole money from fellow Jews, ate on the Day of Atonement, and drank blood.

Finally, after seeing these tortures, Moses observed how sinners were burnt in the section of Hell called Abaddon. There one-half of their bodies were immersed in fire and the other half in snow while worms bred in their own flesh crawled over them and the Angels of Destruction beat them incessantly. By stealth these sinners took snow and put it in their armpits to relieve the pain inflicted by the scorching fire. These sinners were punished because they committed incest, murder, idolatry, called themselves gods, and cursed their parents and teachers.

The Jewish Doctrine of Hell

From this description it might appear that Hell is reserved for those Jews who have disobeyed the Mosaic law. Such exclusivism, however, was refuted throughout rabbinic literature. For example, in Midrash Proverbs R. Joshua explained that gentiles are doomed to eternal punishment unless they are righteous. Asked how a man can escape the judgement of Hell, he replied, 'Let him occupy himself with good deeds', and he pointed out that this applies to gentiles as well as Jews.

Of course, gentiles were not expected to keep all of Jewish law in order to escape Hell; they were simply required to keep the Noachide Laws, that is, those laws which Noah and his descendants took upon themselves. The violation of such laws was regarded by the rabbis as repugnant to fundamental human morality, quite apart from revelation, and was a basis for confinement to Hell. However, there was some disagreement as to the laws themselves. In Genesis Rabbah Noah 34:8, for example, we read that 'The sons of Noah were given seven commands: in respect of (1) idolatry, (2) incest, (3) shedding of blood, (4) profanation of the Name of God, (5) justice, (6) robbery, (7) cutting off flesh or limb from a living animal. R. Hanina said: Also about taking blood from a living animal. R. Elazar said: Also about "diverse kinds" and mixtures (Lev. 19:19). R. Simeon said: Also about witchcraft. R. Johanan b. Baroka said: Also about castration (of animals). R. Assi said: Everything forbidden in Deut. 18:10, 11 was also forbidden to the sons of Noah, because it says, "Whoever does these things is an abonimation unto the Lord".' Nevertheless, despite this disagreement, a gentile who lived a sinful life by violating the Noachide laws was destined to be punished in Hell, and conversely, if he lived in accordance with them, he could gain entry into the World to Come.

5. Deliverance from Hell

In the Jewish liturgy, the rite of *Hazcharath Neshamoth*, especially on the Day of Atonement, is used to save the dead from Hell and bring them to eternal life in God's presence. Though the custom of praying for departed souls is of ancient origin, this rite gained significance through the crusades and the severe persecutions during the seventeenth century and is still practised today. On the Day of Atonement in the Ashkenazi ritual immediately following the Torah reading, the *El Male Rahamim* is recited for the dead after the memorial prayers for relatives. The service concludes with the recital of *Av Harahamim*: 'May the merciful Father who dwells on high, in his infinite mercy, remember those saintly, upright and blameless souls', etc.

In this connection, the belief that atonement for the departed can be attained through their descendants is found frequently in rabbinic literature, as in *Targum Yerushalmi* I to Exodus 40:8 where we read that the merits of mothers save children from Gehenna. According to this passage, the curtain at the door of the Tent of Meeting is spread 'on account of the merits of the mothers of the world, which are spread at the entrance of Gehinnom so that the souls of the young children of the house of Israel should not go up thither'.

CONCLUSION

From this brief survey we can see that the doctrine of Hell is a fundamental tenet of rabbinic Judaism. Whatever horrible descriptions of Hell are to be found in Christian and Islamic sources, these can be matched by equally horrid accounts in Jewish sources. Thus, it is simply not true to say that Judaism rejects the doctrine of eternal damnation.

How has it happened that Jewish scholars have ignored the doctrine of Hell in Judaism? First, it should be noted that the views expressed in the aggadic sections of the Talmud and the Midrashim are not binding. All Jews are obliged to accept the Divine origin of the Law, but this is not so with regard to theological concepts and theories expounded by the rabbis. Thus, it is possible for a Jew to be religiously pious without accepting all the central beliefs of mainstream Judaism. Indeed, throughout Jewish history there has been widespread confusion as to what these beliefs are. In the first century BC, for example, the sage Hillel stated that the quintessence of Judaism could be formulated in a single principle: 'That which is hateful to you, do not do to your neighbour. This is the whole of the Law; all the rest is but commentary.' Similarly, in the second century AD, the Council of Lydda ruled that, under certain circumstances, the laws of the Torah may be transgressed in order to save one's life with the exception of three: avoidance of idolatry, avoidance of unchastity, and avoidance of murder.

In both these cases it seems that the centre of gravity in Judaism is in the ethical, rather than the religious, sphere. However, the Mishnah specifically excludes from the World to Come those offenders who deny the resurrection of the dead, the divinity of the Torah, and those who utter heresies. Commenting on this Mishnaic passage, the medieval philosopher Maimonides formulated 13 principles of the Jewish faith: (1) the existence of God; (2) the unity of God; (3) the incorporeality of God; (4) the eternity of God; (5) God alone is to be worshipped; (6) prophecy; (7) Moses is the greatest of the prophets; (8) the divinity of the Torah; (9) the immutability of the Torah; (10) the omniscience of God; (11) God rewards and punishes; (12) the Messiah; (13) the resurrection of the dead. According to Maimonides, entry to the World to Come is contingent upon subscribing to these beliefs. Other medieval thinkers, however, challenged his formulation. Hasdai Crescas, Simon ben Zemah Duran, Joseph Albo and Isaac Aramai elaborated different creeds, and some thinkers, like David ben Solomon Ibn Abi Zimra, argued that it was impossible to isolate from the whole Torah essential principles of the Jewish faith.

Thus, when formulations of the central theological tenets of the Jewish faith were propounded, they were not universally accepted since they were simply the opinions of individual teachers. Without a central authority whose opinion in theological matters is binding on all Jews, it has been impossible to determine the correct theological beliefs in Judaism. In the words of Rabbi Dr Solomon Schechter, 'any attempt at an orderly and complete system of rabbinic theology is an impossible task', and it is likely that this widespread confusion as to the central tenets of the Jewish faith, coupled with the fact that speculation about the afterlife in Judaism does not have an authoritative status, has persuaded some Jewish thinkers that they are justified in disregarding such notions as the doctrine of Hell.

A second factor which has led to the abandonment of this doctrine has been a gradual this-worldly emphasis in Jewish thought. Before the Enlightenment in the late eighteenth century, the majority of Jews had an indeterminate status and were essentially isolated from their non-Jewish neighbours. When, however, the ghetto was opened, Jews anxiously entered into the mainstream of European life, relishing their social, economic and political opportunities. Yet this emancipation led many to reject traditional Jewish beliefs and practices. Departing from their religious inheritance, these Jews participated fully and actively in secular life. As Rabbi Louis Jacobs writes, 'the desperate struggle to cope with the new problems regarding how Jews could live as Jews in Western society, the allure of new cultural patterns and beckoning ideals, many of them at complete variance with the traditions of their fathers, all these served to make Jews into a this-worldly people'.

A third factor has been the rise of modern Zionism, which has shifted Jewish interest away from theological speculation to the establishment, maintenance and protection of the Jewish homeland. From biblical times the land of Israel has played a significant role in the religious life of the Jew; it is there, according to Jewish tradition, that the exiles will be gathered at the time of the Messianic redemption. At the end of the nineteenth century, however, under the influence of such writers as Moses Hess, Leon Pinsker and Theodor Herzl, love for Israel was transferred from the religious to the political sphere. The establishment of a homeland was conceived as a solution to Jewish political and social insecurity, and thus, from the founding of the State of Israel on 15 May 1948 to the present day, a large number of Jews have regarded the state of Israel as the central focus of their religious and cultural identity.

The fourth factor in the rejection of this doctrine has been the tendency to regard everlasting punishment as morally repugnant. Echoing doubts about the doctrine of Hell voiced by a number of Christians at the end of the nineteenth century, Jewish theologians have maintained that it is a self-delusion to believe that a God of love could have created a place of eternal punishment. In *Jewish Theology*, for example, K. Kohler argues that the question whether the tortures of Hell are reconcilable with divine mercy 'is for us superfluous and superseded. Our modern conceptions of time and space admit neither a place nor a world-period for the reward and punishment of souls, nor the intolerable conception of eternal joy without useful action and eternal agony without any moral purpose'. In this connection Jewish theologians have pointed out that since punishment as retaliation in the vindictive sense has been widely criticised, the notion of eternal punishment seems highly questionable.

The fifth and final factor, a result of the factors already mentioned, is the modern tendency to interpret figuratively the depictions of Hell in rabbinic sources. Since such descriptions are abhorrent to the modern temper, numerous Jewish scholars have insisted that they were never intended to be understood literally. In *Judaism as Creed and Life*, for example, Morris Joseph writes, 'Nor do we believe in a hell or in everlasting punishment. The pictures of penal fires with which some Jewish writers have embellished their descriptions of a future life are purely imaginary.... If suffering there is to be it is terminable. The idea of eternal punishment is repugnant to the genius of Judaism.' Similarly, M. Waxman argues in *Judaism: Religion and Ethics*: 'We can assert that while the belief in otherworldly reward and punishment belongs to the very wrap and woof of Judaism, as expressed through the ages, there is latitude in the conception of their nature and character.'

These writers may well be correct that the depictions of Hell in rabbinic literature were to some extent consciously recognised by the rabbis themselves as projections of vivid imaginations. No doubt the concept of Hell was used to encourage Jews to be faithful to the law; yet given the vast bulk of rabbinic speculation about the afterlife contained in multifarious religious and philosophical sources, it seems likely that such depictions were regarded by the rabbis as serious attempts to pierce the veil of the Hereafter. To regard them as flights of imaginative fancy is to misconstrue the nature and seriousness of rabbinic speculation.

These five factors, therefore, have led modern Jewish apologists to disregard the doctrine of Hell as well as many other doctrines concerning the afterlife. The wheel has thus swung full circle from the faint allusions to immortality in the Biblical period which led to an elaborate development of the concept of the Hereafter in Talmudic times. Whereas the rabbis put the belief in the afterlife at the centre of their religious system, modern Jewish thinkers, orthodox and reform, have abandoned such an other-worldly outlook, even to the point of denying the existence of such doctrines. It may be that these doctrines are outmoded and should be abandoned, but it is a misrepresentation of Jewish theology to maintain that they never had a place in Jewish thought. Their significance in rabbinic times was immense; the power that the image of Hell had over Jewish minds cannot be minimised. When such misrepresentation occurs in introductions to Judaism, students inevitably receive an incorrect picture of the Jewish faith, and it is a sad comment on the state of Jewish life and learning that Jewish apologists feel compelled to hide from the outside world the aspects of Jewish theology that they consider unsavoury.

5

Life and Beyond in the Qur'an

MUHAMMAD ABDEL HALEEM

In the Qur'an life in this world is an inseparable part of a continuum, a unified whole (life—death—life) which gives our life here a context and relevance. In this context the life of the individual is made meaningful and richer inasmuch as it is full of 'good actions'. Life in this world leads to the after-life, a belief which is most fundamental in the Qur'an. The after-life is not treated in the Qur'an in a separate chapter at the end of the book, or as something on its own, for its own sake, but always in relation to life in this world.

Linguistically, it is not possible in the Qur'an to talk about one without semantic reference to the other since every term used for each is comparative with the other. Thus: *al-ūlā* and *al-ākhira* (the First and the Last life); *al-dunyā* and *al-ākhira* (the Nearer and the Further/Latter life). Neither has a name specific to itself that does not refer to the other. Consequently the frequency of occurence of the terms in the Qur'an is the same, in the case of *dunyā* and *ākhira* – 115 times each.[1] There is a reference, direct or indirect, to one aspect or another of after-life on almost every single page of the Qur'an. This follows from the fact that belief in it is an article of faith which has bearing on every aspect of the present life and occurs in the discussion of the creed, the rituals, the ethics and the law of Islam. In discussing it, moreover, the Qur'an addresses both believers and non-believers. The plan of two worlds and the relationship between them is, from the beginning, part of the divine scheme of things.

> It is Allah Who created you, then He provided sustenance for you, then He will cause you to die, then He will give life back to you. (30:40)

It is We Who give life and make to die and to Us is the homecoming. (50:43)

He created death and life that He might try you which of you is best in works. (67:2)

According to the Qur'an, belief in the after-life which is fundamental to the mission of Muhammad was also central to the mission of all prophets before him.[2] Belief in the after-life often comes in conjunction with belief in Allah, in the expression: 'If you believe in Allah and the Last Day'. Believers are frequently reminded in the Qur'an 'Be mindful of Allah and know that you shall meet Him' (2:233) (this is used to urge fitting treatment of one's wife even in intimate situations). 'To Him is the homecoming / the return' (36:83; 40:3 and *passim*). Belief in the after-life being so fundamental in Islam, it is only natural that Muslims are regularly reminded of it not only throughout the pages of the Qur'an but also in their daily life. Practising Muslims in their five daily prayers repeat at least 17 times a day their praise of Allah, 'The Master of the Day of Judgement' (1:4) Being inattentive to the after-life (30:7) or forgetful of meeting the Judgement (32:14) are signs of the Unbeliever. All this heightens the believer's sense of responsibility for actions in this life. In fact the principles and details of religion are meant to be seen within the framework of the interdependence of this life and the after-life and to colour the Muslims' conception of life and the Universe and have a bearing on their actions in this life.

THE IMPORTANCE OF JUDGEMENT IN THE AFTER-LIFE

Divine wisdom and justice necessitate the resurrection in an after-life:

It is not in vain that We created the heavens and earth and all that lies between them. That is the fancy of the unbelievers.... Are We to equate those that have faith and do good works with those that corrupt the earth with wickedness? Are We to equate the righteous with the transgressors? (38:27–8)

> Did you think that We created you in vain and that you would not be returned to Us? Exalted by Allah, the King, the True! (23:115–16)

> We have not created the heavens and the earth and all that is between them save in truth. Surely the Hour[3] is coming. (15:85)

In the Qur'an, as in other scriptures, man is required to labour, doing certain things and refraining from others. Justice requires that labour should be rewarded. Recompense is made not during the period of labour in this world but in the after-life:

> What then can make you deny the last Judgement? Is Allah not the best of judges? (95:7–8)

The resurrection is thus:

> a binding promise from Allah that shall be fulfiled though most people may not know it, so that He may resolve their differences for them. (16:38–9)

Judgement is so essential to man in the Qur'an that Allah has created him with a peculiar, innate permanent judge within himself, that is his conscience, his 'reproachful soul'. Indeed this is marked in a chapter entitled *The Resurrection* in which Allah declares:

> I swear by the Day of Resurrection, and by the reproachful soul! Does man think We shall never put his bones together again? Yes indeed: We can remould his very fingers. (75:1–4)

The 'reproachful soul' foreshadows the judgement and is here placed side by side, in the oath, with the resurrection that precedes the judgement. In answer to the unbelievers' incredulity that scattered bones of dead people can be resurrected into new life, Allah swears that it will be done. Modern interpreters see in the word 'fingers', reference to the power of Allah that moulds the finger prints in a way unique to every individual: He has done it in this life and can do it again in the after-life.

THE POSSIBILITY OF THE RESURRECTION OF THE DEAD

In addition to the necessity and desirability of the resurrection and after-life, the Qur'an deals repeatedly with the possibility of the resurrection. During the Meccan period of the Prophet's mission a great deal of the Qur'an was concerned with the three fundamental beliefs of the Unity of Allah, the Prophethood of Muhammad and other prophets before him, and the resurrection and judgement. The resurrection in particular seemed incredible to unbelievers. In fact, much of what one hears in our present day is reminiscent of what unbelievers said at the time of the revelation of the Qur'an. They found the resurrection biologically impossible and repeatedly asked:

> How after we die and become dust and bones could we be raised again? (56:47)

Against this the Qur'an employs a basic argument which is not difficult to accept rationally, equating two similar things: the power that can accomplish something once can do it again. From the fact that they now exist it is clear that divine power was not incapable of making them: why should it be assumed that such power will be incapable of doing for a second time what it achieved the first? (50:15)

> Indeed a second creation is easier than a first one. (30:27)

The Qur'an repeatedly reminds people that they were made into human beings from something very small:

> Is man not aware that We created him from a little germ? yet he is flagrantly contentious. He raises an argument and forgets his own creation. He asks: 'Who will give life to rotten bones?' Say: 'He Who first brought them into being will give them life again: He has knowledge of every creation; Who has made for you out of the green tree fire and lo! from it you kindle. (36:77–80)

This last point affirms the ability of a power that generates things from seemingly opposite or different things – a fire from green trees and bodies from bones and dust; just as a full grown man is different from the little germ that was his beginning. If they ask:

'What! When we are lost in the earth shall we be created afresh?' (32:13)

the answer comes:

We know all that the earth takes away from them. We have a book which records all things. (50:4)

Another rational argument the Qur'an uses against disbelief in the resurrection is the possibility of the existence of the lesser in analogy with the existence of the greater:

Has He Who created the heavens and the earth no power to create the like of the unbelievers? That He surely has. He is the All-creator; the All-knowing. (36:81)

The Qur'an asserts for those who may not know it:

Certainly the creation of the heavens and the earth is greater than the creation of men, but most men know it not. (40:57)

Perhaps when the unbelievers say it is not possible to turn dust into a new creation, what they really think is that it is not possible for human power like their own; but, after all, they have not created themselves or the heavens and the earth (52:35–6). A greater power than their own has created them once and can do it again, and also created what is greater than them. As the Qur'an argued with the unbelievers, sometimes it even omitted the name of the creator, in order to focus their minds more clearly on the argument itself, saying simply, 'He Who did it first', 'Who created the Heavens', etc.

When the Prophet recited Qur'anic verses that confirm the resurrection in the after-life, the unbelievers of his time challenged him personally:

Bring back to us our fathers, if what you say be true!

The Qur'an directed him:

Say: 'It is Allah Who gives you life, then makes you die, then He shall gather you to the Resurrection.' (45:25–6)

In discussing the resurrection, moreover, the Qur'an cites phenomena very familiar to men to show the power that takes creation through different stages particularly in the life of man and plants.

> People, if you doubt the Resurrection remember that We first created you from dust, then from a living germ, then from a tiny clinging thing, and then from a half-formed lump of flesh, so that We might manifest to you Our power.
> We cause to remain in the womb whatever We please for an appointed term, and then We bring you forth as infants, that you may grow up and reach your prime. Some die young, and some live on to abject old age when all that they once knew they know no more.
> You sometimes see the earth dry and barren: but no sooner do We send down rain upon it than it begins to stir and swell, putting forth every kind of radiant bloom. That is because Allah is Truth: He resurrects the dead and has power over all things.
> (22:5–6)

Indeed the Qur'an uses the very same Arabic verb for 'bringing forth' people from their mothers' wombs (16:78), 'bringing forth' plants from the earth (6:99) and 'bringing forth' people from the earth at the resurrection (30:19).

Not only does the Qur'an present proof of the resurrection, but turns the argument against those who deny it, pointing out that they themselves have no proof for their own stand:

> They say: 'There is nothing but our present life; we live and die; nothing but time destroys us.' Of this they have no knowledge; they merely conjecture. (45:24)

At the resurrection they will know they have lied and will regret it (16:39; 6:31).

BEYOND THIS LIFE

Every soul shall taste of death

(3:185)

Death is the gateway to the return to Allah (6:61–2). Man's body may disperse after death but his soul is not an object of annihilation. By death man enters the stage of *barzakh*, an intermediary state between this life and the resurrection (23:100). The Qur'an says little about this stage: it indicates that the soul will receive reward or punishment (3:169–71; 16:32; 40:45–6; 71:25). Much more is to be found in the traditions of the Prophet.[4] On visiting or passing by a grave or a cemetery, a Muslim greets the dead with the same greeting as for the living: 'Peace be to you', and adds, 'You are our forerunners and we are following after you, may Allah forgive us and you!'

At the resurrection the duration of stay in the grave will appear to men 'as if it were an hour of the day, mutually recognizing one another' (10:45).

The state of *barzakh* will end at 'the Hour', the end of the world, then the resurrection will take place. The time of this 'Hour' is known only to Allah (7:187). Thus when asked by one of his followers when it would come, the Prophet directed him to what is more fruitful by answering:

What have you prepared for it?

Compared to the state of *barzakh*, there is much in the Qur'an about the end of the world, the resurrection, the judgement, and the recompense in the final abode.

THE NATURE OF THE RESURRECTION

Will the resurrection and after-life be only spiritual or bodily as well? Although in the opinion of some, especially Sufis, it would be only spiritual,[5] holding that Qur'anic statements which suggest it is bodily are only manners of expression to be understood by the general readers, the general characteristic of Qur'anic statements indicates that it will be bodily and spiritual. As the Muslim philosopher Ibn Rushd (Averroes) explains, some Muslims consider that existence in the after-life is of the same nature as in this life, only it will be permanent there. Others believe that bodily existence there is different from bodily existence here. As Ibn 'Abbas, the companion of the Prophet, said, there is nothing in this world which it shares with the after-life except the names of things. The Qur'an itself indicates that bodily existence there will be 'a new' creation, so that it will not be the same bodies as we have here (e.g. 56:35, 61). It speaks of the descriptions of Paradise as being parables – *mathal* – (e.g. 13:35; 47:15) and the food there 'appears similar' – *mutashābih* – to what it is here (2:25); and the Prophet says about Paradise:

> There are in it things that no eyes have seen, no ear has heard and what has never occurred to the mind of man.

As Ibn Rushd points out, this view is more suitable for the educated since the spiritual existence is permanent and the concept of the return of the soul in a new body avoids such complications as the objection that the worldly body turns into dust, is fed upon by plants, which are then eaten by other people, from whose bodies come the bodies of their descendants, etc.[6]

The representation of existence in the after-life as being also bodily and not merely spiritual, explains Ibn Rushd,[7] is more suitable as it makes it more understood and more moving for the majority of people; spiritual representation might be suitable only for speculative thinkers in their argumentations, but the majority are the prime targets of religions.

THE JUDGEMENT

There are graphic descriptions in the Qur'an of the end of the world, resurrection and judgement.[8] A most important element is the judgement, when 'people will come to be shown their deeds', each facing judgement 'alone'. 'No soul will carry the burden of another'. Each will be confronted with a book of their deeds:

> Read your book. Your own soul suffices you this day as a reckoner against you. (16:14)

The book shall be laid open, the prophets and witnesses shall be brought in and all shall be judged with fairness, they shall not be wronged. Every soul will be paid in full what it wrought. He knows very well what they do. (39:69–70)

Whoever does an atom's weight of good shall see it, and whoever does an atom's weight of evil shall see it also. (99:7–8)

Whoever brings good, he will have better than it; and whoever brings evil, those who do evil will be requited for what they did. (28:84)

Good deeds can be multiplied as much as seven hundred times. (6:160; 2:261)

Thus the judgement is vital; without it divine commandments would make no sense, observation and violation, good and evil deeds would all be the same:

Are We to equate those that have faith and do good works with those that corrupt the earth with wickedness? Are We to equate the righteous with the transgressors? (38:27–8)

Exalted be Allah, the King, the Truth. (23:116)

RECOMPENSE

There is much description of rewards and punishment. As human beings have bodies, minds and spirits, all of which are, in Islam, gifts from Allah and out of His grace He provided mankind with the means of gratifying all these components in this life, in the after-life He will provide means of gratifying them all to 'those who believed and did good works' (7:32). Bodies, as we have noted, will be 'a new creation' and in Paradise will not suffer the shortcomings of worldly bodies. In Paradise, 'No mortal knows what comfort is in store for them as a reward for their labours (32:17). 'No evil shall visit them' – the Arabic word *su'* includes whatever is undesirable (39:16, 40:7). There is no tedium there, such as sceptics now invoke as an agument against eternal

Life and Beyond in the Qur'an

existence. 'They will live in the land of perfect peace' (6:127). The Qur'an describes food provided there but it is 'of whatever they themselves desire and choose'. It mentions drinks but in such terms as:

> Their Lord shall give them pure beverage to drink (and it will be said to them) 'This is a reward for you, your labour is thanked.' (76:21–2)

They will dwell there 'together with their spouses', receiving whatever they desire, and 'We have more for them', they will be found therein 'with their descendants who followed them in the faith' (36:56–7; 50:35; 52:12). Much is said about spouses in Paradise though no physical relationship is mentioned. Believers in the Qur'an find being 'Together with their spouses' an essential part of good rewards in Paradise. They read in the Qur'an about the relationship between spouses even in this world:

> And of His signs is that He created for you spouses, from among yourselves so that you might repose in them and created between you love and care; surely there are signs in this for people who reflect. (30:21)

Believers in the Qur'an find it difficult to understand why some people wish to insist on excluding material description of the rewards when they are offered in the Qur'an as symbols of Allah being pleased with the good work believers have done. Do we spurn medals and dinner parties given in appreciation for good works in this world? The Qur'an in any case has set a scale for the rewards:

> Allah has promised the believers, men and women, gardens underneath which rivers flow, forever therein to dwell, and goodly dwelling places in the Garden of Eden; and what is greater: Allah's good pleasure: that is the supreme triumph.
> (10:72)

> He will be pleased with them and they will be well pleased with Him. (58:22)

The good company comes first, then Paradise itself:

Enter among my servants! Enter my Paradise! (89:27–30)

An opposite picture is given of punishment, the essence of which is humiliation:[9]

As already pointed out, the Qur'an does not treat the after-life as something theoretical or in a separate chapter at the end of the book. It is embedded in the text throughout and its effect on the reader is enhanced by the vivid and powerful language in the Arabic text. After a short conjunction like 'when' to indicate the after-life, it commonly employs the past and present tense as if it is already here and has happened. There is an obvious interdependence between this life and the after-life. We have seen the terms occur in the Qur'an in equal frequency and how, linguistically, one cannot utter the name of one without semantic reference to the other. Every thing in the Judgement has naturally to do with action in the world. Dwellers in Paradise or Hell sometimes talk about what they did in this world (52:28; 40:47).

THE AFTER-LIFE AND THE PRESENT LIFE

In the Qur'an life in this world has, thus, much more significance. Believers live a much larger life by believing, while living now, that their lives will go on and will not be terminated in dust. They are continually reminded of this (at least 17 times during the day for practising Muslims). The life of the individual continues in the two worlds, but through different stages: from the womb to the world, to the grave, to the resurrection, judgement and lasting life in the final abode – the intervening period in the grave will seem 'a mere part of a day' (23:113).

The Qur'an does not disparage the present life, both lives are created by Allah and

To Allah belong the last life and the first life. (53:25)

He created for you all that the earth contains (2:29)

including beautiful things:

Eat of what your Lord has given you and render thanks to Him. (16:6; 50:7; 34:15; 7:32)

In gathering wealth the faithful are 'seeking the bounty of Allah'. They are directed to do this after finishing the prayer in which they praise 'the Master of the Day of Judgement' (62:10; 65:17; 73:20). In seeking to attain Paradise, people are advised in the Qur'an, 'Do not neglect your share in this world' (28:77).

The Qur'an none the less states (as something earlier scriptures confirm) that the after-life is 'better and more lasting than this life' (87:17-9). Allah objects to

> those who do not expect to meet Us and are well pleased with the present life and content themselves with it and who give no heed to Our revelations. (10:7)

In Islam a believer, while enjoying what is good in this life is at the same time working for the next one and vice versa. Islam does not recognise a clear-cut distinction between what is worldly and what is religious. The Prophet once mentioned that among the 'good deeds' which one can store up for the after-life is having sexual intercourse with one's spouse. A companion exclaimed: 'Prophet, but this is something we enjoy, how can we be rewarded for it?' to which he answered: 'If you were to do it unlawfully, would you not be punished for it?' 'Yes.' 'Conversely you will be rewarded for doing it lawfully.'

The Qur'an emphasises that nobody will escape death, the resurrection or judgement, and that there is no way to salvation in the after-life except through work in this life. The duration of life that is given to any person here is limited, by 'the appointed term' (*ajal* – a word that is mentioned in the Qur'an some 40 times). It is the only chance to work for a good life in the next world (35:37). The urgency is expressed by the frequent use of 'before' (*min gabl an*) death or the hour comes.

> Give of that with which We have provided you before death befalls any of you and he should say: 'Reprieve me my Lord, a while, that I may give in charity and be among the righteous.' But Allah reprieves no soul when its term expires. Allah is aware of all your actions. (63:10-11)

The Prophet said:

> He whose day is no better than the day before it has done himself wrong.

He also said:

> When a son of Adam dies his deeds cease, except through three things: a running charity which he founded, useful knowledge he left behind, or a good child who prays for him.

Of the judgement he said:

> No person will leave the judgement place before being asked about four things: his life span and how he spent it, his knowledge and what he did with it, his body and in which things he wore it out, and his wealth – from where he collected it and how he spent it.

Life in this world is made more significant by the fact that judgement and recompense in the after-life are only for 'deeds' done in this one. Good deeds are good for the individual, society, humanity and all the world which Allah created, appointing man 'a viceroy in it' (2:30) The Prophet of Islam said:

> If the Hour comes while one of you is holding a palm-seedling, if he can plant it before the Hour overtakes him, he should plant it.

We know that the Hour puts an end to the present order of things, yet the 'good deed' should be done. The Qur'an addresses Muslims and followers of other faiths:

> Allah has ordained a law and a path for each of you. Had Allah wished it, He could have made you into one nation, but in order to try you in what has come to you, He has made you as you are. So vie with one another in good works, for to Allah you shall all return and He will declare to you what you have disagreed about. (5:48)

Muslims are taught in the Qur'an to pray:

> Lord, give us good in this life and good in the after-life. (2:201)

Notes

1. M. F. Abdel-Bāqī, *Qur'an Concordance*, in Arabic (Cairo) many editions.
2. See, for instance, Qur'an 3:55, 26:82; 40:27; 71:17–18.
3. 'The Hour' is a term frequently used in the Qur'an meaning the end of the world which begins the resurrection and the after-life.
4. See, for instance, M. A. Khalifa, *Al-Hayāh al-barzakhiyya* (Cairo, 1983).
5. Ibn Rushd, *Manāhij al-adilla fi 'aqā'id al-milla*, ed. M. Qasim, 3rd edn (Cairo, 1969) p. 246, fn.
6. Ibid., pp. 246–7.
7. Ibid., p. 245.
8. See 39:67–75; 56; 75:81; 80:99.
9. Qur'an 83:15; 35:54; 3:192; 9:63; 11:60. There is an excellent and comprehensive exposition of the whole question of recompense in the Qur'an in Chapter 3 of M. A. Draz, *La Morale du Quran* (Cairo: Al-Azhar University Press, 1950).

6
The Indestructible Soul – Indian and Asian Beliefs

GEOFFREY PARRINDER

Some of the most significant discussions about survival of death are found in the Indian Upanishads, dating from about the eighth century BC. It has been said that Semitic thinkers concentrated their attention on God, but the Indians were obsessed by the soul or self, and this made survival of death a central concern. The many forms of Indian discussion may illuminate problems that trouble us today. The texts are complex and sometimes obscure, but selections can be made.

KARMA

The Upanishads are 'sessions', assertions, dialogues, debates and theological tournaments. At first discussion is realistic or sceptical. A great sage, Yajnya-valkya, a kind of Indian Socrates, puts forth a parable with an apparently agnostic conclusion. Man is like a tree, with his members compared to leaves, bark, trunk and sap. When a tree is felled it shoots up again, but from what stump does man shoot up? If a tree is pulled up by its roots it will not shoot again. 'So from what root does man spring up?' This is remarkably like a parable of tree and man in Job (14:7–10), 'there is hope of a tree ... but man dies and wastes away'. The Indian example concludes with an assertion that Brahman (being, or the absolute) 'is knowledge and bliss', but this is enigmatic and may be an orthodox addition.[1]

Earlier Yajnya-valkya was asked, 'When a man dies, what does not leave him?' He replied, 'The name. The name is infinite,

The Indestructible Soul

and by it he wins an infinite world.' This was not very clear and the questioner continued by stating that the voice of a dead man goes into cremation fire, his breath into wind, his body into the earth, his eye into the sun, and so on. But 'what then becomes of this person?' The sage replied that this should not be discussed in public, and he led his questioner away to deliberate privately. 'They said it was *karma*' (action, and its entail). 'One becomes good by good action, bad by bad action.' This moral note comes in again and again in Hindu and Buddhist and other Indian scriptures.

DYING

Observations of the conditions of sleep and dying provide further material. There is the condition of being in this world, and the condition of being in the other world, but 'there is an intermediate third condition', that of being in sleep. When one goes to sleep he takes along the material of this world and 'dreams by his own brightness'. There are no chariots, roads or streams there, but 'he projects from himself' chariots, roads and streams, 'for he is a creator.' In that state he is 'in the embrace of the intelligent Soul', like a man in the embrace of a beloved wife.

The existence of this soul is affirmed, for as a king about to go on a journey 'would prepare a chariot or a ship, even so you have a soul (*ātman*, or self) prepared with these mystic doctrines' (*Upanishads*). The Soul is 'not this, and it is not that' (*neti, neti*). It is indestructible, for it cannot be destroyed, or attached, or bound, or injured.[2]

The process of death is described with analogies. When a man is dying, it is like the creaking of a heavily loaded cart, the bodily soul mounted by the intelligent soul, groaning at the last breaths. As officials and village heads prepare for the arrival and departure of a king, just so do 'all the breaths gather round the soul at the end when one is breathing one's last'.

As a man becomes weaker the bodily faculties gather round, but he no longer recognises forms. They say 'he is becoming one', he does not see, smell, taste, speak, hear, think, touch, or know. The point of the heart lights up and 'by that light the soul departs', by the eye or head or some other part of the body. Intelligence departs with him, and his former knowledge and works (*karma*) follow after him.

REINCARNATION

These considerations lead to the all-pervasive Indian belief in reincarnation, either in the popular sense of a transmigrating soul with its future affected by past actions, comparable to Plato's myth of Er at the end of the *Republic*, or in the Buddhist sense of Karma as the link between two existences.

The Upanishad says that as a caterpillar, when it has come to the end of a blade of grass, draws itself up to take the next move, so this Soul 'draws itself together' for the transition. Or as a goldsmith takes a piece of gold and moulds it into a new and more beautiful form, so this Soul makes a new and better form for itself. This Soul (*ātman*) is Brahman, 'it is made of everything' and the moral emphasis comes again, 'according as one acts, so does he become. The doer of good becomes good, the doer of evil becomes evil.'

A celebrated exposition of reincarnation appears in the first two Upanishads in almost identical terms, witnessing to its importance.[3] A young Brahmin priest is questioned by members of the princely class, who claim to have superior knowledge. Their teachings may have survived from the older pre-Aryan levels of Indian society, before the coming of the Brahmins and composition of the priestly texts in the Vedas, since they also appear in other ancient Indian religions, Jainism and Buddhism.

Young Shveta-ketu is asked whether his father has instructed him, and on answering affirmatively he is faced with questions to which he has no answer: 'Do you know where creatures go from here? Do you know how they come back again? Do you know where the paths of the gods and the ancestors separate? Do you know how it is that the world beyond is not filled up? How can you say that you have been instructed?'

In distress Shveta-ketu goes to his father, who admits that even he does not know the answers. The father goes to the rulers and is told that this knowledge had never come to the priests previously but was the possession of the princely caste. Evidently there was rivalry between priests and princes.

The Indestructible Soul

After some discussion, two ways are asserted that would be followed after death. Those who have the right knowledge and truly worship pass into the flame of the cremation-fire and eventually arrive at the world of the gods, and for them there is no return to earth. But those who believe in sacrifice and merit, pass into the smoke of the cremation-fire and finally arrive at the world of the ancestors. As long as there is a residue of their works, then after a time they return to earth by the same route on which they ascended. They come into space, wind, smoke, mist, cloud and rain. They are born as plants and are eaten as food by human beings (an English version of this process seems to be 'On Ilkley Moor baht 'at').

The condition of rebirth is determined by previous conduct, Karma. 'Those whose previous earthly conduct has been pleasant will enter pleasant wombs, the wombs of women of the priestly or princely or merchant castes. But those whose conduct on earth has been stinking will enter stinking wombs, these of a bitch or a sow or an outcaste woman. This is how it happens that the world beyond is not filled up.'

The theory of reincarnation explains the inequalities of life, once it is accepted, and there are few people in India, or indeed right across Asia, who do not accept it. Demands for proof are rejected, since it is taken as a fact of life.

Two points should be made. First, that in the Upanishads there is no reference to memory for proof of reincarnation. Later writings have countless stories of remembrance of past lives and people still often claim to have lived splendidly in a previous existence (like a claim to an aristocratic ancestor) or to remember their former partners. The Buddhist Jataka, birth stories of the Buddha record some 550 earlier adventures of the Buddha-to-be in animal and human forms, each tale ending with the phrase, 'I was that being.' But in the Upanishads memory is not adduced as evidence of transmigration.

Secondly, the Upanishads assume the indestructible nature of the soul, and this profound conviction provides matter for further discussions and elaborations.

ETERNAL SOUL

A striking story in the Katha Upanishad offers a subtle development. Young Nachiketas is, apparently, slaughtered by his father (a more fatal lot than that of Isaac). The father has sacrificed second-rate cattle to his gods, and the son offers himself as a more worthy oblation. In anger at the implied reproach his father exclaims, 'Oh, go to Hades', and kills him.[4]

Nachiketas proceeds to the realm of Yama, the god of death, but Yama is absent for three days. On his return, finding that Nachiketas has not received the hospitality due to a Brahmin, Yama offers the youth three boons. The first two are granted easily: reconciliation with his father, and the proper kind of sacrifice. The crunch comes in the third.

Nachiketas says: 'There is this doubt when a man is dead. Some say, He exists. Others say, He does not exist. I want to know the truth from you, that is my third boon.'

The god of death, being asked about death, tries to avoid answering. 'Even the gods used to have doubts about this. It is subtle, and not easily understood. Do not press me. Choose another boon. Give up this one.'

Nachiketas replies that if the gods had doubted this, it is not easily understood, and you alone can tell. There is no other boon equal to this one.

Then Death tries to bribe Nachiketas into choosing to have sons and grandsons, cattle, elephants, gold and horses, lovely maidens with chariots and lyres, a great palace and long life. 'But do not question me about dying.'

'All these things are ephemeral', retorts the youth. 'You keep the song and dance and chariots.' Man is not satisfied with wealth, and even vigorous powers wear away 'but this thing on which men doubt, the answer to that secret is my boon. What happens in the great passing-on?'

After further wrangling Death finally comes clean, making two famous statements, in verse, of the nature of the eternal indestructible soul:

> The wise one [soul, *ātman*] is not born nor dies,
> This one has not come from anywhere, or become anyone,
> He is unborn, constant, eternal, primeval,
> He is not slain when the body is slain.

The Indestructible Soul

If the killer thinks he kills,
If the killed thinks he is killed,
Both of these do not understand,
This one does not kill and is not killed.

It is the assertion, intuitive and not argued, that the soul is eternal and unaffected by death. It is post-existent because pre-existent, it is everlasting and unchangeable.

These two verses are quoted, almost verbatim and without acknowledgement, in the famous moral and devotional poem, the Bhagavad Gita, about the third century BC. There the warrior Arjuna is appalled at the prospect of great slaughter in an impending battle. But the god Krishna tells him not to worry, either for himself or others, because the soul is immortal, and those who kill the body cannot kill the eternal soul. It is perhaps cold comfort for those who are being killed, but it is a declaration of the nature of the unchangeable soul.

The Katha Upanishad asserts that the soul is 'smaller than the small, greater than the great', immanent and transcendent. Earlier the Chandogya Upanishad had declared that 'this soul of mine within the heart is smaller than a grain of rice' or even smaller grains, but also 'this soul of mine within the heart is greater than the earth' or atmosphere or sky or all worlds.[5]

Perhaps surprisingly, the Katha Upanishad then goes on to affirm divine action: 'through the grace of the Creator one beholds the greatness of the soul'. This is the first explicit Upanishadic statement of a doctrine of divine grace, and pantheistic commentators tried to explain it away, by varying the text or its interpretation. But the theme is repeated even more theistically in another Upanishad: 'through the grace of the Creator one beholds the Lord and his greatness'.[6]

There are other important and moving verses in the Katha Upanishad, but it ends with a reference back to its opening narrative: 'Thus Nachiketas received this knowledge declared by Death, and all the arts of Yoga. He attained to Brahman, and became free from passion and death. And so may any other who understands what belongs to the Soul.'

THAT ART THOU

The relation of the individual soul (*ātman*) to the universal soul (*ātman* or Brahman) preoccupied Upanishadic thinkers, and the connection was suggested in complex and subtle ways.

In the fourth section of the first Upanishad the origins of things are suggested: 'In the beginning this world was Soul alone in the form of a man. Looking round he saw nothing beside himself and he said first "I am"'. This person or man was as large as a man and woman in close embrace, 'he divided himself into two, and thence arose a husband and wife'. This recalls Plato's androgynous being, and perhaps Adam divided in Genesis 2.

But the same Upanishadic dialogue goes on to affirm that 'in the beginning this world was Brahman, and it knew itself being one only, saying "I am Brahman", and so it became this All'. The verse proceeds to state that 'whoever thus knows that he is Brahman, becomes this All. Even the gods have no power to prevent him becoming thus, for he becomes their own self' (*ātman*).[7]

The second, Chandogya, Upanishad, after declaring the immanence and transcendence of the soul, affirms that 'this soul of mine within the heart is that Brahman. When I depart hence I shall merge into it.'

Later the Chandogya Upanishad goes on to expound famous pantheistic or monistic teachings in nine short examples, each culminating in the assertion of the unity or identity of the individual soul with the universal Soul, in the repeated phrase THAT THOU ART (*tat tvam asi*). This has been taken as the quintessence of non-dualism or monism, though it has been constantly disputed between three principal schools of philosophy. It may be noted that these examples stand alone in this Upanishad, without any connection with preceding or following sections, but they were clearly regarded as of great significance.

The first example is most important for our concern with death and beyond: 'When a man is dying, his voice is absorbed into the mind, his mind into breath, breath into heat, heat into the highest power. That finest essence – the whole universe has that as its soul. That is the Real. That is the Soul. THAT ART THOU.'[8]

Succeeding examples of how the many become the one culminate with the same refrain. Bees collect honey from different trees and reduce their essences to unity, and so the varied creatures in the world become one in the end. Rivers flow east or west, but they become one and indistinguishable in the ocean. A tree has life in various parts and when it is cut down the life leaves it but does not die, for its finest essence is the soul (this is an answer to the earlier parable of the tree). A fig may be divided into seeds and when they are cut open there is nothing within, for its finest essence is imperceptible but real. Salt is placed in water, becomes invisible but pervades the whole. A man may be led away from home with his eyes bandaged, but when he finds a competent teacher he is freed from the bonds of ignorance. A man accused of theft is killed by lies, but if he tells the truth he is released, for the whole world has truth as its soul.

The eighth example refers to death again: When a man is mortally ill his kinsmen ask, 'Do you know me?' As long as his voice is not absorbed into the mind, breath, heat, and the highest power – so long he knows. But when that process has taken place, then he knows not. 'That finest essence – the whole universe has that as its soul. That is Reality. That is Soul. THAT ART THOU.'

MONISM

The most important Indian philosophical schools, the Vedanta (Veda's end), differed strongly in their interpretations of 'Thou art That'. The most thoroughgoing non-dualist or monist was Shankara (788–820 AD). He rejected any duality of human and divine which might imply 'I' and 'Thou', subject and object, for the individual soul was really the same as the universal soul, and when it got rid of *maya* (ignorance or illusion) it would lose its limitations and merge into the divine, realising its own true nature. Shankara said that 'the highest Brahman constitutes the real nature of the individual soul, as we know from passages such as "that art thou", while its second nature, namely that aspect of it which depends on fictitious living conditions, is not its real nature'.[9] Even when commenting on the theistic Bhagavad Gita, with its personal teaching Lord and his disciple, Shankara held to their ultimate identity. His school is called *a-dvaita*, non-dualism, and it has many followers today, even claiming to be India's perennial philosophy.

An equally great philosopher was Ramanuja in the eleventh century, who taught a 'qualified non-dualism.' He taught that the world and the soul are real and not illusions, but they depend upon God and form a unity, since they exist as the body of Brahman. There is a communion or union of souls and God, but they are not identical with him. The soul will always need a God superior to it to adore, as God needs human beings to be objects of his love. Hence Ramanuja was closer to the spirit of the Gita and wrote an important commentary on it, which has been used by the great modern Christian commentator on the Gita, R. C. Zaehner of Oxford.

The third notable Vedanta philosopher was Madhva in the thirteenth century, who taught a frank dualism (*dvaita*) of God and man. He identified Brahman with the god Vishnu, immanent in the world and the Inner Controller of souls, but also transcendent as world-controller. Madhva declared that the famous Upanishadic text should read 'Not-that (*a-tat*) art thou', from a variant reading of the letters. But he tended to extreme rationalism which made him less attractive than other teachers, and he has never had the following of Shankara or Ramanuja.

SOUL AND GOD

There are many other interesting and important elements in the Upanishads, and time would fail to examine them all. The Shvetashvatara is the most theistic of the classical Upanishads, and it identifies God with an earlier divinity Rudra who, as the later Shiva, is sole God to his millions of devotees today.

This Upanishad begins with a series of questions on the origins and nature of life: 'What is the cause? Whence are we born? ... Is it time, or nature, or necessity, or chance? ... It cannot be a combination of these, because of the existence of the soul.' But God is 'the One who rules over all these causes, from "time" to the "soul"'. Later he is regarded as 'the One embracer of the universe. By knowing him as Lord men become immortal'.

Again, 'some sages discourse of inherent Nature, and others of Time. Both are deluded. It is the greatness of God in the world, which causes this world of being to revolve.' Hitherto transmigration was regarded as so fundamental as to be an automatic or natural process, but now it is asserted that God is 'the cause of reincarnation and of liberation from it'. And, 'by knowing God, one is released from all fetters'. At the end of this short but profound Upanishad these matters become manifest 'to one who has the highest devotion (*bhakti*) for God'. The great emphasis upon loving devotion, which became popular in the Gita and in the following ages, finds its first mention in this theistic Upanishad.[10]

This brief survey of Hindu philosophical teaching about life here and beyond death must end by emphasising the constant concern with the indestructible soul: in transmigration and release from it, in the unity of individual and universal, and in the conviction that intelligent mind is the source of the universe, sustains it, and transcends both individual lives and the cosmos itself.

JAIN SOULS

From about the eighth century BC there was intellectual ferment in India, with many religious and philosophical thinkers speculating on the existence and activities of gods and immortal souls. One of the most ancient was Jainism, which survives today with some three million followers in closely knit communities.

Jainism rejected both theism and non-dualism, for the world is eternal. Yet while they did not believe in an original Creator, Jains were devoted to superhuman beings. Jain temples are some of the most magnificent in India and all contain statues of the twenty-four Jinas, 'conquerors', after whom the religion is named. To these Jinas devotions are addressed, and although they are rapt in meditation and have attained Nirvana, they are said to be compassionate towards the needs of their worshippers.

For Jains, the facts of experience are the material universe, and the existence of innumerable living beings or souls (*jivas*). Souls are distinct from matter, they are eternal but embodied through Karma. All beings, animal and human, are living souls, and devout Jains take many precautions against injuring any living being. A distinctive virtue is 'harmlessness' (*ahimsa*) or non-violence which involves not taking life and, therefore, not only pacifism but vegetarianism. The way for salvation or 're-lease' is through three 'jewels' of right faith, knowledge and conduct, through which the souls seek to rise to the ceiling of the universe and gain Nirvana.

Belief in the plurality of souls led to constant Jain attacks on the monistic or non-dualistic philosophers of Hinduism: 'If the soul were only one, then it would be of one and the same character in all bodies. But the soul is not like this. There are many souls, just as there are many pots and other things.' Again, 'If we assume the non-dualistic hypothesis there can be no liberation or bondage, for the soul is uniform like space. Assuming non-dualism there can be no soul enjoying final bliss, for there are many maladies in the world, and thus the world-soul can only be partly happy.'[11]

Jains, therefore, believe in transmigration and the goal of final Nirvana ('blowing out', extinction of desire and defilement). Death is but a stage, a fact of life, for the soul itself is life. By self-denial, refraining from taking life, subduing anger and fear, the Jina may ultimately reach Nirvana and attain supreme knowledge, omniscience and comprehension of all conditions of being.

BUDDHIST QUESTIONS

Buddhism emerged into history in India about the same time as Jainism. Its founder, like Mahavira of the Jains, was not a Brahmin priest but belonged to the warrior–ruler caste. The one who is commonly called *the* Buddha is believed to have come in a succession of Buddhas, like Jinas, and to have become a Buddha, 'an enlightened one', for this present long eon. His personal name was Siddhartha, of the Gautama clan in the Shakya tribe, and he is often called Gautama or Shakya-muni, 'the sage of the Shakyas'.

Whereas Jains believe in immortal souls, and monistic Hindus postulated an all-embracing world-soul, the Buddha seems to have taught a Non-soul or Not-self doctrine. Yet he also believed in transmigration, so that death is but a stage in the round of existence.

The Indestructible Soul 91

Although he is said to have debated with Jains and Brahmins, it is questioned whether the Upanishadic doctrine of the soul (*ātman*) was known to, or had much influence upon, the Buddha. He was opposed to the egotism implied in the use of 'I' or 'mine' by ordinary people but as a great authority, Edward Conze, remarks, 'the Buddha never taught that the self "is not", but only that it cannot be apprehended'.

In repeated canonical dialogues the Buddha declared that 'the body is not the soul (self). For if the body were the soul it would not be subject to sickness.' The feelings are not the soul, etc. Perceptions are not the soul, etc. Impulses are not the soul, etc. Consciousness is not the soul, etc.

Not canonical, but of great importance in the expositioin of Buddhist thought, are the Questions of Milinda, a supposed Greek King, Menander, debating with a Buddhist monk Nagasena. When the king asks about the person he is told that it is none of the five elements named above. But, 'it is in dependence upon them that there takes place this designation, this conceptual term of person. In ultimate reality, however, this person cannot be apprehended.'[12]

The Buddhist attitude seems to have been agnostic, preferring negatives on disputed questions, though with affirmation of its own views. This attitude appears in the Ten Indeterminates or Open Questions. To each of these fascinating and much debated problems the Buddha replied 'That is a matter on which I have expressed no opinion.'

The questions were: Is the world eternal? Is it not eternal? Is the world finite? Is it infinite? Is the soul the same as the body? Is the soul one thing, and the body another? Does one who has reached the truth live again after death? Does he not live again after death? Does he both live again, and not live again? Does he neither live again, nor not live again?

To every query came the same reply: 'That question is not profitable. It is not concerned with the truth. It does not help to right conduct, or to detachment, or to purification from lusts, or to tranquility of heart. It does not lead to real knowledge, or to insight, or to Nirvana.'

Even on the existence and nature of the celestial Buddha there are enigmatic answers. King Milinda asks whether the Buddha still exists, and is told that he does. Then he wants to know whether the Buddha can be pointed out, as here or there. The monk replies that the Buddha cannot be pointed out. 'The Lord has attained final Nirvana, so that nothing is left which could lead to the formation of another being. . . . The Lord has gone home, and it is not possible to point to him or say that he is here or there. But it is possible to point to the Lord in the body of his Doctrine, for the Doctrine was taught by the Lord.'

Nirvana, too, is abstract and indescribable. 'One cannot point to its form or shape, its duration or size, either by simile or explanation, by reason or by argument.' It is like the wind, one cannot point to it, but one knows there is wind. 'Just so, there is Nirvana, but one cannot point to Nirvana, either by its colour or its shape.'[13]

Popular Buddhism was not content with abstractions and, like Jains and Hindus, Buddhists built countless temples, stupas and pagodas. Such sacred places are alive with statues, candles, decorations, incense and worshippers. There is no supreme God but there is the figure of the central Buddha and, in northern Mahayana Buddhism, many other celestial beings like Amida or Kwanyin. The Buddha is not a god, indeed that would be an inferior condition for him since the gods also are caught up in the round of transmigration. But the Buddha is regarded as 'teacher of gods and men', above them all, the functional supreme 'deity'.

Buddhists, like Hindus and Jains, see death as a stage in transmigration. There is a round of births and deaths, like a chain from which one must seek release. Milinda is taught: 'To be born here and to die here, to die here and to be born elsewhere, to be born there and to die there, to die there and to be born elsewhere – that is the round of existence.' Eventually, it is hoped that there will come salvation or release, escape from the round of births and deaths into the timeless bliss of Nirvana.

Buddhism became the first great missionary religion, cutting across caste and race, taking this Indian gospel right across Asia. It remains a powerful influence upon the thought of countless people in south-east Asia, Tibet, China, Korea, Japan, and from there to the Buddhism of the dispersion in America and Europe.

PERVASIVE BELIEFS

Indian convictions of the transmigration of souls after death into other existences, affected religions beyond Hinduism and its sects, and Jainism and Buddhism. Sikhism was founded in the Punjab in the fifteenth century AD, combining elements from Hinduism and Islam with distinctive teachings of its own gurus. Rebirth was taken for granted. Human beings are creations of the one God, but they become attached to temporal values with their Karma, and the consequence is passage from one life to another. The only way to achieve liberation is by turning from worldly things and becoming God-filled, aware of his inner presence, by his grace and that of his gurus.[14]

The Parsis (Zoroastrians) who came from Persia and are an ancient but small element of Indian religious life, also believe in reincarnation. The progress of souls is through a chain of being, achieved by practices of self-denial which are more suggestive of Hindu asceticism than of the traditional practical methods of orthodox Zoroastrianism.[15]

Islam, like Judaism and Christianity, has taught the future destiny of human beings in heaven and hell, but all three of these religions in India and neighbouring lands have found it hard to resist the insidious appeal of belief in the transmigration of souls. This has been particularly evident among Sufi mystics and Shi'ite sects. In the thirteenth century the Persian mystic Rumi wrote, 'I died as mineral and became a plant, I died as plant and rose to animal, I died as animal and I was man. Yet once more I shall die as man, to soar with angels blest.'[16] In India, the Shi'ite Ismailis, and especially the followers of the Aga Khan, hold not only to reincarnation but to the divinity of their leader.

Beyond death, in general Indian and East Asian belief, there is certain life, in higher or lower forms according to Karma. Hindus, Buddhists and others believe in many heavens and hells, but these are temporary and the final goal is complete release from all impurity and ignorance, in the peace of Nirvana. This is by merging with the Absolute, as in non-dualism, or with God or the Buddha-nature, or in existence in a galaxy of liberated souls.

The appeal of such beliefs has been constant and is diffused across the world today. But concepts are often mixed in their travels, as may be illustrated from Sir Edwin Arnold's popular poem *The Light of Asia*. After giving a verse rendering of teachings of the Buddha, he ended his paraphrase with an aspiration that was more Hindu than Buddhist:

> The Dew is on the Lotus – Rise, Great Sun,
> And lift my Leaf and mix me with the wave.
> ... The Sunrise comes,
> The Dewdrop slips into the shining Sea.

Notes

Reliable selections can be found in *Hindu Scriptures* by R. C. Zaehner (Everyman, 1966) and *Buddhist Scriptures* by E. Conze (Penguin, 1959).

1. Brihad-aranyaka Upanishad 3:9,28; 3:2,13.
2. Ibid., 4:2 and 3
3. Ibid., 6:2l; Chandogya 5:3f.
4. Katha Upanishad 1–2.
5. Chandogya 3:14.
6. Shvet-ashvatara Upanishad 3:20.
7. Brihad-aranyaka 1, 4, 10.
8. Chandogya 6:8f.
9. Vedanta Sutras 1, 3, 19.
10. Shvet-ashvatara 1:1; 6:1; 6:23.
11. For Jain selections see *Sources of Indian Tradition*, ed. W. T. de Bary et al. (Columbia, 1958) p. 81f.
12. E. Conze, *Buddhist Scriptures* (Penguin, 1959) p. 149; and see his *Buddhist Thought in India* (Allen & Unwin, 1962) p. 39.
13. E. Conze, *Buddhist Scriptures* (Penguin, 1959) p. 159; see Digha Nikaya 1, 187; Milinda 77.
14. See W. O. Cole and P. Singh Sambhi, *The Sikhs* (Routledge, 1978) p. 68f.
15. See M. Boyce, *Zoroastrians* (Routledge, 1979) p. 198.
16. R. A. Nicholson, *Rumi* (Allen & Unwin, 1950) p. 103.

7
Death's Rituals
VICTOR DE WAAL

In Mexico on the Days of the Dead (All Saints Day and All Souls Day, 1st and 2nd November) the church bells are tolled, and sweet-smelling flowers and incense invite the dead to come home for a few hours to rejoin the living in a feast. The best foods are set out on an elaborately decorated altar table in the house, more lavish than can be afforded at other times of the year, and the departeds' favourite drink is there too. For dead children (*angelitos* – little angels) that may be a bottle of coca-cola, and there will also be toys, though the dolls and footballers will have the faces of skeletons. The souls enjoy the inner essence of the offerings, and on the next day the living, their family and neighbours, feast in communion with them on the outward appearance. The sweetmeats in the form of skulls are especially delicious.[1]

The Museum of Mankind's exhibition on 'The Day of the Dead in Mexico' is one of two on attitudes to death seen in London in 1991/2. The other was 'The Art of Death' at the Victoria and Albert Museum, which brought together objects designed for death rituals in post-Reformation England between the sixteenth and early nineteenth centuries.

Two quotations serve as texts for this exhibition, and might have served equally well for the other also. The first greets the visitor as he enters. It is from Jonathan Swift:

> It is impossible that anything so natural and so universal as death should ever have been designed by Providence as an evil to mankind.

The second is from Henry Vaughan, addressing death itself:

> Yet by none art thou understood.[2]

The rituals surrounding death have to do with our need as human beings to cope with those moments, stages of our existence, which we experience as particularly risky and dangerous, the times when we have to cross a threshold from a state with which we are familiar to a new and as yet unknown one. Of these liminal moments, these dangerous transitions, when we cross the threshold from one existence to another, death is the paradigm. For it is noticeable how similar in many cultures are the rites surrounding birth, the attainment of adulthood, marriage, religious profession, to those associated with death. The borrowings, the analogies, work both ways: features that find their obvious meaning in one are adopted for the other. Washing, anointing, stripping and the putting on of new clothes, and feasting after the event recur throughout. In passing from one state of life to another – from the womb to the cradle, from childhood to puberty, from the single to the married state, whether the marriage be to a partner or to God, the passage is marked by a symbolic dying to the old and resurrection to the new. In all but the first instance this is for the benefit of awareness both by the individual concerned and by the community. In Western society the symbolism may be no more than the new white dress and the taste of champagne, but in other cultures also today, new-born babies will be given special food before being introduced to the mother's breast, adolescent boys and girls will nakedly submit to painful initiation rites, ordinands and novices will lie prostrate before their admission to a new way of life.

Christian baptism in its original and most expressive form exemplifies this theme dramatically – baptism being understood as a second birth, being born again following on a voluntarily anticipated death. The practice of the early church, itself a development of widespread baptismal custom in the Judaism of the period, is reflected already in St Paul's exhortations to newly converted Christians in the course of his letters. The focus is on death and resurrection, the relinquishing of their former way of life in favour of a new ethic, mirrored in and effected by union with Jesus' dying and rising again. Jesus himself referred to his passion and death as his forthcoming 'baptism', and it is by their own baptism that new Christians participate in his conquest of death. In a classic passage in the Epistle to the Romans Paul writes,

> We died to sin: how can we live in it any longer? Have you forgotten that when we were baptised into union with Christ Jesus we were baptised into his death? By baptism we were buried with him, and lay dead, in order that, as Christ was raised from the dead in the splendour of the Father, so also we might set our feet upon a new path of life. (Rom. 6:2–4)

The most vivid working out of this imagery in practice is in the instructions given by St Cyril of Jerusalem to the newly baptised towards the end of the third century. They are assembled in the Church of the Holy Sepulchre at the reputed spot of Jesus' actual burial and resurrection. So Cyril can point his hearers to the tomb and remind them how it resembled the font into which they had descended and from which they had re-emerged. They had come to the church on the night of Easter and, facing the darkness in the West had repudiated the devil and the vanities of their past life in the world; they had stripped naked (Paul in Colossians 3:9 had written of 'discarding the old nature with its deeds') and stepped down into the water. There facing East in the light of the baptistery they had been interrogated and confessed their three-fold faith, each time immersed, 'buried' under the waters. Emerging, 'raised to life with Christ' (Eph. 2:6), they were rubbed with oil – the conventional anointing after a bath of those times here interpreted as being 'christened' by the descent of the Spirit to be adopted sons and daughters (Rom. 8:15) in the likeness of the Messiah, to whom at his Baptism the voice had spoken, 'Thou art my beloved Son' (Mark 1:11). Then in clean white clothes (Paul had written of 'putting on the new nature which shews itself in a just and devout life' (Eph. 4:24), or in Galatians 3:27 simply of 'putting on Christ') they enter the church and join the community in the eucharistic banquet. It is a foretaste of the marriage feast of the Kingdom of Heaven, and there may be for them an additional cup of milk and honey as a sign that they have entered the promised land.[3]

* * *

If rites of passage in the course of a person's lifetime are marked by rituals borrowed from dying and death, in the most daunting of the threshold experiences to which we inevitably all come, the reverse is also the case. Dead bodies are washed, as a newborn baby is washed; then like the baby, like the bride, like the novice about to become a nun, the corpse is wrapped in white, or where the shroud is no longer in use then in best clothes; and as marriage is followed by a wedding breakfast so the funeral is often completed by a Requiem eucharist and very generally by a 'wake', usually a surprisingly cheerful celebration. At these the departed are in a sense 'present' in a way reminiscent of the feasts on the Mexican Days of the Dead. How else to explain the readiness of friends and relations of the dead to travel long distances to the funeral of someone whom they had not taken the trouble to visit perhaps for many years during their lifetime? Indeed it became customary in England in the eighteenth century to send out elaborate invitation cards to funerals in the same form as we still do to a wedding. And we take for granted the daily announcement alike of births, marriages and deaths in the personal columns of newspapers.

In these ways the fear of Death the Unknown is mitigated by underlining the continuity with the ever-changing processes of life itself. In a symbolically rich society this ritual echoing corresponds to the awareness that from the moment of birth we are dying people, and this nourishes a healthy attitude which makes the most of living. 'Live to die' says one memorial spoon in the V & A exhibition, and its pair reads 'Die to live'. 'Holy Living' was inseparable from 'Holy Dying', and to die well was itself a practised art in which the dying person hoped to be in command, not least importantly in the proper making of a will. Hence the anxious petition in the Prayer Book Litany, 'From sudden death: Good Lord deliver us' – from a death unprepared.

The whole message of the exhibition in fact revolves around the theme of *memento mori* – ranging from the gentle exhortation on a child's sampler and the (to our way of thinking) macabre gold locket which when opened contains a miniature skeleton, through illustrations of good and bad deaths – such as Hans Holbein's *Dance of Death* which can strike anyone, high or low, at any time – to impressive memorials, on some of which the living represent themselves well before their own death, rather as Joseph of Arimathea prepared his tomb in his own lifetime. Here is the monument of William and Mary Evans in Hereford Cathedral. It shows both man and wife and was erected in 1660 on Mary's death; but William himself lived another eight years, and no doubt contemplated his own effigy each time he came to church.

Such an acceptance of death in life is rarely found in Western societies today outside monastic houses. In the Cistercian monastery in Snowmass, Colorado, high up in the Rocky Mountains, there hangs on the right side of the altar a simple wooden cross – the cross that will stay there until it is taken down to mark the grave of the next monk to die. Until then it remains, so that whenever the brothers turn towards the altar they will face also this simple and immediate symbol of their own death – a visual statement of St Benedict's saying in his Rule, 'Keep death daily before your eyes' (4:47). Far from being a morbid and depressing thought, it is in fact life-enhancing, making both for the fulfilling of every moment of earthly existence and for the encouragement of the monks to 'look forward to holy Easter with joy and spiritual longing' (49:7).[4]

In societies like that of Britain today, the consciousness of death is remote and shrouded in euphemisms. The rituals of death have been divorced from everyday social experience. So when someone dies the matter is quickly handed over to the professionals in the funeral business and the old wisdom that the living could learn from the experience of death has faded. The embarrassed bereaved are barely able to focus on the rituals of the burial services, which, as in the Book of Common Prayer, seek to reiterate that lesson. The muzak of the crematorium is a poor substitute for the powerful funeral music of earlier times, whether it be a Catholic Requiem or the evocative melodies, simple or solemn, of Croft or Purcell. Though an evening congregation might still sing Bishop Ken's hymn in which, lying awake at night, he reflects on his 'bed as little as my grave'. Where folk rituals are concerned, we are infinitely far from seventeenth-century Herefordshire, for example, where a 'sin-eater' would consume the sins of the deceased by eating a loaf of bread and drinking a bowl of ale over the corpse as it journeyed to the grave, being paid sixpence for his services.⁵

In his book *The Meanings of Death*, John Bowker describes the attitudes to death and its associated rituals in the world's major religions, and in doing so sets our post-modern society on the way to recover, in terms appropriate to our own times, the values of death as they are and were perceived in other cultures and in our own past history. He demonstrates that far from being rooted in the denial and evasion of death, as early psychology and anthropology used to maintain, religions have universally asserted 'dramatically that there are no other terms on which we can live except those of death', and that in recovering value in death, religion asserts precisely the value of human life and relationships. And he goes on to shew the congruence with this understanding of the heart of religion with contemporary scientific understanding of the nature of life. The common factor in both is sacrifice. Our very existence depends on the sacrifice of life *for* life, 'life giving way so that other, more complex, life can come into being.'. Take hold of your hand and look at it.

> Not so very long ago (at least in the time scale of the universe) most of the atoms in that hand were burning in the depths of some distant star.... There can be no development of life without evolution.... There could not be a you, and there could not be a universe, without death, the death of stars and the death of succeeding generations of organic life. If you ask, 'Why is death happening to me (or to anyone)?', the answer is: because the universe is happening to you; you are an event, a happening, of the universe; you are a child of the stars, as well as of your parents, and you could not be a child in any other way.... What that means in relation to death and why it occurs, becomes very clear: it is not possible to arrive at life except via the route of death.⁶

The awareness of death as an incentive to full and creative living may still to be found today among artists and poets as it was two centuries ago when Henry King wrote that, 'The beating of thy pulse (when thou art well) / Is just the tolling of thy Passing Bell.'⁷ And that awareness is not confined to those who believe that there is something beyond death. Thus Paul Theroux in his contribution to *Hockney's Alphabet* writes

> We are dying every second and that unstoppable tick of our mortal clock can fill us with such anxiety that our fear may make us brilliant and ingenious. Throughout history people have invented ways to defy death, by creating works of art, imagining strange gods, taking risks, making sacrifices, attempting to appease its terror, even constructing a whole kingdom beyond death in order to bestow immortality on ourselves.... Oddly, we take hope from the seasons – the rebirth of spring after the death of winter – or from the rising and setting of the sun. But no spring, no dawn beyond death has ever been proven. Death is an endless night so awful to contemplate that it can make us love life and value it with such passion that it may be the ultimate cause of all joy and art.[8]

The *memento mori* in artefacts and memorials serve to unite the living with the dead and the dead with the living. They remind the living that they are all the while 'dying': for those who are alive they preserve the memory of the departed. In that sense the dead have a continued existence, and can indeed profoundly influence the present. In many primal cultures the ancestors have a central place, and their invoking, and the respect due to them, makes for the prosperity of their descendants and gives meaning to the community's self-understanding and direction to its existence. The cult of the saints in Christianity, spiritual ancestors of the church so to speak, has the same purpose and consequence. They may be spoken of and invoked as contemporaries whose prayers are known to be efficacious.

Thomas Traherne, Anglican priest and poet in the seventeenth century, brings together these two strands of natural and supernatural ancestry, and in his way anticipates the conclusions of John Bowker's study in the form of a thanksgiving:

> They are the Root of our being. We are the Branches of theirs. They are the fountain of many benefits. We are the objects of their Love. And they of ours. They are Blessed in their seed, And we in our forefathers.... They love us I think more than

themselves. For children are their fathers Bowels, & the Apple of their Eye, yet Grandfathers love their Grand-children, more than fathers their children, live in them & feel in them, as we see by their kindness: so the further off we go, the more naturally their Love doth increase, & the more they delight in our Blessedness.... I love my Ancestors, because they gave me my Being; & I owe all that I am or have to them: for my Hope had been Extinct, had any of them perished before I had been conceived.... There is not a Morsel of bread which they did ever eat, but it served us in feeding them....

All the Goodness of GOD to them is Goodness to us....
The Ages in my Ancestors afford
Me many predecessors, that prepared
The way, as if my God did still regard
In making them my Soul alone, who am
The very End.⁹

As I stand here and now, conscious of myself as the End, the end point of an immeasurably long past, I know also that I stand at the threshold between past and future, equally immeasurable, a future to which I am given to contribute all that I have received together with all that I myself have made of value. In that sense this is for me The Day of the Dead, the day in which I discover The Meanings of Death and so learn to practise The Art of Death.

Notes

1. Catalogue by Elizabeth Carmichael and Chloe Sayer of the British Museum's Museum of Mankind exhibition *The Skeleton at the Feast: The Day of the Dead in Mexico* (1991).
2. *The Art of Death: Visual Culture in the English Death Ritual c.1500–c.1800*, catalogue by Nigel Llewellyn (Reaktion Books, 1991).
3. Hippolytus, *Apostolic Tradition*, 21; cf. E. C. Whitaker, *Documents of the Baptismal Liturgy* (London: SPCK, 1960) pp. 5f.
4. Esther de Waal, *Living with Contradiction* (Harper Collins, 1989) p. 122.
5. Rowland Johnson, *The Ancient Customs of the City of Hereford* (London, 1868) pp. 159–60, citing John Aubrey (p. 90); quoted in Llewellyn, op. cit. (p. 74).

6. John Bowker, *The Meanings of Death* (Cambridge: Cambridge University Press, 1991) pp. 37ff; 211ff.
7. Henry King, 'My Midnight Meditation', *The Metaphysical Poets*, ed. Helen Gardner, 2nd edn (Harmondsworth, 1972) p. 114; quoted in Llewellyn, op. cit., p. 81.
8. 'D is for Death' by Paul Theroux in *Hockney's Alphabet* (Faber, 1991).
9. Thomas Traherne, 'Ancestor', Commentaries of Heaven; reprinted from an unpublished MS in A. M. Allchin *et al.*, *Profitable Wonders* (The Amate Press, 1989) pp. 54ff.

8
Mourning: The Song is Over but the Memory Lingers On
MARTIN ISRAEL

It may be true that no one knows for certain what happens to the person after death, but few of us can be in any doubt about the fate of those closest and dearest to him or her. An enormous wound has been inflicted on the psyche and, like bodily wounds, the initial pain can be of overwhelming intensity. Time alone can allow the healing process to take effect, but whereas a physical breach is usually repaired within a matter of days or certainly weeks, the psychological damage sustained after bereavement can take a full two years to recover.

Bereavement is a recurrent human experience; we know it whenever something or somebody close to us is irretrievably removed and is intrinsically irreplaceable. In a minor way it confronts a parent, especially the mother, when the child moves into ever-widening independence, eventually leaving home and fashioning its own abode and way of life. It acquires an increased poignancy when a married couple separate and one partner is left alone; when the employment one has known and loved to the extent of its being a marker of self-identification is taken from one at the time of retirement, especially when this is premature and one is summarily dismissed as being redundant; when a basic faculty like sight or hearing fails and a radically new way of life is forced on one. It attains its zenith when a loved one is separated from us in the mysterious process of death. Whatever views we may have about the survival of the essence of personality, it cannot be denied that we relate as physical creatures while we live in this world, and the body is our means of recognition and communication. The irreplaceable loss of someone we love is the most terrible experience of bereavement that we can know, and few of us are likely to escape it. The psychological, especially emotional, pain caused by bereavement is called grief, and the process of its unfoldment is called mourning.

THE INITIATION OF MOURNING[1]

Immediately after the fact of bereavement has made its impact upon us, we register a state of shock; it is as if our emotional reactions are numbed. We simply cannot take in the magnitude of the situation. This state of numbness insulates us from the intensity of our deeper feelings, and we may appear to cope remarkably well at least to the casual outsider. Indeed the numbness allows us to get on with details of funeral arrangements and other immediate concerns, such as barely keeping alive in radically altered circumstances. Sometimes attacks of panic intrude as we are suddenly confronted with the enormity of the situation: we feel afraid and suddenly cannot cope. Of course, our protector (wife quite as often as husband in conjugal bereavement) is no longer there to do the accustomed work, and now a load of responsibility falls squarely upon us, especially if we have dependants around us. There may also be outbursts of uncontrollable anger due to our helplessness, rather like the baby's cry when it feels neglected by its mother. Though our apparent stoicism may impress others, it is most important that we are attended by friends in the pursuance of our immediate needs, especially those involved in the funeral arrangements.

After this period of days, occasionally a few weeks, has passed, we become fully aware of our situation and grief really shows itself. Modern psychoanalytic thinking stresses the importance of personal attachment; it is even asserted that close attachment to one or more people is just as important as food and drink.[2] The infant gains this strength through its mother, so that when independence becomes inevitable with the passage of years, it still has an anchor of security. In due course other focuses of attachment are developed: friendship and especially marriage provide them. If the individual has had a good family background of love when young, he or she will be better able to cope with later loss than if the family attachment has been faulty. In this case there will be a tendency either to an obsessive attachment to someone in later life or else a difficulty in committing oneself to any attachment at all. Grief is as natural a response as hunger or thirst; what matters is how it is expressed and what comes from it. If one is morbidly attached to another person the experience of grief will be accentuated, and very likely require professional bereavement counselling.

THE EXPERIENCE OF GRIEF

As the shock wears off, so the terrible pain of sorrow reveals the magnitude of our loss; its persistence demonstrates its irrevocability. The principal emotional concomitants of grief are anger, bitterness, guilt and shame.[3]

Anger comes in flashes but can sometimes be quite prolonged. The anger is vented alternately on the deceased and on God, on the medical attendants and on providence. We are angry with the dead one for leaving us alone and often so suddenly and inconsiderately, without due preparation for the single or solitary life ahead of us. He could at least have shown me how to conduct my financial affairs; she might have had the foresight to teach me how to cook for myself. The medical staff were not interested enough in his condition until it was too late, the God whom we worshipped so ardently has let us down. Why did it have to happen to me? All this is very common, very childish, and all too human. The important thing to realise is that it is a natural part of the work of grieving (Freud called it 'grief work'[4]) and must in no way be suppressed. It carries no shame with it. It also reminds us that anger, though included among the seven deadly sins (the others are pride, covetousness, lust, gluttony, envy and sloth), is by no means to be summarily condemned. Without it a disastrous *status quo* could prevail in society, and standing injustices tolerated indefinitely. Unexpressed anger is dangerous since it may recede into the depths of the psyche and precipitate a depression. Unacknowledged anger is likewise to be avoided since it may flare up into destructive hatred.

Bitterness is an amalgam of sorrow and anger.[5] We all know it at some time in our lives when our schemes fail, our expectations are not fulfilled or our trusted friends let us down (often forgetting how frequently we have behaved selfishly to others in the past). All that we have striven for has collapsed around us and our lives seem to be mere failures. We often forget that the ultimate judgement of any life is what we have given to others and how much we have grown in love and wisdom; by contrast earthly possessions and power are evanescent.

Guilt is a more subtle emotion and needs careful analysis. It is natural to mull over the past in the solitude of bereavement, and then we come to see how selfishly we have behaved to the deceased. The prefix 'if only' comes persistently to our consciousness: if only we had paid more attention to the deceased's health before it was too late, had shown him or her how much we really loved them, had been less selfish about our own interests and more considerate about those of the departed one, had listened to the professional advice of our doctor, had not insisted on going on that particular holiday when the accident occurred. The list is endless and is sometimes compounded with the guilt of surviving at all when so many others died in an accident or a massacre. Unresolved guilt is common in grief and must be faced squarely, if necessary with a counsellor.

Closely related to guilt is regret that one had not fully enjoyed the simple pleasures of life with the deceased one. It is not so uncommon for a couple to retire to a pleasant bungalow, often near the sea and quite idyllic, and then one of them develops inoperable cancer or a progressive disease of the nervous system. Sadness, anger and regret colour the life of the survivor. If only we had used our holiday times more imaginatively, travelled the world and seen the sights; and now it is too late. To all this is added the scarcely tolerable truth that our love was not as sincere as we thought (I am not speaking of infidelity in this regard), that the dear one was less easy than we would like to acknowledge. We often over-compensate by turning him or her into a minor saint. How often have I counselled people who were plagued with troublesome relatives or colleagues, only to find that when these people died, only good could be remembered of them. This situation is in its way admirable, and a sharp riposte to Shakespeare, who in *Julius Caesar* makes Mark Antony comment, 'The evil that men do lives after them, the good is oft interred with their bones'. If one were to be somewhat cynical, one would see this devaluation as an almost inevitable part of the memorial of a celebrity once sensation-hungry biographers got under way. But the newly dead, whether humble or exalted, tend to be highly regarded. It is important for the bereaved one to start to see the truth, lest he or she becomes attached to the memory of the loved one to the extent of being unable to form any subsequent relationship that might at least help to assuage the pangs of loneliness. If their love were real, surely the departed ones would want the survivor to be as happy as possible and to fulfil the remainder of his or her earthly existence before they came together again later.

Shame is a more obscure emotion, but it is common enough: the bereaved one simply cannot face his or her acquaintances and retreats from any signs of sympathy. This feeling of shame is more than merely one of possibly reduced social status as a single person and therefore of less use to the social life of one's friends and colleagues. It is intrinsic to the grief work, and is probably an outcome of loneliness, so at least does the psychoanalyst Erich Fromm believe: 'The awareness of human separation without reunion by love is the source of shame'.[6] Hence it is especially valuable for grieving people to share their feelings with others.[7]

Despite inevitable personal variations, the course of grief is remarkably uniform; the emotions change quite rapidly and in the passage of a single day a person may feel sharp physical pain and then a sense of devastating loss with copious weeping, then a nagging sense of guilt followed by anger.[8] Between these strong emotional outbursts there may be relative calm. These strong emotions are not merely to be tolerated, but are to be positively acknowledged as part of the healing process; they serve to cleanse the wound and promote its healing. Nevertheless, some people have periods of irrational behaviour almost psychotic in intensity. In the course of such an episode destructive actions may be performed, such as getting rid of all articles that were once used by the deceased. Later on, in more balanced mood, this destruction of mementos may be bitterly regretted. It can also be hard to leave old habits in the past; one may act as if the deceased were still there. The intellect tells the bereaved person one thing but the emotions have difficulty in assimilating the unwelcome truth. It is certain that important decisions should be delayed during the mourning agony; the accompanying apathy and depression can further lead to unwise actions. A trustworthy relative or friend is invaluable in gently steering the bereaved person through the present darkness in which unwise actions may be performed. One should not actively interfere, but merely speak words of wisdom in loving concern.[9]

Grief also has its physical concomitants. The person sleeps badly, has a poor appetite, may suffer indigestion, and tends to lose weight. While the emotional ravages of grief can be quickly allayed by anti-depressants and drugs that promote sleep, it is generally agreed that these should be used only as a last resort, because they interfere with the work of grief. They afford comfort rather than support. The real work lies with the person, aided if necessary by the counsellor and psychotherapist.

THE END OF MOURNING

After several months to about two years the reality of death has finally sunk in and the bereaved one is in a position to let the beloved go, to go both to that place in the afterlife which we can dimly imagine, and to go from the constant attention of the mourner. We are moving to recovery when the deceased is no longer the primary focus of our thoughts.[10] The tempo of the bereaved one's life begins to change, and there is a desire to fill the gap left by the departed one with present social concerns. Indeed, sometimes this desire and its fulfilment shame the mourner (and his or her friends) into doubting the depth of affection really felt for the deceased one, but this is merely a healthy recuperation after a severe injury. Furthermore, there may be periods of regression when all seems to be proceeding so well; these times of grief are usually associated with significant anniversaries or when a particular event or symbol brings the beloved sharply to mind. The grief does not last long, but is a reminder of the depth of the loss. Hope takes the place of grief as a new life opens for the bereaved one. The nature of this hope may vary, from a new type of social life with or without marriage (if the bereaved has been a spouse) to a spiritual awakening of great magnitude.

It should finally be said that not all bereavement is accompanied by the type of grief that has been outlined. If the deceased has suffered a longdrawn period of illness, much of the grieving may have occurred while the sufferer was still alive and, indeed, death may be seen as a merciful release for both parties. People of deep spiritual awareness, which is decidedly apart from conventional piety or gnostic élitism, tend to accept death positively, while the elderly, who may have had earlier experiences of bereavement, tend to be less affected than their offspring when disaster strikes the family.

THE TASKS OF GRIEF WORK

The first task is the acceptance of the loss, something that may take a little while in a shocked person. Then comes the deeper acknowledgement that the loss is irrevocable. This seems so obvious to the uninvolved onlooker, but although the intellect may accept the fact of death, that fact has to penetrate through to the heart, to the emotional nature. In the depths there sometimes lingers the pathetic hope of a reprieve or that a mistake has been made. This is where direct contact with the dead body is so helpful; if the corpse has been badly mangled in an accident it is still worth while making it as presentable as possible for the bereaved one to see. The same applies in the case of stillborn babies. All this makes the grief more concrete, and then the bereaved can respond in the usual way by heartfelt tears.

Weeping is of the utmost value in a grief situation. Not only must the tears not be staunched, but their flow should be encouraged. Tears have a relieving effect on the stress produced by loss or injury. There is the rather shallow weeping of the baby who uses this mechanism to draw attention to itself, and the much deeper weeping of those who are doing their grief work properly. It is unfortunately 'not done' in some social groups to cry when an adult, but this is really because those around the weeper would feel embarrassed as they had to face their own sadness. In the end the truth will come out, and bereavement shows us how undeveloped our emotional life so often is. Of course, not all crying has this liberating effect; some is pure self-pity or even exhibitionism. Its shallow nature is as apparent as its shallow emotional content.

Mourning

Then comes the need to acquire new skills in contacts with people and in accomplishing practical tasks; the widow, for instance, learning how to cope with details of the Income Tax or the widower in looking after the children. The people or 'network' around the bereaved one are the friends and relations. They have to learn how to listen and support without offering comfort (rather like the drugs already mentioned). Comfort merely maintains the *status quo*, whereas support gives the sufferer strength for the future. In this way the person learns to act in new ways; we remember that the object of the exercise is the letting go of the deceased and the entrance into a new life.

This leads us to the fourth and final task, the reinvesting of emotional energy in new relationships and in new ways. It is important to bid a final farewell to the dead one. A letter, a ceremony, or the empty-chair technique of Gestalt therapy[11] are all very acceptable approaches. It should always be stressed that the beloved will never cease to remain in the person's memory, but now as a focus of blessing and an encouragement to new endeavours. The process of grieving has its own momentum; it cannot be speeded up, but it can be retarded disastrously by those who refuse to acknowledge the loss by showing a brave face to the outside world. In due course they will suffer a serious breakdown either mental or physical. If they survive this they will have to go through the full process that they thought they had evaded. Bereavement counselling is certainly a specialty in its own right.

PARAPSYCHOLOGICAL ISSUES

It is not very uncommon for the recently bereaved person to have a direct encounter with the deceased. This is often a morbid hallucination, and all such experiences tend to be written off in this way. However, it may be wiser to be more circumspect, at least in some instances. If the bereaved one seems fairly composed mentally and claims a single circumscribed apparition, it is at least within the bounds of possibility that the appearance is a valid one. An hallucination is simply a private sensory experience without a corresponding external object, and on occasions it may be valid for the person concerned. 'Phantasms of the living' have been well-described in the literature of psychical research,[12] and similar appearances involving the dead are also well known.[13] If the appearance becomes a repeated performance, it is very probably in the bereaved person's mind, but a sporadic event should not necessarily be summarily dismissed; at the very least it may support the person during a particularly dark period. Needless to say, such experiences are spontaneous, and should not be sought.

Some bereaved people visit mediums and get comforting messages from the dead. The whole question of mediumship is not within the mandate of this chapter, but from what has already been written it should be clear that communication with the dead person, should this indeed be possible (the validity of mediumship as evidence of survival after death is open to question, though the practice has its enthusiasts), can only serve to delay the process of letting go and starting a new life (this could well apply to the deceased one also). Therefore on purely psychological grounds, without reference to the biblical prohibitions against trying to communicate with the dead (Lev. 19:31 and Deut. 18:11), this practice is to be avoided. To be fair though, some mediums do have a supportive effect on their clients when other people seem ineffective. It is the medium's personality that proves helpful, as was recorded after King Saul's visit to the woman of En-dor (1 Samuel 28:8–25). It incidentally points out how ineffective traditional religion and its ministers so frequently are in a bereavement crisis. It is quite in order that mediums be investigated by responsible parapsychologists.

SPIRITUAL IMPLICATIONS[14]

Suffering brings us close to the core of our being by rendering us naked of all previous conceits. The mourner comes to a personal reality that may shock in its intensity; truth cannot be evaded when we are alone, unshielded by another's support. We see how much we have evaded life's deeper issues by losing ourselves in the pleasures of the passing scene; these in themselves are not to be scorned, but they do tend to produce a comfortable self-absorption until the facades of security have disintegrated. Bereavement brings us to our full measure; it makes us be open to our ourselves in all our frailty. The void can be terrible in its expanse.

Sometimes it is filled with a religious faith, and if this is of a mature type it can help us greatly in the work of suffering from whatever cause. But often it is immature and ill-conceived. We lose it when it proves inadequate to restore the loss or reverse the disappointment. Such a loss of faith need not necessarily be deplored; it is at the least an indication that the person is growing into the truth of the situation divested of all comforting delusions. If the end is an embittered, destructive agnosticism, it can easily sour the personality and lead to a gradual impoverishment of well-established human relationships, but if the person proceeds onwards in the spiritual darkness with courageous intent seeking nothing less than the truth, we should applaud these efforts.

The story of Job, one of the world's supreme spiritual masterpieces, is one of bereavement properly mourned, but in the end the debate moves in dark silence: human wisdom reaches its end as the traditional teachings of the sages about the fruits of righteousness are seen to be not so much wrong as inadequate. And what then? God in overwhelming majesty makes a direct entry, showing Job the vastness of creation, so that human wisdom stands merely at the foothills of reality. Job now understands how paltry are his complaints compared with God's providence: 'I know that you can do all things and that no purpose is beyond you.... I knew you then only by report, but now I see you with my own eyes' (Job 41:1–6). Job has been given no explanation about the cause of his pain, but he has been privileged to see God so clearly that his entire view of reality has been changed. The final chapter of the book may seem something of an anticlimax, since it brings the tale back to the world with Job's fortunes restored. But he, like us all, must live on this planet until he dies, and so there is no scandal in his later happiness, but one can sense a quiet assurance in his family life that contrasts with his fear of disaster at the beginning of the book.

Earlier in this chapter the importance of personal attachment was stressed, but there comes a time when the limited attachment to a particular person has to broaden until it achieves a universal scope. True love between people starts the process, since it cannot help pouring out to others, but finally the bereaved one has to see the features of the beloved in the faces of everyone else too. I have always found the most moving and convincing resurrection appearance of Christ to be that of the stranger the two disciples on the road to Emmaus meet (Luke 24:13–32): his presence warms their hearts as he expounds the scriptures to them. And he is the perpetual stranger in our midst. We cannot understand the full meaning of our transient life in this world; death is its final end, and sometimes this may be so horrifying, like the many mass murders of our own century, that we are, like Job, tempted to renounce all hope whether in the human, the world or the Deity. In the great family religion Judaism, the dead are unceasingly commemorated in the Kaddish, a prayer of exultant praise of God. It is also prayed that God's kingdom will come speedily to Israel (and by extension to the whole world), and that peace from heaven and the gift of life be granted to us all. It ends with the prayer that God who makes peace in the highest may bring his peace upon us and upon the whole world (again using the name Israel as a metonymy for the whole divine creation). Peace (*shalom*) means wholeness of life, a full integration of all parts of the individual personality as well as an integration of all creatures into the world of reality. Then there can be no disharmony or warfare. Love is indeed the fulfilment of the Law (Rom. 13:10).

I believe that all prayer for the dead has this universal intent; the Holy Spirit works through the intercessor to the soul prayed for in the great fellowship of life that extends further than we here can understand. The beloved is enveloped in a love so profound that we here could not bear to face its power to reveal the innermost secrets of the heart and to forgive them. We may pray for those whom we knew while they were here with us, but now our prayer extends to the whole of creation so that nothing is left out of the scope of God's providence. But then intercession for those still alive in the flesh works likewise. All this stresses the fellowship of all that lives whether here or in regions far beyond our knowledge.

Notes

1. C. M. Parkes, *Bereavement: Studies in Grief in Adult Life* (London: Tavistock, 1972); J. Tatelbaum, *The Courage to Grieve: Creative Living, Recovery and Growth through Grief* (London: Heinemann, 1981); N. Leick and M. Davidsen-Neilsen, in *Healing Pain: Attachment, Loss and Grief Therapy* (London: Tavistock/Routledge, 1991).
2. J. Bowlby, *Attachment and Loss*, vols I–III (New York: Basic Books, 1969, 1973, 1980), see esp. vol. I: *Attachment*.
3. Leick and Davidson-Nielsen, op. cit.
4. S. Freud, 'Mourning and Melancholia', vol. II: *On Metapsychology* (London: Pelican Freud Library, 1984).
5. Leick and Davidson-Neilsen, op. cit.
6. E. Fromm, *The Art of Loving* (New York: Harper & Bros, 1956) p. 14.
7. Leick and Davidson-Neilsen, op. cit.
8. Ibid.
9. Tatelbaum, op. cit.
10. Ibid.
11. Ibid.
12. R. Heywood, *The Sixth Sense* (London: Chatto & Windus, 1959). The book was later published in 1966 in London by Pan Books.
13. Churches' Fellowship for Psychical and Spiritual Studies, *About Bereavement* (1983). This booklet, published by the above Fellowship, is available from The General Secretary, CFPSS, 44 High Street, New Romney, Kent TN28 8BZ.
14. I. Ainsworth-Smith and P. Speck, *Letting Go: Caring for the Dying and Bereaved* (London: SPCK, 1982); C. S. Lewis, *A Grief Observed* (London: Faber, 1961); M. Israel, *Living Alone: The Inward Path to Fellowship* (London: SPCK, 1982).

Part II

New Perspectives

9
Death and Immortality: Towards a Global Synthesis
PAUL BADHAM

Belief in life after death is one of the things almost all religions have in common. J. G. Frazer's research in the last century showed that it was simply taken for granted by the adherents of the primal religions,[1] while in the major world faiths it forms an essential part of their belief structure. In Christianity, and Islam, belief in a future hope is a natural consequence of their belief in an all-powerful creator who has fashioned human beings for an eternal destiny with him. In Hinduism and Buddhism the belief in Karma requires the concept of a succession of lives as its necessary condition. Hence it seems reasonable to claim that the most widespread religions unite in affirming that this present existence does not constitute the whole of reality, and that human life should be seen in a cosmic perspective. The same is also true of Judaism, Sikhism, Zoroastrianism and most of the so-called 'new religions'. It is only for purposes of convenience that I confine my attention to four major traditions.

At first sight it might appear as if agreement ends at the statement of a future hope. For the traditional ways of expressing that hope, and for articulating in what sense 'we' live on, reveal significantly different emphases. Taken simply at face value, belief in the immortality of the soul, the resurrection of the body, reincarnation in successive earthly lives, absorption into the absolute, or entry into *parinirvana* do seem to represent a variety of mutually incompatible schemas deriving from fundamentally different world views. But I suggest that if we probe deeper and explore what these various doctrines are seeking to articulate, we may find a surprising measure of common ground lying behind these apparent disagreements, and a global synthesis may begin to emerge.

Let us consider first what happens at the moment of death itself. Traditionally, the world religions unite in affirming that at death some essential part of our identity continues. Hindus speak of the *atman*, or essence of each person, continuing with the individual's intellect, vitality and mind carried forward in a 'subtle body', (*suksma-sarira*), which forms the 'link' between one life and the next;² historic Christianity, and Islam talk of the soul 'going on'. Buddhists prefer to speak more cautiously in terms only of some 'connecting psyche', (*patisandhi vinnana*),³ and deny that a person should be identified with some eternal and unchanging soul-substance. In this latter stance they have attracted a great deal of sympathy from many contemporary Christians who are also troubled about the language of the soul. Nevertheless, both traditional Buddhists and liberal Christians do seem ready to affirm that there is some sense in which we go on, even though they are concerned about how to give this concept adequate expression.

What worried the Buddha was some presentations of the Hindu concept of *atman*, namely that there was in us a permanent, and unchanging essence, unaffected by the traumas of life, and that this is the self which proceeds through a succession of lives. As Buddha said: 'The speculative view that ... I shall be *atman* after death – permanent, abiding, everlasting, unchanging, and that I shall exist as such for eternity, is not that wholly and completely foolish.'⁴ But this 'no-self' doctrine should not be interpreted as ruling out any sense of personal continuance through death. Certainly Buddha himself did not take that view. Indeed, he even described the view that death meant extinction as a 'wicked heresy', and as something which was precisely what he did not teach.⁵ Buddha affirmed a dynamic, developing, ever-changing concept of the person. His understanding of Karma was associated with such a view, for the Buddha believed that the idea that what we do now affects what we become later, only makes sense if we are capable of change, and yet at the same time capable of being in some other sense continuous with our past. Hence Buddha affirmed a middle-path between those who suggest that death does not really affect our real selves, and those who affirm that death means total extinction. This middle path includes the notion that in some sense we continue, and such an understanding is given very great weight in the Tibetan and Pure-land forms of Buddhism, as well as finding expression in the Theravada tradition.

Contemporary Protestant Christianity has had comparable worries about the concept of the soul. Much western philosophy of mind is strongly anti-dualist, and at the same time biblical scholars have re-emphasised the psychosomatic monism of ancient Old Testament Judaism. The combination of these two features has led many Christian writers to seek to disassociate themselves from belief in the immortality of the soul, and to put the whole weight of their emphasis on the doctrine of resurrection. However, the same writers tend also to understand resurrection as affirming only the necessary embodiment of future human persons, rather than the literal raising up of the corpse laid in the tomb.[6] Hence while looking for the future resurrection of a 'spiritual body', they also talk of 'personality', 'mind', or 'the essential part of what we are' as also continuing, so that the new life will be authentically 'our life'. Hence some concept corresponding to talk of the soul seems in practice to be inescapable, even when the word itself is shunned. Within Catholicism the position of the Holy See is absolutely clear: 'the Church affirms that a spiritual element survives and subsists after death, an element endowed with consciousness and will, so that the "human self" subsists, though deprived for the present of the complement of its body. To designate this element the Church uses the word "soul", the accepted term in the usage of Scripture and Tradition.'[7]

All religions affirm that the continuation of soul, consciousness, or connecting principle, is a temporary stage, a bridge between two worlds. St Thomas Aquinas in the Christian tradition has drawn attention to the limitations of such an existence as an 'imperfect state' for a human person because of the necessary limitations of an existence without the flow of sense-experiences to stimulate its mental life.[8] H. H. Price, a former Professor of Logic at Oxford University, has spelt out how useful a mind-dependent state might be for reflection, recollection, and reformation, and this view has been developed within modern Christian theology by John Hick.[9] Al-Ghazali in the Islamic tradition has described the next stage of existence as the world of *'Barzakh'*, a mind-dependent state shaped by our thoughts and feelings, where we reflect on our past life before the day of resurrection.[10] What Al-Ghazali says of *Barzakh* seems akin to what the Tibetan Book of the Dead says of the *Bardo* world to which the consciousness-principle moves on the death of the body,[11] and this in turn seems akin to the ancient Hindu concept of a world of desire (*Kama*

Loka) which is understood as a mind-dependent state reflecting our desires and memories.[12]

So there appears to be a global agreement that the immediate stage after death is a mind-dependent world. Yet all agree that this is only a temporary state prior to resurrection in the Christian and Islamic traditions, and to reincarnation in the religions of the East. A strong contrast is often drawn between these two beliefs, especially when resurrection is understood in a very literal sense as the precise restoration to life of the physical corpse, and when reincarnation is understood as entering a new body on this earth which might not even be a human one. However, these are not the only ways these doctrines can be understood.

Most contemporary Christians have abandoned a literal understanding of resurrection, in favour of a hope for being clothed with a new and glorious body for a totally new mode of life in heaven. As the Church of England Doctrine Commission puts it: 'We ought to reject quite frankly the literalistic belief in a future resurrection of the actual physical frame which is laid in the tomb ... none the less ... in the life of the world to come the soul or spirit will still have its appropriate organ of expression and activity, which is one with the body of earthly life in the sense that it bears the same relation to the same spiritual entity.'[13] Most discussions of resurrection by Christian theologians emphasise their hope for a radically new mode of existence in an altogether more glorious and resplendent mode of being. Similarly, within Islam the main emphasis in the descriptions of the hereafter (*al-'akhira*) is to emphasise the otherness and wonder of the life of heaven (*al-Janat*). And although resurrection is often thought of in very physical terms, it is interesting to note the terminology actually used in the Quran. Unbelievers had questioned the possibility of resurrection saying, 'When we are turned to bones and dust shall we be raised to life?' The Quran's response is clear 'Do they not see that Allah, who has created the heaven and the earth has power to create their like?'[14] Not literal resuscitation, but a new creation is here implied, and this ties in with the Quran's insistence that very different physical conditions will apply in the life of heaven. Modern Muslim scholars insist that the 'nature of the life of heaven is beyond our comprehension.'[15] It is certainly not a straightforward continuation of earthly style existence.

Many Christian theologians have argued that to understand

heaven as a limitlessly open future would involve so great a change that it would be hard to think of it as a potential future for us. Hence they have suggested that many lives in many worlds might be a better way of understanding it. Though this view is nowadays most commonly associated with the speculations of Professor John Hick, it is interesting to recall that William Temple, the best-known Archbishop of Canterbury this century, interpreted a saying of Jesus as meaning this. In John's Gospel (14:2) Jesus is reported as saying: 'in my Fathers house there are many resting-places, I go to prepare a place for you'. Archbishop Temple points out that 'these resting-places (*monai*) are wayside caravanserais – shelters at stages along the road where travellers may rest on their journey.... We are still far from perfect fellowship with the Father ... we have a long journey ahead.... But there are, by God's mercy, many resting-places. Otherwise of what avail would be the promise? ... If it were only in the realm of ultimate attainment would Christ mock us with the promise of a welcome there?'[16] This is no new theory. St Gregory of Nyssa, who drafted the 'Nicene' Creed which Christians recite at their Communion Services, had a similar perspective in mind when he wrote 'Moving from one new beginning to the next the soul makes its way towards the transcendent.'[17]

From the Islamic tradition, Dr Salih Tug seems to be thinking in comparable terms. He has argued that the life hereafter should be likened to a journey with many stages to pass through as the soul travels onward. He believes that 'A quasi "spiritual hospital" called hell ... will be one of the stages in the process of evolution for the soul that has not utilised the opportunities provided for it in its earthly sojourn. It stunted its faculties becoming diseased and corrupted, but after cure it shall come out of that state and start on its evolutionary journey.'[18]

It is clear that many Christians and Muslims now interpret resurrection, not in terms of getting their old bodies back, but of receiving new bodies, suited for the continued expression of their personality in the life of heaven. It is also clear that some thinkers are prepared to think in terms of progress and development after death involving perhaps a succession of different lives. These developments very significantly move the understanding of resurrection closer to some important elements in the Buddhist concept of re-birth, and the Hindu understanding of reincarnation.

The greatest difference remaining is that in popular Buddhist and Hindu thought reincarnation is conceived of in terms of re-embodiment on this earth. Since in 99 per cent of cases there is not even a claim to be able to remember a past life, such an understanding of what we may expect after death has always been rejected by most Christian and Muslim scholars. Even in the handful of cases where there are apparently well-attested 'memories' pertaining to a supposed earlier life, difficulties still remain. I have no explanation to offer for the peculiar fact that sometimes a young child may, for a few years, possess up to fifty correct memories of the life of a deceased person. But what I do claim is that the possession of such memories is not a sufficient basis to conclude a former person is now living in that child's body.

However, in many Hindu and Buddhist texts reincarnation is said to take place in other worlds. If this modification of the doctrine were to become universal, then there would seem little remaining difference between this understanding of reincarnation, and the contemporary Christian and Islamic reinterpretation of resurrection. In fact the description of life in Buddha's 'pure-land', and the Christian vision of heaven have a very great deal in common. When one tries to articulate a contemporary understanding of either resurrection or reincarnation in terms which are acceptable today, both doctrines tend to be modified to incorporate insights already present in the other. A global synthesis is already emerging.

Part of the justification of belief in life after death is that the world religions believe that human life needs to be seen in a cosmic perspective where there is the possibility for progress beyond the limits of this life. For this to happen, some concept of judgement and reflection upon our past lives would seem essential and this is in fact part of the tradition of each religion. Horrifying images of hell abound in all world religions. Today, however, there is an increasing tendency in each religion to move away from such images and to emphasise instead the need for moral reflection and progress in the life beyond. We have already noted the judgement of Dr Salih Tug, the Dean of Theology at Istanbul, that hell is a hospital for wounded souls. A comparable view is now increasingly widespread within Christianity, and even so conservative a leader as the present Pope believes that, 'in the light of the truth that "God is love"' we should contemplate 'tentatively reaching out towards some later phase in the history of salvation – not disclosed in revelation and the scriptures – which might put an end to this separation between those who are saved and those who are damned'.[19] Other Christians would put this much more positively and, apart from the most extreme fundamentalist groups, there is now a consensus that hell should be interpreted as a form of purgatory, a stage on the way towards salvation. In Buddhism and Hinduism, hell has always been understood as a temporary state leading to purification, and many writers have insisted that the horrifying imagery should be interpreted symbolically rather than factually. So once again a global synthesis is now emerging.

Finally we turn to what the world religions see as our ultimate destiny. For Muslims, life after death should be seen as 'a life of unlimited progress' towards God.[20] For Christians too, God is our ultimate destiny, and the beatific vision as described by the mystics is a state where we are ultimately completely at one with God and rest in his eternal changelessness.[21] Within the Hindu traditions, 'Liberation, according to Vaisnavism, is union with God and enjoyment of perfect freedom and bliss in the celestial world.'[22] For the Buddhist, the ultimate goal is Nirvana. This has been interpreted in a negative way as the disappearance of the existent entity. But when Buddha himself heard this interpretation being given he insisted that 'this is just what I do not say'.[23] Rather, he interpreted Nirvana as a state of joy, happiness and peace; an experience of 'bliss unspeakable'.[24] According to Takeuchi Yoshinori in the Kyoto school of Buddhist philosophy 'Nirvana' is the equivalent of what western mysticism understands as the "being of beings", the supreme and one reality, the absolute, the divine. . . . Nirvana is the infinite, the eternal, the uncreated, the quality-free, the ineffable, the one and only, the highest, the supreme good.'[25] If this interpretation is correct, one can suggest that the unitive vision of the Christian mystic, and the hope of *parinirvana* of the devout Buddhist are alternative ways of expressing the same Reality. And this Reality is the goal towards which the world's great religions are pointing as the ultimate destiny of humanity in the life beyond.

Notes

1. J. G. Frazer, *The Belief in Immortality and the World of the Dead*, vol. 1 (London: Macmillan, 1913) pp. 138–9.
2. R. Balusubramanian, 'The Advaita View of Death and Immortality', in Paul and Linda Badham, *Death and Immortality in the Religions of the World* (New York: Paragon House, 1987) pp. 109–25.
3. Saeng Chandra-Ngarm, 'Life, Death, and the Deathless, in Theravada Buddhism', in Paul and Linda Badham, *Death and Immortality in the Religions of the World*, p. 131.
4. Cited in Walpola Rahula, *What the Buddha Taught* (London: Gordon Fraser, 1967) p. 59.
5. Samyutta-Nikaya XXII 85, cited in Sarvepalli Radhakrishan and Charles A. Moore, *A Sourcebook in Indian Philosophy* (Princeton: Princeton University Press, 1957) p. 286.
6. For full documentation of this see Paul Badham, *Christian Beliefs about Life after Death* (London: Macmillan, 1976) Chapter 5.
7. J. Neuner and J. Dupuis, *The Christian Faith in the Doctrinal Statements of the Catholic Church* (London: Collins, 1983) p. 691.
8. St Thomas Aquinas, *Summa Theologiae*, 1a. Question 89.
9. John Hick, *Death and Eternal Life* (London: Macmillan, 1976) p. 270.
10. Salih Tug, 'Death and Immortality in Islamic Thought', in Paul and Linda Badham, *Death and Immortality in the Religions of the World*, p. 88.
11. W. Y. Evans-Wentz (ed.), *The Tibetan Book of the Dead* (London: Oxford University Press, 1957) p. 98.
12. John Hick, *Christianity at the Centre* (London: SCM, 1968) p. 110.
13. *Doctrine in the Church of England* (London: SPCK, 1962) p. 209.
14. 'The Night Journey', *The Quran*.
15. Sulayman Nyang, 'The Teaching of the Quran concerning Life after Death', in Paul and Linda Badham, *Death and Immortality in the Religions of the World*, p. 83.
16. William Temple, *Readings in St John's Gospel* (London: Macmillan, 1963) p. 218.
17. John Hick, *Death and Eternal Life*, p. 422.
18. Salih Tug, 'Death and Immortality in Islamic Thought', in Paul and Linda Badham, *Death and Immortality in the Religions of the World*, pp. 88–9.
19. Pope John-Paul II, *Sign of Contradiction* (London: Hodder, 1979) p. 180.
20. Salih Tug, 'Death and Immortality in Islamic Thought', in Paul and Linda Badham, *Death and Immortality in the Religions of the World*, p. 88.
21. John Hick, *Death and Eternal Life*, Chapter 21.
22. R. Balusubramanian, 'The Advaita View of Death and Immortality' in Paul and Linda Badham, *Death and Immortality in the Religions of the World*, p. 121.
23. Majjhima Nikaya 1.140 (Buddhist Sacred Text). Cited in John Hick, *An Interpretation of Religion* (London: Macmillan, 1989) p. 285.
24. Rudolf Otto, *The Idea of the Holy* (1917, London: Penguin, 1959) p. 53.
25. Takeuchi Yoshinori, *The Heart of Buddhism* (New York: Cross Road, 1983) pp. 8–9. Cited in John Hick, *An Interpretation of Religion*, p. 287.

10
Beyond Death: The Case of New Religions
PETER CLARKE

DIVERSITY AND NEWNESS OF NEW RELIGIONS

An estimated 800 new religions have emerged in Western Europe since the Second World War. In the United States the number is much higher, some specialists in the field suggesting that it is around 3000.[1] There is no reason, however, to suggest that the United States is more fertile soil for new religious movements than Western Europe. Statistics are often produced to show that church attendance is much higher in the United States than in Europe and the conclusion drawn that the former is more religious and open to the spiritual than the latter and hence more likely to provide a more congenial environment for the growth of new religions.

This line of thinking overlooks the level of interest in the spiritual in Western Europe and the relatively widespread search for, and experience of, the 'supernatural'.[2] Moreover, although it was largely in the United States that the New Age has found its most powerful advocates and spokespersons, historically it owes much, as do many new religions, to the ideas and writings that originated in Western Europe. The writings of the English medium Alice Bailey, for example, are an important source of New-Age thinking. Europe has also been an important source of materials for the modern occult revival. Indeed, this revival is historically largely the creation of, among others, the Austrian Franz Mesmer, Emmanuel Swedenborg from Sweden, and Britain's Aleister Crowley. However, many of the post-Second World War new Christian missionary movements found in Western Europe, among them Youth for Christ International, Youth with a Mission and Young Life, arrived from the United States. Overall, there are some

200 such American missionary agencies in Western Europe today.

The new religion's scene is an extremely varied one and bears out, at least in part, Durkheim's observation that, although there are no gospels that are immortal, there is no reason for believing that mankind is incapable of inventing new ones.[3] The diversity is immense, consisting of varying kinds of Neo-Pagan and New Age, and new Hindu, Buddhist, Christian and Islamic movements. Such diversity naturally makes any generalisations that one might offer on the subject of death and the beyond, or for that matter on any other existential question, from the perspective of new movements extremely tentative, something I hope will be borne in mind by the reader of this contribution. Not only is diversity a problem, so also is the application of the term 'new' to many of these movements. By new religions is meant here religions new to the West, that is religions that have either emerged in the West during the past thirty years or so, or have arrived there from elsewhere. Scientology is an example of the first kind. Originally a form of psychotherapy known as Dianetics and founded by the American fiction writer L. Ron Hubbard, it became the Church of Scientology in 1954. The reasons for such changes are often many and varied and include the desire to acquire charitable status.

An example of a 'new' religion that would claim to be old is the International Society for Krishna Consciousness or Hare Krishna which was introduced to Europe via India and the United States in the late 1960s. Hare Krishna would claim that it is not a new religion in any chronological sense of the term, but part of a long tradition of spirituality dating back to Chaitanya Mahaprahbu, an early sixteenth century holyman and social reformer from Bengal who is believed to have been an incarnation of Vishnu. Chaitanya is said to have popularised the type of devotion seen today practised on the streets of Western capitals by Hare Krishna devotees.[4]

A relatively large number of new movements are 'old' in the Hare Krishna sense, in that they are linear descendants of a long tradition of teaching, spirituality and practice. Soka Gakkai or Value Creation Society falls into this category, basing its doctrines and rituals on the writings of the thirteenth-century Japanese monk Nichiren Daishonin. But once again, like Hare Krishna, Soka Gakkai, which is growing steadily in the West, is new in that it only began to establish itself there in the 1960s. It is also new as a separate lay organisation distinct from the priestly based Buddhist movement known as Nichiren Shoshu. In other respects also, the modern versions of these older spiritualities and philosophies are by no means identical in every respect with the parent body. In their Western garb they may at times appear so different as to be unrecognisable in the original context, as was the case with the Rajneesh movement in Poona, India, where the local people found it at first extremely exotic if not esoteric. Moreover, the packaging of the older traditions to suit the needs of the modern world can give rise to very marked differences between the original tradition and its modern version. Most Japanese new movements, and the same holds for modern Self-Religions such as Scientology, Sufi-, Hindu- and African-derived new religions, are knowingly and expressly syncretistic as they reach out to modern society.

New movements, then, while not necessarily new in a doctrinal or ritual sense do, of necessity, adapt and change to the new contexts in which they find themselves and arrange and present their philosophy accordingly. This is true of the New Age movement which in many respects is a lineal descendent of various nineteenth-century philosophies, including the American Metaphysical Movement, the New Thought Movement and Positive Thinking.[5]

Some movements, furthermore, in an effort to convince the world of their newness surround themselves with the paraphernalia of science to show that their claims can be verified in the modern way, that is by recourse to empirical and rational methods and techniques such as the E-Meter of Scientology. Other movements construct models of paradise where they display the heavenly symbols and delights of the modern world: golf courses, stress-eradicating pastimes and such leisure pursuits as may be had by means of wealth in the best areas of California.

THE APPEAL OF NEW RELIGIONS

As in many other religions, people are often drawn in the first instance to new religions not because they provide them with the meaning of life or with answers to the great existential questions. It is often the practical dimension of a new religion that first attracts people; the techniques it might offer them to cope with anything from the performing of everyday, routine duties to coping with stress, to bolstering their self-confidence or to feeling better about themselves. Soka Gakkai members speak of how chanting before the Gohonzon or sacred scroll enables them to do their normal tasks with greater vigour and commitment and shoulder responsibility for their lot. New religionists are not necessarily concerned with overturning the present order or with radical self-transformation. Some simply want more religion in their life and are not too concerned about the content which can range from the extremely simple to the highly developed.

While there is often a strong desire among those who join new religions to do even better in what they are already engaged in rather than to strike out on a radically new path, there are also, among new religionists, 'the renouncers' or 'rejectors', those who have turned against the wider society in pursuit of a totally new understanding of the self and of a completely different value system. Other new religionists might be termed 'gradualists'; they have a much more measured view of change both at the personal and societal levels.

New movements, often charged with being inward-looking, narcissistic and obsessed with the self, do concern themselves with 'real' issues affecting the wider society. New Agers are the greens of the new religious scene. They are also convinced that a new order will be ushered in by a profound change in consciousness in which all will come to recognise that we are one people living in one world that shares a common destiny. This realisation will have revolutionary effects and make for a complete transformation of the planet. Other movements that have become deeply engaged in environmental and peace issues include the Brahma Kumaris movement and Soka Gakkai, while Scientology has focused on, among other things, problems of interpersonal communication which it sees as one of the main concerns of modern society.

By contrast, some movements have taken the same path as mainstream politics, for example in the early 1980s. The Unification Church, or Moonies, is but one example of a stridently and militantly anti-Communist new religion, and the Church Universal and Triumphant is another.[6]

THE QUESTION OF THE SELF AND ATTITUDES TO DEATH

Many new religious movements fall into the category of Self-Religions and are essentially a response to the search for an answer to the pressing question of personal identity, and to the search for a path to self-development. Self-Religions, as Heelas, the author of the term, points out 'offer participants the experience of god . . . what they experience is the god within'.[7]

Numerous people believe that they are not as they should be. In other words, they have been constructed by family, school, sometimes but not always by church, and by society at large, and exist as a product of these socialisation agencies whose values they have internalised and to which they may have given notional but never real consent. They will not hear of brainwashing at the hands of gurus but instead insist that, given a certain combination of circumstances, experiences and encounters, they have come to embark on a process of self-deconstruction in an attempt to discover the nature of their real self and move on from there to self-development.

It is at this point that ideas of and attitudes toward death can be decisive. While new religionists as individuals do seriously confront these questions and many find that the *Tibetan Book of the Dead* provides them with most valuable insights, it needs to be pointed out here that many new movements rarely mention death and what lies beyond. Some talk of the impending Apocalypse to be followed by the reign of the just and righteous and others speak simply of the imminent arrival of the millenium. But with the notable exception of such movements as the Worldwide Church of God and the Unification Church, there are few developed eschatologies and little about death *per se* and the future beyond the grave. As already indicated most new movements are millenarian in a decidedly this-worldy sense. There are, none the less, movements that give a central place in their teaching to death and beyond. Although the point has been made that a large part of their concern is salvation from immediate or present evil in the form of stress and other everday difficulties, a range of the previously mentioned Self-Religions, including the Rajneesh movement, are also preoccupied with the issue of death as it relates to self-development and tend overall to adopt one or other variant of what might be termed the oriental interpretation of its meaning and consequences.

CONQUERING DEATH TO LIVE

The belief that there is such a thing as once and for all physical death which is final in terms of one's spiritual well-being and progress is largely rejected. Indeed, it is more than rejected, it is ridiculed and placed in the same category as the monotheistic idea of a God who stands above and passes judgement on human beings. According to a leading member of the Friends of the Western Buddhist Order, such a God destroys the creative potential of the human being, paralysing and reducing them to slaves.[8] Physical death, likewise, if seen as the end of human endeavour, disempowers individuals; it becomes an instrument of oppression that generates such fear that it becomes impossible to live and develop spiritually. There are those new religionists who believe that Western society has achieved remarkable material growth but only at the expense of spiritual progress, thus giving rise to an unbalanced, immature outlook and attitude toward what constitutes the purpose and meaning of life. This has motivated seekers to pursue spiritual development as an essential prerequisite of full human development. Such seekers are also persuaded that it can be a very long process, and as such is incompatible with the idea that such development ends with physical death.

Spiritual development as understood in the Self-Religions is essentially concerned with understanding the previously mentioned process of deconstructing the received understanding of the self in order to discover the real self. Such a discovery can be a very long journey involving numerous lives.

Much new religion makes a distinction between the ego and the true self and one of its basic premises is that while the former is subject to death the latter is indestructible and can never die. The Indian Guru Bhagwan Shree Rajneesh, founder of the Rajneesh Movement which began in Bombay in the early 1970s and soon moved to Poona, is but one of a number of spiritual masters who taught his followers, or sanyassins as they are known, to view death in this way. He told his disciples:

> Death is one of the holiest of the holies. People have completely forgotten how to live and they have completely forgotten how to die. They have been taught that death is the enemy of life, the end of life, so they are scared and cannot relax. . . . Their life is ugly and their death is ugly. Death should be welcomed. It is one of the great events in life.[9]

According to Rajneesh, teaching death in the sense of the destruction of the ego has a two-fold purpose: first of all it enables us to reach a full understanding of who and what we really are and secondly it enables us to live to the full now. Thus, death should not be a taboo subject. There is no need to fear physical death, to shun it, to refuse to talk about it, to avoid contact with it. The whole problem of death lies in the way it is perceived, that is as something negative. And this misperception is reinforced by the fact that the care of the dead in modern society is, for the most part, in the hands of professionals, with the result that most people, even the closest of kin of the deceased, have little direct contact with it. While in the not too distant past death was a regular experience within the domestic situation, as most people died among their relatives at home, in contemporary Britain an estimated fifty per cent of people die in hospital and in the United States some eighty per cent of the population experience what is termed institutional death. Death consists of approaching physical death in a negative way; for it is essentially this approach that gives it its power and mastery over one's thinking and behaviour. Instead of regarding death as a means to an end, as a way of achieving those positive and constructive goals mentioned above, it becomes a barrier to creative, dynamic action and an unsurmountable obstacle to self-development and self-realisation.

DYNAMIC MEDITATION, SYMBOLIC DEATH AND FREEDOM TO BE

Changing deeply-ingrained and psychologically and spiritually damaging views of, and attitudes toward, death is a most important part of the spiritual therapy of a number of new religions. Dynamic meditation was one of several techniques used by the Rajneesh movement for this and other purposes. By means of it the sanyassin symbolically experienced the joy and freedom that came from conquering death.

The following rather lengthy quotation from a former member of the movement explains rather graphically how this technique helped her to come to terms with death:

> I had been doing Dynamic Meditation almost every day when I was in the States, but doing it on the beach in Bombay at six

o'clock in the morning with a group of sanyassins was a totally different experience. My catharsis in the second stage of the technique went deeper than it had ever gone before. I lay on the sand; I screamed, I cried. Wetness poured from my eyes, my nose, my mouth. . . . I lost myself completely in the catharsis. My body jerked and writhed in epileptic-like movements. I vomited, and kicked the sand ferociously to cover the mess I had made. Anger came up. I punched the air, I growled like a lion, I killed my mother and my father and the beggar I had seen on the street that morning and a multitude of strangers I'd never met.

I fell to my knees. In my hand was a dagger. I raised my hands above my head, both of them clutching at the dagger. Tears poured down my face. . . . I had to kill. One quick stroke and it would be done . . . my death accomplished. My arms shook . . . but they wouldn't drop. . . . Finally, finally – Ahhhhhhhh! The stab. The death. I crumbled on the ground. Tears of relief. Tears of sadness. Tears of joy. I had done it. I had killed myself. It was done finally. I couldn't stop crying. Tears of relief that washed me. Cleansed me; I was drenched in them.[10]

No guarantees were given that this or any other technique would work in every instance, and in some cases they clearly did not. Another meditation technique recommended to those seeking to drive away the fear of death and make it serve its true purposes of enabling life to be lived to the full and true self-understanding reached was that of 'watching' death. The practice was to watch the people one loved, especially children, die and to meditate on their death. To quote again from the above source on this technique:

You go through their (your loved ones) death. . . . Everything that lives is bound to die. The beginning is the end, your first step is your last, your birth is your death. . . . If one can live through the death of one's children one can live through anything. It's not death itself that is so bad; it's the fear of it. The technique worked for Krishna (a sanyassin) as it hadn't for me. He felt cleansed by it. Death – his own or that of someone he loved – no longer held any fear for him.[11]

To master the death of the ego is to begin to live in freedom. Furthermore, it is to take full responsibility for oneself. New movements among the so-called Self-Religions such as Scientology, Buddhist movements of Japanese origin including Soka Gakkai, or Hindu-derived movements like Hare Krishna, emphasise that individuals are fully responsible for all that happens to them, including their death. What is being taught here, with some variations, is basically the law of karma whereby nothing happens to a person that is not in some sense the result of that person's action in this or a past life. Thus, one reaps what one has sown. *Samsara* is the continuous process of dying and being reborn for many different lives and in many different conditions of existence that are the result of previous actions conforming to a law of similarity between action and result. Such existences are deemed to be unsatisfactory compared with the ultimate spiritual goal of *nirvana* (supreme tranquility) or *moksha* (liberation) from the cycle of birth and rebirth.

It is worth noting that an estimated twenty five per cent of the people of Western Europe believe in one form of reincarnation or another and, more generally, what appears to be happening is the construction in the religious sphere of a new syncretism derived largely from Christian and Eastern, mainly Hindu and Buddhist, beliefs and rituals.

The appeal of reincarnation lies in part in the added space it provides for spiritual growth, in which the seeker moves beyond the limitations of physical death in pursuit of the real self.

CONCLUSIONS

In the teaching of the Self-Religions, dying is an essential ingredient of being a complete person. The right way to approach death is to accept it, for what dies is the ego not the real self which, as previously noted, is eternal. To refuse to contemplate death, to put it to one side, to hide from it, to live in fear of it, is to destroy the chance of attaining that wholeness for which a person is born.

All of this reflects a desire people appear to have to find something permanent and stable to hold on to, something that cannot be destroyed. And to find it they turn not towards the notion of an immortal soul that will live forever in a paradise beyond the grave, but inward to within themselves where, they believe, the divine is located. This outlook is expressed by one sanyassin when she speaks of her ageing, sick father's attitude to death:

> My father is seventy, he has never been a well man, but when I mention death to him, and the need to find something within himself that won't die with his death, I'm bringing up something that he would rather ignore.... We live in fear of death, we don't welcome it. It's our panic in the fear of death that makes it so ugly.[12]

The main text then of the new religions' understanding of death and beyond is that death is the way to life and the subtext is that as god, the individual is responsible for determining the manner and content of both.

Notes

1. J. G. Melton, *Encyclopaedic Handbook of Cults in America* (New York: Garland, 1986).
2. D. Hay, *Religious Experience Today* (London: Mowbray, 1990).
3. E. Durkheim, *The Elementary Forms of the Religious Life*, trs. J. Ward Swain (London: George Allen & Unwin, 1915) p. 286.
4. K. Knott, *My Sweet Lord* (Wellingborough: Aquarian Press, 1987).
5. M. O. York, 'The New Age and Neo-Pagan Movement', PhD thesis, King's College, University of London (1991).
6. Ibid.
7. P. Heelas, 'Western Europe: Self Religions', in S. R. Sutherland and P. Clarke (eds), *The Study of Religions: Traditional and New Religion* (London: Routledge, 1991) p. 167.
8. Dharmachari Subhuti (A. Kennedy), *Buddhism for Today* (Salisbury: Element Books, 1983).
9. Ma Satya Bharti, *Death Comes Dancing* (London: Routledge, 1981) p. 49.
10. Ibid., pp. 25–6.
11. Ibid., pp. 48–9.
12. Ibid., p. 49.

11
Death and the Afterlife: New Approaches to an Old Question

ARTHUR BERGER

A six-year old girl wrote to God: 'Granny is very sick. Mommy says she will die, What is death? I don't want her to die and I don't want to die. But I would like to know what death is.' We don't know whether God replied to her question but we do know that, young or old, the question raised by the little girl is the oldest and most persistent and absorbing of all in its interest. What is death: extinction? or is there some sort of afterlife?

The Survival Research Foundation is an internationally known nonprofit organisation exclusively devoted to the search for scientifically valid evidence to throw light on this question. This chapter will deal with why our investigation is important, what we mean by the 'afterlife', where we look for evidence and the sorts of methods we use.

PRINCIPLE OF CLOSEDNESS

I believe that most of us who are interested in this question would subscribe to what John Hick in *Death and Eternal Life*[1] called 'the principle of openness to all data'. I construe this as meaning that when we begin to ponder and try to answer the question of an afterlife, we ought to take into account the data and investigations relevant to this question and consider them another means of helping us understand our ultimate destinies. I think also that the principle of openness is the mark of the rational mind.

Yet among many educated and intelligent people there persists the opposite principle of what we might call 'closedness' to all data. When some scientific investigators claim that it may be possible to obtain data suggesting an afterlife, these closed-minded people are amused and incredulous: they make sarcastic remarks about soft-headed and gullible investigators who believe in ghosts, mediums and haunted houses and they either bring the conversation to an abrupt halt or steer it toward more agreeable subjects such as the weather or the latest scandal in the White House.

But I don't believe that these educated critics would dismiss investigations into the problem of the afterlife so readily if they knew that ever since the beginning of these investigations in England in 1882 and America in 1885, many eminent scholars and scientists have been associated with the research. They do not know of the extremely careful investigations and analytical reports made in the past by William James of Harvard, Eleanor Sidgwick of Newnham College, Richard Hodgson of Cambridge, James H. Hyslop of Columbia and, more recently, by Ian Stevenson of the University of Virginia and the late Robert H. Thouless of Cambridge and the Survival Research Foundation. These were and are critical and sceptical people. They were and are not soft-headed or gullible. Anyone reading their papers or the journals of the societies for psychical research will see how rigid the standards of evidence are.

IMPORTANCE OF RESEARCH

Those who do sneer at scientific research into the question of an afterlife may wonder what purpose it serves. They may ask: Isn't this a religious question? Shouldn't we leave it to religion?

For all who subscribe unquestioningly to the dogmatic teachings of religion, theirs is not an unreasonable position. But even the most devout might concede the importance of scientific research if they realised that strong empirical evidence of the continuation of some spiritual element of the human being would be an almost lethal dose for materialism, which postulates that the human being is no more than the physical body. This evidence also would supply the fundamental precondition of the eternal life promised by Western religion or the rounds of lives promised by Eastern religion. Such evidence also would demonstrate that religious teachings of a future life are consistent with scientific findings and are credible.

I think also that such evidence could have great practical importance. Death comes to us all. Any enlightenment we can be given about it and whether it is a wall or a doorway would go far towards allowing us to assume a rational stance towards it. Should it appear to be a doorway, this knowledge would be of utmost importance to widows, widowers, parents, lovers and friends who have lost someone dear. There should be great consolation and a lessened sense of grief if there were evidence of an afterlife. In addition, if we were to learn that the line is not drawn at the grave, people might become aware of their responsibility for their actions. This changed attitude should have moral importance for both the individual and society.

FIELD OF EXPLORATION

To avoid confusion, it might be well to clarify what the Survival Research Foundation means by an 'afterlife'. The question it investigates is whether any conscious remembering and identifiable component of the human being continues beyond death for any period of time. The field we explore may be described as 'pareschatology', the word John Hick adopted for distinguishing between eschatology, the study of the ultimate state about which religion has much to say, and the study of the state between death and the ultimate one. So the Survival Research Foundation is not concerned with immortality, nor eternal life, nor resurrection. The question we investigate has nothing to do with reward or punishment, heaven or hell. Not is it a philosophic conception, such as John Hick's, of a transpersonal self or *atman* transcending the empirical self and personally developing and spiritually progressing toward God. Nevertheless, our exploration has great relevance for all these religious and philosophic post-mortem states, because they depend on the existence and continuance after death of some nonphysical component of the human being which can became immortal, can enjoy eternal life, can be clothed in a new body in the world to come, can enter heaven or hell, can go on to progress in spiritual development toward God, as Hick argues. It is this minimal fact the Survival Research Foundation is after: does some nonmaterial and disembodied principle in us survive physical death? It is the essential first support for any of these teachings or concepts.

Ours, therefore, is not a religious or philosophical approach. The Survival Research Foundation explores for empirical facts which may *suggest* that a human personality or consciousness has survived death. I have chosen my words carefully. Please notice that I said 'suggest' survival, not 'prove', because I think it is impossible to adduce any proof of survival that is incontrovertible, The Survival Research Foundation is not searching for that one watertight case, that one indisputable fact, that will conclusively resolve the question. Rather, we are looking for evidence, if it exists, that will 'suggest' an afterlife and make it more probable than not.

Where do we look? Obviously, no facts commonly understood as normal or any of orthodox science now, prove an afterlife. If they did, there would be no question of whether or not there is an afterlife and no need for research and you would have better things to do than to read about afterlife research. So, if the Survival Research Foundation is to discover any facts suggestive of an afterlife, they must be found among those phenomena and faculties called the 'paranormal', that is, beyond the normal scheme of things. It is here that our approach is made and from this zone of the paranormal that those data will come, if they come at all. And we should be open to them because they may provide us with an understanding of what lies ahead of us.

METHODS OF EXPLORATION

The Survival Research Foundation has developed some new ways of exploring paranormal phenomena. Allow me to give you an analogy to help you understand the nature of these approaches. Recently my wife and I went to Scotland. We took a side trip to Loch Ness where a great creature is supposed to dwell in the depths of the lake. No, we didn't see Nessie. But we saw what the scientists there are doing to try to determine if it exists and I realised that their work was similar to what the Survival Research Foundation is doing to try to see if there is evidence of life after death. They send out boats on the lake to get photographs of the monster, send down submarines to get radar readings and even dolphins with cameras on their backs to try for underwater photos. Then they try to observe the monster from the shores of the lake and interview eye-witnesses who claim to have seen it from their automobiles or houses. These scientists attack their problem by water and by land.

We also attack the problem of the afterlife from different angles and with different methods. One method takes us to the dry land of real life, to dig for scientifically acceptable evidence among the strange spontaneous experiences people have in daily life. There are intriguing anecdotes to investigate: of children who claim detailed recollections of previous lives; of haunted houses; of victims of automobile accidents who say they have looked down on their crushed bodies lying in the wreckage. But experiences in which we are particularly interested are cases of dying patients or patients who have been declared clinically dead but have been resuscitated and who report visions of deceased people who convey verifiable information about their identities or personalities.

I am an experimental thanatologist with a leaning toward the second method which takes us out on the ocean of experimental research to explore for new empirical data. By experiment I mean that we are trying to see if certain paranormal events will happen under conditions we control and in a form we have selected. We use the tool of experiment in the hope of getting better evidence and better understanding of the problem and in an experiment we can avoid the danger of being thrown off by chance coincidences because we know what to expect by chance and will not accept evidence unless it is better than that. In the type of experimental investigation we are now conducting throughout the United States and in many other countries, we are seeking evidence of the afterlife in the form of a secret item of information which will identify a deceased person. To picture the experiment, think of a puzzle left by a person during his lifetime with the Survival Research Foundation. Only this person and no one else in the world knows the solution to the puzzle. Only this person knows the item of information or key that will solve the puzzle. To maintain complete secrecy the key is not told to anyone and is not written down. It is remembered. It is only in the person's mind. The person intends to try to communicate the key after death and to show his or her survival and identity by communicating the only key that will solve the puzzle. Without this secret item of information, the puzzle cannot be solved. Elsewhere[2] I have described this experimental method and a puzzle of my own design with odds against chance guessing of 1 in 600,000. If the puzzle-solving key were to be communicated after death, a counter-explanation that psychics had gotten it from the mind of a living person would not be reasonable because no living person could have known it and a further counterexplanation that a psychic had obtained it by clairvoyance would not be reasonable, either, because the key had not been written down. The design of my experiment also calls for conducting ante-mortem experiments with psychics who try repeatedly to learn the key by telepathy while the person leaving the puzzle is still alive. Since it would seem easier to obtain the key by telepathy while the person is alive rather than after the person's death, failures of ante-mortem tests followed by a post-mortem success will make less likely the additional counterexplanation that the key had been obtained telepathically from the person while alive.

Ideally, the puzzle should be prepared and left by a person who appears to have the qualities of a powerful post-mortem communicator. To find who had these qualities, I analysed several areas of inquiry and two population samples and came up with the profile of the 'ideal' communicator.[3] For greater assurance of success in solving a puzzle and of obtaining strong experimental evidence of the afterlife, those preparing the puzzle should replicate as many as possible of the factors associated with the 'ideal' communicator.

A second method returns us to the dry land of our present life, to dig for scientifically acceptable evidence among the experiences reported by dying patients or by patients who have been declared clinically dead but are resuscitated.

It appears that many involve an out-of-body experience, a sense patients have of detachment from their physical bodies. These out-of-body experiences are divided into two kinds: 'autoscopic' in which patients observe their own physical bodies, physical objects, resuscitation attempts and other details; and 'transcendental' experiences which seem to involve entering another world of light peopled by religious figures and the spirits of the dead. Of course, it is the 'transcendental' experience that has relevance to the problem of an afterlife. But virtually every case can be put down to cerebral anoxia, wish-fulfillment dreams or schizoid episodes allowing patients to cope with life threatening situations by hallucinating fantasies of a different world. The Survival Research Foundation's approach is to see if a type of 'transcendental' experience can be collected which would combat the naturalistic explanations just offered and which might be evidence of an afterlife. Our new approach here consists of an effort to collect this kind of experience through the distribution of 5000 questionnaires to American nurses who attended dying patients or those declared clinically dead but were resuscitated.

Based on some older cases, here is a hypothetical example of the kind of case we are looking for:

A man in great physical distress hears himself declared clinically dead by his doctors, He hears a loud buzzing noise and simultaneously has the feeling of travelling out of his physical body and through a dark tunnel. Then he sees his dead uncle. The uncle speaks to him: 'Look for my old overcoat. I sewed a large roll of bills in my inside pocket and the money is still there'. Later, the man recovers from his illness, the overcoat is found and the money is discovered in the inside pocket.

In this case, a fact, namely, the presence of money inside a sewn pocket, was known only to the dead person and not to any living person.

Now we'd expect a person under the stress of dying to hallucinate. We'd expect dying or nearly dying patients to have wish-fulfillment dreams or to react with schizoid fantasies against life-threatening situations. Indeed, many visions or dreams of people in such situations may be the results of such factors and so are not evidence of an afterlife. But what about a dream suggested by the nineteenth-century English poet Samuel Taylor Coleridge:

What if you slept? And what if, in your sleep, you dreamed? And what if, in your dream, you went to heaven and there plucked a strange and beautiful flower? And what if, when you awoke, you had the flower in your hand? Ah, what then?

Cerebral anoxia, wish-fulfillment dreams or defensive schizoid reactions could not explain such a dream because something objective, in this case the flower, was brought back. In the case of the man who saw his dead uncle, these naturalistic factors could not explain his vision because the experience gave him objective information: the existence of a roll of money sewn in an overcoat pocket.

This kind of case would be challenging and might provide evidence suggestive of continuation after death. If such cases exist, wouldn't it be worthwhile to find them? But there has been no organised effort before the Survival Research Foundation's initiative to collect this kind of case. We would welcome direct accounts of such experiences from patients who have recovered from clinical death. We would also welcome descriptions of such experiences from family members, doctors and nurses who have attended dying patients.

It took science three hundred years to get ready for its accomplishments of the last few decades and it took medicine the almost 2500 years since Hippocrates to get ready for its technology and transplants of today. While we of the Survival Research Foundation may hope that empirical evidence of the afterlife, by either method described here, will be obtained while we are still alive to appreciate it; we also realise that we do not have the resources of science and medicine and that the task we have set for ourselves may take much longer and will require great patience and dedication.

Notes

1. John Hick, *Death and Eternal Life* (New York: Harper & Row, 1976) p. 26.
2. A. S. Berger, *Aristocracy of the Dead* (Jefferson, NC and London: McFarland, 1987).
3. Ibid.

12
Are Near-Death Experiences Really Suggestive of Life after Death?
CHRISTOPHER CHERRY

I

I shall be tiresome and borrow the familiar (but useful) device of making a couple of preliminary remarks before launching into my topic proper.

First, I have to say that I've not myself had a near-death experience – though to judge from the abundant literature on the subject (to which I admit to having contributed) just about everyone else has. I am, on balance and somewhat unworthily, relieved rather than dismayed about this. My point, however, is that if I had, I should probably not be writing this essay – partly (I hope) through a natural reluctance to bore you with autobiography, but mainly because it is most unlikely I should still believe that the question I've chosen to investigate is an open one. For almost everyone who has had such an experience (at any rate, of a substantial and authentic kind) emerges with an unshakeable conviction that *of course* there is life hereafter – a life to which that near-death episode has afforded privileged, albeit fleeting, access. Now, whilst it would be presumptuous to disparage or dismiss such convictions, their status – what truths (if any) they intimate – is problematic. Having noted them, therefore, I shall set these convictions *qua* convictions on one side; for I chiefly want to discover where philosophical scrutiny can lead. In short, direct acquaintance with near-death experiences is likely to be intrusive rather than advantageous.

Secondly, I must acknowledge straight away that many philosophers would not dream of debating my topic. This is not because they doubt the existence – or even the richness and therapeutic value – of near-death experiences and their phenomenology. It is rather because they suppose, for reasons unconnected with and far more general than any having to do with such experiences, that the merest *idea* of (personal) post-mortem survival is subtle and seductive nonsense. Their grounds are very broadly ones about the conceptual limits of and conditions on identity and personhood. Now, if the notion of life beyond death is incoherent, then it is likewise incoherent to seek evidence for (or against) it, including evidence from near-death experiences. I happen to think that these – and related – philosophical difficulties can be met; and I shall henceforth assume, without further argument, that we may – and indeed as rational beings must – examine post-mortem evidences in an open spirit. This is far easier said than done. For even those who allow that there could be such evidences are often confused about what they are looking for, and tend to make excessive or extravagant demands which cannot possibly be satisfied. This will emerge, I hope.

I also hope – my third point – that the approach I take will show, implicitly if not explicitly, certain things about the nature of parapsychology in its relationship to philosophy.

II

My first task is to describe as briefly as possible what near-death experiences are. I shall then turn to the more austere and difficult business of enquiring where they point.

It is certain that many, and perhaps most, people who find themselves in life-threatening situations of one sort or another have remarkable experiences of a kind which have come to be known as 'near-death'.[1] The phenomenon is abundantly (not to say excessively) documented and analysed in a vast literature, specialist as well as popular, which has piled up over recent years. Now, it must be said immediately that there is some disagreement and confusion about the significance of the *occasion* and *context*, as distinct from the *content*, of such experiences: must an experient actually *be* 'near death', or merely think he or she is?; and if the former, what shall count as a 'near-death' state? Must it meet rigorous clinical criteria, or will some less strict and more intuitive test suffice? The answers we give to these questions are very important and I shall return to them later. For the moment, however, we can get away with saying that near-death experiences typically occur on those occasions when competent observers are convinced (erroneously in the event) either that the subject is dead, or else that death is imminent or certain as a consequence of trauma from, for instance, falling, drowning, road accident or cardiac arrest. We are allowed to be as vague as this because we *already* have the primary and obvious way of identifying experiences as near-death in terms of the characteristic and quite extraordinary content reported. For even though subjects – and more particularly those who write on the topic – differ somewhat in their accounts of what a near-death experience is like, there none the less remains a remarkable degree of basic agreement.

There are more and less elaborate ways of classifying the phases (or stages) of near-death experiences. The one I adopt here is a somewhat simplified version of Kenneth Ring's.[2] He distinguishes five stages: *peace*; *body separation* (*out-of-body experiences* and *autoscopy*); *entering the darkness* (*or the tunnel*); *seeing the light*; and *entering light*. Each of these five stages can be further sub-divided and described in greater detail. It is particularly significant that experients often report phenomena such as *panoramic recall* (or *life review*); meeting and perhaps communicating with a '*bearing of light*'; and encountering and conversing with *deceased* friends and relatives. As Susan Blackmore[3] remarks, the five stages tend to unfold in order, with the first by far the most common (60 per cent of Ring's sample) and the last the least common (10–12 per cent). And this, along with other features, seems to imply, at least to those who have had the full experience, a progressive disclosure of what it is – or will be – like to be dead. The experience strikes them with what, in a rather different context, the great philosophical sceptic Hume calls 'a force like that of sensation'.

Now, however remarkable the experience, it is clear that by no means all its features bear directly upon the matter of post-mortem survival. The initial serenity and post-experiential euphoria commonly reported certainly do not; and panoramic recall and autoscopy in themselves probably do not, unless and until they are placed in a context of beliefs already held. By contrast, certain features are suggestive: we learn, for example, that some subjects seem to discover paranormally in the course of their near-death experience that, and how, friends and acquaintances have died *subsequent to* the onset of their own experience. In effect, it is as we would expect: the aspects of near-death experiences which are strongly suggestive of survival are found in the later, less common phases – the 'transcendent' stages, to use an older and partisan description. And most people who have had 'transcendent' near-death experiences retain the conviction that they have been vouchsafed a glimpse of how it will be for them after death, no matter what their persuasions beforehand. Here is an excerpt from one unusually detailed and sustained, but otherwise typical, 'transcendent' case:

> Then suddenly, I saw my mother, who had died about nine years ago. And she was sitting – she always used to sit in her rocker, you know – she was smiling and she just sat there looking at me and she said to me in Hungarian [the language her mother had used while alive], 'Well, we've been waiting for you. We've been expecting you. Your father's here and we're going to help you'. And all I felt was a tremendous kind of happiness, of pleasure, of comfort. And then somehow she took me by the hand and she took me somewhere [pause] and all I could see was marble all around me; it was marble. It looked like marble, but it was very beautiful. And I could hear beautiful music; I can't tell you what kind, because I never heard anything like it before.[4]

I shall set on one side the issue of whether the artlessness of the sentiments makes the report more or, alternatively, less impressive and plausible, and merely observe that for those already disposed on prior grounds to believe in some form of life after death, experiences like these are bound to provide further evidence (if it is felt to be needed), or indeed confirmation.[5] Our business, however, is to enquire how far they may take us *without* any such prior beliefs. This I now turn to.

III

An apparent root difficulty for all survival claims is elegantly (though question-beggingly) stated by David Hume:

> What must a philosopher think of those who so far reverse the whole course of nature, as to render this life merely a passage to something farther; a *porch*, which leads to a greater, and vastly different, building; a prologue, which serves only to introduce the piece.... *Present* phenomena never point to anything further, but must be exactly adjusted to them.[6]

And again:

> By what arguments or analysis can we prove any state of existence which no one ever saw, *and which no way resembles any that ever was seen?* ... Some new species of logic is requisite for that purpose, and some new faculties of the mind, that they may enable us to comprehend that logic.[7]

Hume, of course, intends a *general* point about the conditions on one central 'species of logic': analogical inference must be made and validated within – 'exactly adjusted to' – a context with which we are acquainted and familiar. Nevertheless, his metaphors of the porch and the prologue, and the argument-pattern in which they feature, would seem to have a peculiarly fitting target in common talk of near-death experiences as anticipations, previews, of what it will be like for us when we die. For the literature of near-death is laden (how could it be otherwise?) with references to 'entrances', 'windows', 'thresholds', 'vestibules', 'avenues' and 'steps'.[8] Yet if we heed Hume's words, are we not forced to admit that porches and prologues can be identified and labelled as such only because we are *already and independently* acquainted with numerous specimens of the items they introduce? The things with respect to which they are porches and prologues are incontestably 'present phenomena', familiar artefacts, and not 'anything further' – which is precisely what putative post-mortem states seem to be. In short, how dare we aspire to infer from 'transcendent' experiences enjoyed fleetingly by (a small number of) *living* subjects to lasting, let alone everlasting, analogues of those experiences enjoyable by some or all persons *after death*? How can we possibly hope to extrapolate from experiences which are sublunary to post-mortem ones which, *ex hypothesi*, emphatically will not be?

In more formal terms, the application of Hume's argument to near-death experiences seems to leave things like this: we have, as matter of empirical fact, a frequent but not invariable conjunction of subject (A) in near (or clinical) death state (S) with an experience (E) having certain regular though not constant features.[9] Now from

(1) For many (but by no means all) cases of S, A has E we may infer (e.g.):
(2) Probably X in S will have E; and
(3) Probably Y in S had E which he did not subsequently report; and poignantly,
(4) Probably the deceased Z had, prior to true (brain-stem) death, E which he had no opportunity to communicate; and so on.

From even this rough schematisation it looks at if (2)–(4), although mildly interesting and conceivably consoling, can make no *post-mortem* promises. The inferences are all to what have happened, or may happen, to the near-dead, that is to say *the living*, in temporarily altered states of consciousness, irrespective of whether (normal) consciousness was, or will be, regained. Yet what is looked for is a conclusion of the following sort:

(5) When in death 'state', S_1, probably A has some analogue of E, namely E_1, perhaps of a relatively continuous and extended kind.
But if Hume is right, (5) is something we can never get to. Well, is he right?

He is wrong in that he seeks to exclude too much far too soon. For why exactly are we forbidden *in any circumstances* to proceed to tentative inferences about post-mortem experiences on the basis of certain (which incontestably do occur) pre-mortem, as in near-death, situations? Surely whether or not we may do so here depends upon whether or not we find ourselves able to give sense and substance to the suggestion that *near* and *true* death are sufficiently and relevantly alike to permit us to conclude that certain experiences closely associated with the former will, in all probability, accompany the latter also. After all, this is precisely the sort of reasoning which, in more humdrum applications, we exploit every day of the week. To be sure, we may decide it does not work in the present case. But if so it will be because we do not, after all, discern the appropriate kind and degree of resemblance between near and true death that its successful application demands.

So what we ought to conclude about the evidential worth of near-death experiences turns upon how close a resemblance we are prepared to allow between the conditions of near and actual death. This, to refer back to something I emphasised at the beginning, is an issue about the *context* rather than the *content* of near-death experiences, about the circumstances in which they occur rather than what they are like when they occur. I have fairly positive views about this matter of resemblance, and shall return to it a little later. By contrast, Hume's view is entirely negative: we cannot possibly 'prove any state of existence which no one ever saw, *and which in no way resembles any that ever was seen*...'. But what he so confidently rules out of court is of course the very issue I have suggested *does* confront us: is there or is there not resemblance between the states of actual and near death of such a kind as to make what often accompanies the latter a good guide to what is likely to accompany the former? If there is, and if some near-death subjects have experienced something of what it is like to be dead, then (but only then) a *different* claim of Hume's does indeed hold good. But it is a claim about the *content* rather than the context of the near-death experience. Thus, if it is established that near-death experiences do tell us about experiences postmortem, our claims about the latter must, in Hume's words, 'be exactly adjusted to' what has been experientially presented in the former. That is to say, what we are entitled to say about experiences beyond death is confined to what we have experienced beforehand, in near death. We have no licence to elaborate and embellish what we have been given. (More strictly, near-death phenomena provide no such licence though other things conceivably may.) This confinement may disappoint some. For it forces us to conclude that the best near-death *on its own* could evidence is *experiences hereafter* and not *experiences of (and 'in') a hereafter*. And many near-death apologists have looked to something richer and more 'solid'.

I shall say a little more about this at the end. But before that I have two other things to do. The first is to suggest a deeper reason why Hume – like so many others – took it for granted that no matter how great the ostensible evidence, nothing could be said about 'a future state'. The second is to try and resolve the issue which has been left open: *does* death in fact resemble near death in enough relevant respects to allow us to conclude that experiences of the kind we know to be associated with the latter are likely to accompany the former?

IV

Hume confuses the claim (1) that to assert anything whatsoever about experiences hereafter would necessarily be to go beyond all legitimate bounds of inference, with the claim (2) that to assert anything about experiences hereafter beyond what may be given pre-mortem (as with near-death experiences) is to go beyond such bounds. The first is false, the second arguably true. Why does he make this mistake? For this reason, I think: he sets a condition on the admissibility of evidence for survival which is, in all conscience, remarkably stringent and then proceeds to interpret it in such a way that it cannot conceivably be met. The condition is made a hurdle which cannot possibly be cleared. The condition itself is this: the only data admissible as evidence for survival are reports by living persons of their own, first-hand experience of what it is like to be dead. Well, we may reasonably say that if anything seems to meet such a requirement it is precisely (certain) near-death experiences. After all, we have noted their distinctive – and possibly unique – feature of first-hand testimony. However, the condition is now *interpreted* in such a way as to debar even the experiences which seem best able to satisfy it. For it is construed as the requirement that an experient should *really and truly* die and subsequently return to the world of the living to report back on his or her death experiences. The requirement demands, in effect, that the following two propositions should be true together:

(i) At t_1, A is dead; and
(ii) At t_2, A is alive and communicates with other living persons.

But since whatever grounds we have for asserting the one proposition are grounds for denying the other, (i) and (ii) are contradictory; and so a condition which looked very much as if it might be met by near-death experiences is decreed logically unsatisfiable. Like everything else they, too, are made evidentially worthless.

It is not just philosophers who thus put the hereafter out of reach. The same unmeetable condition is implicit in much expert writing on near-death itself. Here are just a few examples:

You can't subject these [near-death] experiences to a scientific test – in other words, you can't kill people off and then bring them back.[10]

Death remains, in Hamlet's words, 'The undiscover'd country from whose bourn/No traveller returns...', The near-dead are not dead; and the dead, whether surviving in some form or not, can be left to thanatology and eschatology.[11]

No one has yet returned from the dead and given an account of his experiences.[12]

Other than possibly and questionably Lazarus, no one has truly died and returned and offered a documentable accounting. All reports... are anecdotal, and until technology is appropriately developed, the verbalization of experiences will continue to be anecdotal. The state of death is impossible to conceptualize. Therefore, since being dead cannot even be imagined, a void evolved that must be filled with superstitions, fantasies, and religious and poetic creations.[13]

In my opinion, anyone who claims that near-death experiences prove or give scientific evidence of an afterlife is only betraying his ignorance of what terms like evidence or proof mean (... [M]y purism stems from the fact that I was a professor of philosophy and of logic before I went to medical school...)[14]

Now, constructing impossible evidential conditions is bad enough, but there is more – and it is revealing. We can explain why people should demand, impossibly, that a subject now living and reporting first-hand on what it is like to be dead must at some prior time have actually died only on the supposition that they *already* take it for granted that no *uninterruptedly* living person can possibly have experiences of what lies beyond death. But this is the very point at issue with near-death experiences: *do* the uninterruptedly living (albeit in a bad way) have experiences of what lies beyond this life?

The point I am making is of great general importance. We cannot decide in advance to exclude certain putative experiences from any and every living subject's experiential repertoire even if the candidate's experiences were ones *ordinarily* available only to the dead. If there are states to be enjoyed (or suffered) post-mortem, we cannot just decree that they are accessible to the dead but never ever to the living. The same goes for Kant's, or Plato's, or Plotinus's, or Julian of Norwich's or Swedenborg's 'worlds'. If post-mortem – or 'intelligible' or 'noumenal' – worlds exist they are *there* for the apprehending. What is certainly true is that, as a matter of fact, they are rarely or never apprehended because most or all of the living are biologically (sensorily) ill-equipped or impoverished. What makes this just about bearable is the possibility that the occasional deviant, better endowed than the rest of us, should be experientially privileged and report back.[15]

Well, are near-death subjects among the privileged? This returns me to the second of the tasks I mentioned above: to try to settle the question of whether death and near-death are sufficiently akin to entitle us to conclude that experiences associated with the latter will in all probability be associated with the former. I confess I do not think I can actually resolve the matter but (the next best thing) indicate how it could be resolved.

V

One who is prepared to give sense and substance to the suggestion that the state of true death resembles, in sufficient relevant respects, the state of near-death will accept something like the following formula:

> Given that E is regularly conjoined with S, and given that S_1 (abundantly) resembles S, it is rational to conclude that *probably* E_1 is regularly conjoined with S_1, where E_1 stands in the same relation (or degree) of resemblance to E as S_1 does to S.

But *should* we be prepared to? There are connected problems. In the first place, the very notion of resemblance is here obscure. (Does a fantasy 'resemble' the real thing? Does being remembered and valued by others after one's death 'resemble' survival?) It is these things at least partly because – a second difficulty – the concept of near-death, even in specialist medical literature, is intuitive and impressionistic in ways in which that of death proper is not. It affords no more than gross similarities between S and S_1 which seem far too superficial to license the critical move from E to E_1, the move to experiences hereafter. And in any case, should they not be taken as secondary to a dissimilarity – possibly the only dissimilarity undubitably common to all instances: the latter's irreversibility? Some will be inclined to discount this dissimilarity as irrelevant precisely *because of* its inescapability; but it strikes many otherwise.

There is a third and familiar set of problems bound up with the two I have noted. Much specialist analysis of near-death experiences is devoted to elaborating or else disputing clinical similarities between near-death states and a variety of pathological conditions – cerebral anoxia, toxic psychosis, clinical depersonalisation, failing information-processing systems and so forth – characteristically associated with experiences which are unproblematically confused and non-veridical. These kinds of delusive or hallucinatory experiences carry (for the most part) no post-mortem implications, and yet their richness and immediacy inspires in their subject a confidence, as misplaced as it is short-lived, that they are perceiving real existents and real states of affairs. The more immediate implications for survivalists are unclear and perhaps unsettling. In particular, if near-death experiences were akin, in their phenomenology and aetiology, to these and associated pathological conditions they would indeed be suspect.

Now, research on near-death experiences at least suggests that they do differ in kind from other experiences; and, furthermore, that their phenomenology is peculiar to circumstances of near death (no one, so far as I know, has claimed that such circumstances suffice to generate them, only that they are necessary). And this, of course, brings us back to the issue of what shall count as the near-death condition with which these unique experiences are, apparently, exclusively and intimately associated. For we need to determine precisely *what it is* which true death either does not 'sufficiently resemble' in order to know whether or not conclusions may be drawn to the post-mortem. Now, it is obvious that for these purposes the contextual criteria for near death will have to be clinical – specifically: neurophysiological – in nature. I do not pretend to be able to formulate a perfect test; but it would be along the lines drawn (though never more than hazily) by certain of the more medical-minded students of near-death experiences.[16] Crudely, a subject is to be accounted near-dead if and only if he or she manifests total absence of all discernible *brain* function for a period before resuscitation. The test is thus one of electro-cerebral silence, of the flat EEG; but we need not worry here about the technology. My point is that if, after an appropriate period of time, the subject is resuscitated and recounts experiences of the sort I have described we have, as far as can possibly be ascertained, an instance of *mental* activity without its alleged universal causal correlate, *brain* activity. There remains much detail to work out, of course. Furthermore, I do not suppose that doing this would be of any great medical or therapeutic value. What I do suspect is that had it been possible and practicable to apply such an ideal test very many near-death experients would have been seen to pass.

To show why a 'contextual' test of this sort is needed, let me list its merits in ascending order of importance:

(1) In providing an objective, 'scientific' account of the (brain) state of a subject it enables us to give a precise, non-intuitive sense to what shall be accounted a near-death context – not, of course, to help the medical profession but the near-death experience researcher.

(2) Because (1) allows us to identify near-death *independently* of a subject's experiences we can investigate the nature and degree of the association between 'physical' and 'phenomenal' near-death and, in particular, the frequency with which the mental events reported by ostensible near-death subjects occur in dissociation from brain events, Now it *may* just turn out that they never do, in which we – or at any rate, I – shall have to think again. This, however, seems to me extremely unlikely. I very strongly suspect that what distinguishes authentic (paradigmatic) near-death experiences from other varieties of experience is that they, uniquely, *are* unaccompanied by brain activity.

(3) By virtue of (2), we are better equipped to resist moves to 'explain away' near-death experiences in reductivist, naturalistic terms. For, put simply, there is nothing very suitable – like anomalous brain activity – in terms of which to explain anything away.
(4) By virtue of (1)–(3) we can give not just sense and substance, but a positive answer, to the crucial question: does true death *resemble* near-death in sufficient relevant respects for what goes on in the one kind of case to be a pointer to what will go on in the other? The answer is yes, just so long as there are instances of near-death satisfying my criterion. For if there are, they will share with true death a feature which renders all dissimilarities shallow and irrelevant: *a total cessation of brain activity.* (That in the one case the cessation is temporary and in the other permanent of course remains true but now beside the point). This being so we may rationally anticipate hereafter experiences of the sort sometimes available here and now to the near-dead.
(5) (1)–(4) permit us to speculate, perhaps somewhat wildly, about causes – and perhaps agents – acting *directly* upon the mind. Taken together they at least suggest that the brain is, in certain respects, disempowering – an impediment to certain sorts of experience. This is a consoling thought to many who fear death; and I return to it, though very briefly, in my conclusion.

VI

What I have sought to do is determine how far analogical argument can carry us. My cautiously optimistic conclusion has been that it can carry us far further than Hume and many others have supposed. Now, this optimism rests upon a conviction of which many have felt the force without fully understanding the logic. The conviction is that near-death and actual death, for all their apparent differences, are alike in such a way that what is intimately linked with the one will in all probability be intimately linked with the other. As so often happens, there is a price to pay which I hinted at earlier. It is this: the logic of the argument I have traced does not allow us to say anything more about prospective experiences after death than what is on offer at near-death. This is all we have to go on, and we must not try and take out anything more than we (that is, the near-death experients) have put in. These limits are, so to speak, hard-wired into any rational apologetic. (This may of course encourage some to seek elsewhere; but if so it will be outside – or beyond – argument.) For instance, if near-death experiences were, typically, of drinking cups of tea or watching videos or attending local government meetings these and these alone would be the sorts of experiences we could look forward to after death. It is a quite remarkable fact that near-death experiences have *the content* they do – that what they promise seems almost too good to be true; but it is not a fact any analogical argument is greatly interested in.

That said, *what* they have experienced has certainly led near-death subjects to assume, almost as a matter of course, that they have had advance experiences, previews, of a hereafter rather than – the most they are entitled to infer – experiences in circumstances which suggest they will have further similar experiences after they die. But at best, near-death experiences seem to intimate experiences hereafter and not experiences of a hereafter. The difference is immense, but – understandably – not one which near-death subjects bother themselves with. They commonly talk as if they have made a round-trip to an after-*world* – a world which, like the present one, is tolerably coherent and continuous, and causally responsible for the experiences they have enjoyed at near-death. And they usually feel certain that when they actually die they will return, this time on a one-way ticket, to the *same* independent world they have already fleetingly accessed. Unfortunately, near-death experiences provide no evidence for such a solid, objective and shared hereafter. The vestibule is *itself* the mansion, the prologue *itself* the drama. By the same token, however, they provide none against. Such matters lie quite beyond their reach.

Just as the ontological differences between experiencing *a* hereafter and experiences hereafter are enormous so it is with their prospective attractions. The first prospect is of a hereafter with which being dead will afford a leisured, progressive and lasting acquaintance. It is rather like a yet-to-be explored country in which one – everyone? – will later take up residence, and of a tiny part of which a few of the living have already been vouchsafed a glimpse. The second, of experiences hereafter, is by contrast the prospect of an indefinite series of pretty similar experiences which, no matter how agreeable in themselves, are neither referrable to, nor constitutive of, a reality independent of the post-mortem experient. The near-death experience is just the first member in the series; and the whole is rather like having the same dream over and over again – or, Marienbad-like, walking the same corridors without end.

As I have said, near-death experiences at best evidence the second and not the first of these two prospects. One thing this means is that those who want more must look in a different direction. And of course many do hope for more. They want their experiences hereafter to be experiences of *a* hereafter, not just a succession of subjective states. They want to have experiences of being with dead friends and a Being of Light because they actually *are* with dead friends and a Being of Light. (It is surprisingly little consolation to be told that the difference won't really matter when the crunch comes since it won't, *ex hypothesi*, be apparent to the dead subjects themselves!) Since all this is so, let me end with a gesture in a different direction but from the higher ground now achieved.

When, above, I roughed out the 'silent-brain' test I speculated under (5) that from the near-death perspective the brain might be perceived as selectively disempowering the mind. Suppose now that you accept my test, or something like it: the cause of near-death experiences becomes deeply problematic. Since it is one operating despite brain inactivity, why should we not take a further, bolder step of proposing that it does so *because of* it, that cerebral is *necessary* (whether or not it is sufficient) for the experiences? On this proposal such experiences can result only from direct action upon a mind – action perhaps exercised by another mind (or Mind). (The more sceptical may care to think of less unfamiliar sorts of direct intermental communication such as telepathy and perhaps clairvoyance.)

This idea that a silent brain facilitates the occurrence of near-death – and possibly of post-death – experience by allowing the operation of causes which could not otherwise operate can be situated in a venerable tradition, that of seeing the material and corporeal as in essence estranging, deforming and confining. I like and approve of the corporeal, and wish to take from this tradition only the speculation that the bodies we have – and more particularly our central nervous systems – make it horribly difficult to discover anything much, or to say anything very useful, about what it may be like after we have died. If this is not hopelessly unconvincing, it may be supplemented with the further suggestion that the depressing distinction, drawn above, between experience of a hereafter and experience hereafter is more illusory than real. For suppose someone asks: even if whatever (or Whoever) occasions near-death experiences continues to operate after our death, how can *it* (or He, or She) underwrite the veridicality of those persisting experiences? How, that is, can it help to guarantee that there is in fact anything like a post-mortem world or reality 'out there', corresponding to them? One answer might be this: It is no longer clear what the doubting question means because, given the non-cerebral, non-material nature of the contex*t*, it is no longer clear what could possibly count as a *failure* to correspond. What, for example, could in such circumstances count as a delusion-inducing or scrambling agent? In such encounters it seems very much as if whatever acts directly on the mind just *has to be* whatever the mind experiences. Cause and object necessarily become one and the same, for we have now gone beyond the point at which they may intelligibly be held apart. And if this is so it probably heralds the dissolution of another familiar pair of opposites: subject and object. But this, to my relief, is a further story.

Notes

1. Though only a relatively small proportion have the 'fully-fledged' variety. The best recent general works on the phenomenology and implications of near-death experiences are: K. Osis and E. Haraldson, *At the Hour of Death* (New York: Discus, 1977); K. Ring, *Life at Death* (New York: Coward, McCann & Geohegan, 1980); M. B. Sabom, *Recollections of Death* (London: Corgi, 1982); G. Gallup and W. Proctor, *Adventures in Immortality* (London: Corgi, 1984). The most meticulous and detailed research into specific aspects of near-death is to be found in medical and psychological journals. For near-death experiences and survival after death, see I. Stevenson and B. Greyson, 'Near-Death Experiences: Relevance to the Question of Survival after Death', CCXLII (1979) 265–7. For incidence of near-death experience occurrence, see G. O. Gabbard, S. W. Turemlow, and F. C. Jones,

'Do "Near-Death Experiences" Occur Only Near Death?', *J. Am. Med. Assoc.* CLXIX (1981) 374–7; J. E. Owens, E. W. Cook, and I. Stevenson, 'Viewpoint', *Lancet*, vol. 336 (1990), 1175–77. For an overview of near-death experience incidence and frequency, see I. Stevenson, and B. Greyson, 'The Phenomenology of Near-Death Experiences', *Am. J. Psychiatry*, CXXXVII (1980) 1193–6.
2. Ring, op. cit.
3. 'Visions from the Dying Brain', *New Scientist*, 5 May 1988.
4. Ring, op. cit.
5. Whether of the discarnate or quasi-embodied variety I leave open. I should add that I incline to share the conviction.
6. David Hume, 'Of a Particular Providence and of a Future State'. Adapted from *Hume on Religion*, ed. Richard Wollheim (London: Collins, 1963) pp. 238–9.
7. David Hume, 'On the Immortality of the Soul' (my italics; ibid., pp. 269–70).
8. See in particular Gallup and Proctor, op. cit.
9. For the near-death apologist, some of these features will be centrally relevant, such as autoscopy and encounter with a 'being of light', and others peripheral.
10. Gallup and Proctor, op. cit.
11. Editorial, *British Medical Journal*, vol. II (December 1979) p. 1530.
12. R. Noyes, *J. Psychiatry*, vol. 35 (1972) pp. 174–84.
13. N. Schnaper, 'Comments Germane to the Paper Entitled "The Reality of Death Experiences" by Roding', *Journal of Mental and Nervous Diseases* (1980) vol. 168, pp. 268–70. Despite frequent allusions to Lazarus in near-death literature, the reanimation of corpses has nothing to do with *evidence* for the post-mortem.
14. Moody, op. cit.
15. Here, I take it, I part company with thinkers like Ring. The longstanding and extraordinarily difficult issue of an 'intelligible' world lying beyond – or behind – 'appearances' is broached, in neuropsychological terms, by Ring in *Heading Toward Omega* (Chapter 12, (New York: William Morrow, 1984).) As I understand him, he proposes, following Karl Pribram amongst others, a holographic model, arguing that 'primary' reality is composed of frequencies only, in respect of which it makes no sense to speak of space, time and causality. From such frequencies the human brain constructs an intersubjective world of appearances – by implication, 'secondary' reality. Near-death experiences usher subjects into the primary, holographic domain of frequencies, and the accompanying altered state of consciousness is termed a 'holographic state'.

Now, is this 'holographic domain' meant to be the one 'true' reality, or at all events a closer approximation to (representation of) it than is the secondary world of appearances; or merely another, alternative reality? Ring is not clear. On occasion he implicitly identifies the 'frequency domain' (the domain of 'higher vibrations') with 'primary' reality; on other occasions, he describes it as 'another world of appearances' – though presumably a less distorted one than that perceived by human beings in a *normal* state of consciousness. (The account is made more obscure by his reference to the *mind* [sic] as a laser, to Hell as a 'lower frequency domain', etc!)

Unless we are blinded by novel scientific models we shall realise that Ring's discussion raises the problems posed by Plato and Kant: what entitles us to speak of an *underlying* reality, and to equate it with (for example) the 'frequency domain'? Isn't the latter at best a world of other appearances? And if so, in what way can it be ontologically or metaphysically privileged? Again, if it *is* true that near-death experients enjoy a holographic state of consciousness (and I'm not sure what this means) which affords them a holographic 'conception of reality', in what way would this make them epistemically and sensorily privileged? Finally, how do the descriptions of their experiences offered by near-death experience subjects lend themselves to this construction? After all, their *concepts* remain very much anchored to, and interpreted in terms of, the familiar world of 'appearances'.

Pribram's account of the holographic domain (Bohm's 'implicate order' as contrasted with the 'explicate order' of the 'world of appearances', 'world of objects') is primarily addressed to memory: its encoding, storage and retrieval. He does, however, speculate cautiously about extending it to explain the ostensibly paranormal (including, in particular, the Jungian idea of 'synchronicity'). Thus:

> [Mystical experiences] bespeak the possibility of tapping into that order of reality that is *behind* the world of appearances. . . . I wonder if somehow those people haven't hit upon a mechanism that lets them tap into the implicate order.

However, Pribram seems not to want to claim any metaphysical *primacy* for the implicate order, as the remarks below suggest (despite the unsuccessful illustration):

> The world of appearances is certainly a real world. But it is *not* the *only* order of reality. . . . We directly perceive only one order. Yet we know from other sources that the world is round. The fact that in the world of appearances it seems flat doesn't contradict the other reality, its roundness.

(Both quotations are from Pribram's discussion with Daniel Goleman of 'Holographic Memory' in *Psychology Today* (February 1979) pp. 83–4.)

16. See, for instance, M. B. Sabom's *Recollections of Death* (London: Corgi, 1982) pp. 21–5. (Sabom is a heart surgeon.) He discusses, scrappily, the ideas of near-death, clinical death and brain death, but settles for 'Physical Near-death': 'Any bodily state resulting from an extreme physiological catastrophe, accidental or otherwise, that would reasonably be expected to result in irreversible biological death in the majority of instances and would demand urgent medical atten-

tion, if available. In general, these conditions would include cardiac arrest, severe traumatic injury, deep comatose situations from a metabolic derangement or systemic illness, and the like.'

Those who are interested in the concept of clinical brain death and its application to the devising of a more rigorous test for near-death experiences along the lines I propose should see, for instance, the Health Department's Working Party's *Code of Practice for Cadaveric Organs for Transplantation* (1983); 'Death', *J. Med. Ethics*, vol. 16 (1990) pp. 3–13; the International Federation's recent report on 'EEG Instrumentation Standards and Cessation of Cerebral Function'; and G. Roberts and J. Owen, 'The Near-death Experience', *Br. J. Psychiatry*, vol. 153 (1988) pp. 607–17.

Anyone who believes that mental events *are* brain events will be unimpressed by most of what follows.

13

The Near-Death Experience: A Glimpse of Heaven and Hell?

DAVID LORIMER

The near-death experience (NDE) is a challenging and even disturbing phenomenon: it calls into question the assumptions of a materialistic science and medicine which insists that mind is a by-product of brain function and that it cannot, therefore, conceivably survive the disintegration of the brain; it also impinges on the ecclesiastical territory of the afterlife – or at least of its threshold – by purporting to describe the transition from a material to a nonmaterial reality. Some Christians would be inclined to dismiss the whole episode as an elaborate and fanciful piece of self-deception engineered by the fallen angel of light, Lucifer himself; but 'by their fruits shall ye know them', and in the aftermath of the NDE many experiencers undergo a radical transformation of being and values scarcely associated with evil influence.

So what exactly is the NDE? It can be thought of as the continuation of conscious experience while the person is clinically dead – no heartbeat, breathing or skin resistance response and, in some cases, no detectable EEG activity. The awareness of the conscious self is focused in two dimensions: at first a parallel space (often with no ordinary feeling of time) in which it is possible to perceive events in the vicinity of the physical body or elsewhere – such reports of veridical ESP are well-authenticated by survivors and their clinicians, often to their considerable amazement, not to say alarm. An intervening stage of awareness is the so-called 'tunnel experience', going through a dark tunnel at high speed (or else floating more gently) towards a light at the end. This phase seems to mark the separation from the parallel reality and entry into an inner space out of which a whole environment may unfold.

Before proceeding any further, we will make a cultural excursus to sketch in some cultural background to traditional concepts of heaven and hell. Traditional societies, with the continuity implied in communion with the ancestors, seem to have a natural belief in immortality, although their ideas of post-mortem existence extend the social hierarchy rather than demarcating individual destinies by using moral criteria. Frazer observed that a life after death 'is not a matter of speculation and conjecture, of hope and fear; it is a practical certainty which the individual as little dreams of doubting as he doubts the reality of his own existence.'[1]

The idea of a post-mortem judgement emerged only gradually, becoming more insistent as an exclusively this-worldly moral order broke down and questions of theodicy came to the fore. The classic example of this process is to be found in the Book of Job, to which I shall return in a moment. Early forms and images of post-mortem judgement include ordeals, crossing a dangerous bridge, the weighing of the soul, and the opening of the Book of Fate in which are inscribed all the deeds of an individual life.[2]

We now come to traditional Christian eschatology, the 'Last Things' of Death, Judgement, Heaven and Hell. In the Old Testament the idea of a desirable afterlife evolves very slowly in the face of apparent individual injustice and collective disaster epitomised by the book of Job and the Exile: if these calamities are unmerited or disproportionate punishments, the question of compensation arises quite naturally; and if there is no compensation in earthly existence, it must be postponed to the after-death state, at least for the Righteous Remnant of good individuals. The enemies of Israel, and latterly the wicked more generally, will have an uncomfortable time in store. At first Sheol was the common fate of all, a gloomy underground cavern where a vapid half-life was pursued, similar to the Hades of Homer. Only later does Sheol come to have compartments (in Enoch) and does the idea of resurrection appear, at first metaphorically and subsequently more literally. It takes place on the Day of the Lord, the trumpet-sounding apocalypse where the nations are gathered for the general reckoning.[3]

In the New Testament apocalyptic tradition typified by Matthew 25, the Son of Man separates the sheep from the goats, the sheep inheriting the kingdom and eternal life, while the goats are cast into the punishing fire. Elsewhere, the images of fire and brimstone are repeated, while Heaven is ascribed many mansions. And in Luke we find the story of the rich man and Lazarus, each of whom find themselves in a compensating state after death, with an unbridgeable gulf between: in the bosom of Abraham (not a very explicit image for the twentith century), and tormented by flames and thirst in Hades. The powerful moral of the tale is that the rich man's brother will simply disbelieve any report of his fate – a scepticism only too apparent in our own day when one considers many reactions to paranormal spiritual phenomena.

More generally, the imagery of heaven and hell presents a dualism of light and darkness (especially in St John), love and hatred, bliss and torment, hope and fear. The later Catholic development of purgatory as a proving ante-chamber to heaven, uses fire as the purifying agent, a fire to be distinguished from the everlasting fire of hell, that brutal stick of Mediaeval preachers. In the eighteenth century, Swedenborg's graphic *Heaven and Hell* depicted the Divine Light of the heavenly Sun and the forbidding and damp darkness of hell, while Dante's geography is even better known. Dr Carol Zaleski, in her book *Otherworld Journeys*, shows how powerfully these traditional images were reflected in mediaeval stories such as the vision of Knight Owen on St Patrick's Purgatory. Owen himself is cast into the bottomless pit, falling until he remembers the name of Jesus; he also witnesses Bosch-like scenes of sinners being devoured by dragons, 'set upon by serpents and toads, fixed to the ground by red-hot nails, baked in furnaces, immersed in boiling cauldrons . . .'.[4] Then, at length, he comes to the gates of paradise, where a flame comes down from heaven and 'he felt such a sweet sense of delight in his body and his heart that he could scarcely tell, for the delight of the sweetness, whether he was living or dead'.[5] This ineffability recurs in modern experiences, as we shall see, and is referred to by Dante when he says that his vision was greater than his speech and that his memory failed at such an excess.

With the rise of the modern scientific outlook in the seventeenth century we can trace the gradual eclipse of the spiritual world-view and a growing disbelief in any form of afterlife. The trend of scientific hypotheses has been towards a thoroughgoing materialism which explains mind and consciousness as a by-product of matter. Scientific method has concentrated on examining and measuring things from the outside with ever-more sophisticated instruments: thus the inner is explained in terms of the outer, the subjective by means of the objective, mind as a manifestation of the brain.

More specifically, it is assumed that consciousness is actually produced by the brain: therefore it perishes at brain death, and visions of heaven and hell are relegated to the status of superstitious fantasies. There is another option, though, which explains the close correlations of mind and brain equally well, but which leaves room for so-called paranormal experiences, including the NDE. In contrast to the 'productive' theory of consciousness, this other theory is 'permissive' or 'transmissive', claiming that the brain does not so much produce consciousness as transmit it or permit certain kinds of consciousness. This view can be traced back to William James, Henri Bergson and F. C. S. Schiller at the beginning of the century.[6]

The most compelling evidence in favour of the 'transmissive' view comes from veridical out-of-body experiences (OBE) during an NDE, that is cases where the subject can give accurate visual reports of what was going on around them at the time when they were clinically dead. In one recent example from Holland, a patient was brought into the emergency unit completely unconscious, and underwent a series of resuscitation procedures. An attendant nurse happened to remove his false teeth and place them in a glass. Without ever recovering consciousness, the patient was transferred to intensive care and, ten days later, came back into a ward. He immediately recognised the nurse and asked her what she had done with his false teeth! It is important to stress that the patient had never physically seen the nurse before, and that there is no normal means by which he could have perceived the resuscitation procedures.

Returning now to the twentieth-century NDE, we can examine a number of themes in connection with 'heavenly' and 'hellish' experiences: the encounter with the Being of Light or sensing of an evil force, the life review, and entering a heavenly or hellish environment. We shall then make a few interpretative comments. It is worth pointing out at the outset that some 95 per cent of reported NDEs are positive or heavenly; I say 'reported' advisedly as one evangelical researcher, Dr Maurice Rawlings,[7] speculates that a good many negative experiences are repressed in the unconscious. The encounter with the Being of Light often follows the 'emergence' from the 'tunnel'. The light is 'brighter than a thousand suns', but does not hurt the 'eyes', it is also infused with other qualities such as love, peace, joy, beauty, energy and warmth; the experience is timeless and ineffable. A couple of extracts from Kenneth Ring[8] give the flavour: 'it was a total immersion in light, brightness, warmth, peace, security . . . it's something which becomes you and you become it. I could say I was peace, I was love and 'as I reached the source of light I could see in. I cannot begin to describe in human terms the feeling I had at what I saw. It was a giant infinite world of calm, and love, and energy, and beauty'. This second account is less unitive than the first, but is still ineffable. Other experiencers speak of the being as like a person but not a person – a mass of energy and love which engulfs the subject. Still others experience the being of light as Jesus, the source of their lives or their Higher Self. In any event the sublime loving radiance brings about an experience of supernal bliss.

If the positive NDE is characterized by sensations of rising into love and light, the negative experience begins with a sinking feeling suffused with panic, anguish and fear.[9] The environment is dark and hostile, and the subjects may even feel that they are being dragged down by an evil force accompanied by visions corresponding to the wrathful deities of the Tibetan Book of the Dead. They struggle and fight to keep a grip of life, immersed in isolation and perhaps smelling foul stenches around themselves. They may also come up against a monster which threatens to overpower them. At this stage, however, a curious phenomenon may occur as they suddenly realise that the monster is a projection of their own fear or anger. As these feelings are overcome, so the proverbial lion shrinks to cat size and wanders away. Such episodes recall the teaching of the Tibetans that these monsters are productions of the percipient's own mind, thought-forms which have been built up and can equally be dissolved. As in similar confrontations in nightmares, the negative NDE provides a scenario for the subject to face these creations and move beyond them. The simplistic notion that good people have pleasant experiences and evil people unpleasant ones is not borne out by the evidence, although both positive and negative experiences have transformative effects. A major drug criminal was amazed to have a blissful experience (it changed his life!), while a negative experience reported in a medical journal seemed to be a dramatisation of resuscitation procedures with the doctors in the role of fiends bringing the patient back to the pains of his earthly life.

We pass now to the life review, often experienced in the presence of the being of light, that is to say in an atmosphere of unconditional love and forgiveness, but at the same time with clear-sighted honesty in one's insight into ambivalent motivations; the lesson is frequently quoted as the need to learn to live a loving life as opposed to merely accumulating experiences or possessions. There is the sensation of one's life passing before one and the inability to hide anything. It also becomes apparent that the 'judging' is done by the individual, or an aspect of the individuality – the Higher Self or Witness Consciousness, an impartial and all-knowing awareness. Sometimes the experience is a more exclusively emotional one, so that one senses not only one's own emotions but also those of others who were directly or indirectly affected by the thought, word, feeling or action of the personality. The point of comparison is, as mentioned above, the feeling of pure logical consequence. This process reveals an awesome degree of responsibility, clarified by the grace of love. The Love may forgive you, but can you forgive yourself? The experiencer now has direct insight into what Maslow calls B-values, the values of being which underlie material phenomena, the spiritual qualities which we encountered in the being of Light: Love, Peace, Wisdom, Joy, Beauty. It is these qualities which many experiencers subsequently seek to realise in their lives, and which makes them sceptical of conventional material values of acquisitiveness, ambition and fame.

In entering the heavenly environment, experiencers feel the same qualities as in the encounter with the Being of Light. The building may seem to be made of golden light, there is a feeling of unity and peace, of activity, and it seems that some live in worlds which are more make-believe than others. One subject concludes: 'In heaven there is light, peace, music, beauty and joyful acitivity, but above all there is love and within this love I felt more truly alive than I have ever done before'. There is also reunion with loved ones, without whom no account of heaven would be complete, although this implies a continuation of deep spiritually bonded relationships of those closely attuned to each other rather than friendship of a more superficial level. I have already said more about the negative environments with all their accompanying desolate and cold landscapes and figures – and noise rather than music. These impressions reinforce the dualism of light and darkness, joy and anguish, with which we began our treatment of Christian imagery.

In a recent study of childrens' NDEs 'Closer to the Light', Dr Melvin Morse recorded the experiences of young children, some of which explicitly contradicted their parents' belief systems. Apart from some remarkable OBEs, a number of the children described encounters with the heavenly light: one said that he had been 'climbing a staircase to heaven . . . it was such a good and peaceful feeling'.[10] Another met a being about seven feet tall in a long white gown: 'His hair was golden, and although he didn't say anything, I wasn't afraid because I could feel him radiating peace and love.'[11] Another said: 'Then everything became dark, until I saw angels. I was in a beautiful place, where everything was white like it had its own light.'[12] The descriptions are direct and touching, 'visions with a power to heal', to use Dr Morse's words. He leaves the last word to the children themselves: 'I wasn't afraid to live again, because I knew that some day I would be with that Light.'[13]

In that famous quatrain Omar Khayyam concludes: 'I myself am heaven and hell'. Few people think of heaven, purgatory and hell as actual places on various storeys of a multi-tiered universe, but the imagery is deeply embedded in the Western psyche. In this brief space it is not possible to enter into all the issues raised by NDEs and the cross-cultural research by Ian Stevenson which suggests that different patterns may obtain in Hindu India. A few concluding remarks, however, may be helpful:

(1) The early stages of the NDE, corresponding to out-of-the-body experiences, some of which are objectively verifiable, suggest that the conscious self is able to perceive and remember independently of the physical brain. Some researchers would dispute this, but mainly those maintaining materialist world-views in the face of the ESP evidence which they prefer to brush aside as statistically insignificant.

(2) The subjective existence of continuing experience and inner worlds is attested by all experiencers. Practically none of them now fear death, while almost all (I can think of only one sceptical exception) are convinced that they went through the first stage of the death process and are equally convinced that they will survive the transition. We can therefore say that experiencers certainly think that they have caught a glimpse of the afterlife.

(3) The question of the objective or subjective status of the experiences of 'Heaven and Hell' needs to be considered in the light of the fact that all experience is mental: while our normal waking consciousness is focused outwards to the material world, we also have experiences of other states of consciousness which are less dependent on the material world and point towards the creative role of the mind or imagination in constructing our realities. Although forms of idealist philosophy have a bad press in academic circles, they are now being propounded by neurophysiologists familiar with the field. One precursor was Professor H. H. Price with his lecture on 'Survival and the Idea of Another World'.[14] This is not to deny the 'reality' of the physical world, but to sound a note of caution when people deny the possibility of other worlds or realities.

(4) We may perhaps derive a clue from Swedenborg when he asserts that places in the spiritual worlds are in fact states of mind – which may or may not be shared and hence intersubjective. The places or states are unquestionably real to the experiencer, and many do correspond to the traditional archetypes of heaven and hell. But the deeper question is whether these states represent transitory phases of postmortem experience rather than fixed destinations. I have already discussed this proposition with regard to negative experiences, and now turn to heavenly experiences. It is undeniable that such experiences represent a capacity of the human soul or spirit – perhaps the highest or deepest capacity. But can it be sustained by those who find it literally overwhelming? The Tibetan Book of the Dead thinks not; the dying person first encounters the Clear Light, but few can live with it, so that the Light is replaced by lesser lights, until they correspond with the person's state of being. Similar considerations occur in Swedenborg when he comments that many people are unable to stand the presence of the highest celestial angels and gravitate towards lower realms – perhaps like the fabled foreigners who prefer lectures on heaven to heaven itself. In brief, one must have the Kingdom of Heaven within one if one is going to be able to sustain the gaze. Only those imbued to the core with Love, Wisdom, Truth, Beauty, Peace and Joy will be able to contain such bliss. The rest of us will contract away from it

until we learn to expand our minds, hearts and wills into the Mind, Heart and Will of God – but that opens another Chapter....

Notes

1. Quoted in David Lorimer, *Survival?* (London: Routledge and Kegan Paul, 1984) p. 20.
2. See David Lorimer, *Whole in One* (London: Arkana, 1990) Ch. 5.
3. See Lorimer, op. cit., Ch. 3.
4. Carol Zaleski, *Otherworld Journeys* (Oxford, New York: 1987) p. 36.
5. Ibid., p. 37.
6. See Lorimer, op. cit., pp. 130–4.
7. Maurice Rawlings, *Beyond Death's Door* (London: Sheldon, 1978).
8. Kenneth Ring, *Heading toward Omega* (New York: Morrow, 1984) pp. 53 ff.
9. See, for example, Margot Grey, *Return from Death* (London: Arkana, 1985) Ch. 5.
10. Melvin Morse, *Closer to the Light* (London: Souvenir Press, 1990) p. 27.
11. Ibid., p. 29.
12. Ibid., p. 31.
13. Ibid., p. 181.
14. See *Proceedings of the Society for Psychical Research*, vol. 50, part 180 (1953).

14

Human Survival of Death: Evidence and Prospects
ARTHUR ELLISON

INTRODUCTION

Many people think that the business of whether or not we survive death can only be a matter of religious faith or guesswork because 'nobody has ever come back'. That does not appear to be the case. We can and do have good factual evidence concerned with human survival of bodily death, as we shall see. The rabid materialist or literal realist would say, of couse, that statements about human survival of death must be incoherent nonsense because one can hardly survive if one is dead: it's a contradiction in terms. For the question to be coherent we shall need evidence that a human being is more than just an electrochemical machine. That evidence is available and clearly is relevant, indeed fundamental, to survival. I shall not refer much further to religious faith because faith does not seem necessary when facts are available. Nor shall I refer much to the idea of a human being as no more than a machine because the evidence that this is not the case is so strong.

Another important preliminary point concerns the defences that surround our belief systems. The materialists to whom I referred earlier refuse even to look at the good-quality scientific evidence for survival because they consider that they know already that it must be delusive because they are quite certain that a human being is no more than a machine. They defend this view by false logic and emotion. Some religious zealots also refuse to look at scientific evidence for survival because they already have firm beliefs, just as strong as those of the materialists, that it is irreverent or indeed positively evil, and perhaps even dangerous, to make such investigations and indicates a lack of religious faith even to have interest in evidence. I have met many exponents of these views amongst both scientists and religious believers.

I propose then to discuss the scientific evidence for survival which I consider is now sufficiently strong to impel acceptance by any reasonable person and shall consider a little of what a life after death might be like. I shall not take further space on prejudice, whether it be scientific or religious; but I shall consider the experiences of psychics (who are often also spiritualists – but I shall ignore the religious side of spiritualism); the out-of-body experience, together with the near-death experience, with which it has something in common; the reincarnation evidence (as, obviously, if one reincarnates then one has necessarily survived death); and the so-called cross-correspondences, which appear to provide the strongest scientific evidence for survival.

SCIENTIFIC FACTS

But first, what are scientific facts? Scientific facts, indeed all facts, are no more and no less than human experiences – the experiences of normal people uninfluenced by such things as illness, the effects of drugs, or hypnosis. Those experiences are purely mental. They are patterned and interpreted in terms of 'mental models' which 'make sense' of the experiences, which correlate them with other experiences and which enable us to feel that we 'understand'. The largest mental model (or paradigm, as Thomas Kuhn calls these models) is the physical world. That model makes sense of a high proportion of the experiences we have. In terms of that 'mental model' our language has been constructed.

Most of the explanations of science are based on sub-models of this big overall model and descriptions are in terms of this model. This is the 'unquestioned paradigm' on which 'normal science' (Thomas Kuhn's term) is based. ('Normal science' he defines as 'puzzle solving within an unquestioned paradigm'.) Items in this big model (based on the philosophy of realism) are, for example, space, time, sky, land, tables, chairs, our own bodies (with their five senses and brain) and other people, all 'directly known' via the five senses. Items in sub-models of this big model, deduced from sensory experiences, are such things as electrons, electromagnetic fields and chemical elements. It is important to note that no philosopher, so far as I know, would suggest for a moment that it is possible to prove that the physical world 'really exists', independently of our perceptions of it, in the sense asserted by the materialists or realists.

Our culture has explanations of how we 'know' of the existence of the objects of the physical world. Electrochemical pulses travel to the brain, the results of the operations of the senses in our realism model. How these pulses, arriving at the cortices of the brain (considered as a sort of computer) lead to the objects of the physical world, is not explaind. The experience of apparently looking out at the world through windows in the front of the head is particularly mysterious. This was usually not pointed out to us when the functioning of the eyes and other senses was explained by 'authority figures' in our school days. Indeed, the fundamentally mysterious nature of ordinary perception seems never even to occur to many otherwise thoughtful people.

PSYCHIC EXPERIENCES

The difficulties in understanding ordinary perception are compounded when we consider the rather more extended range of experiences of those many, otherwise normal, people we refer to as psychic. They have all our usual normal experiences, which they interpret in the same way as the rest of us do and they refer to objects 'out there'; but in addition they have extra 'paranormal' experiences which a majority of people do not have. These 'psychic experiences' they explain with the use of a different model, as the physical world model is clearly inadequate. The model which they use to pattern and order most of the psychic experiences is referred to as the 'astral world', interpenetrating the physical and extending all around and which has in it their own 'astral body' (with astral senses) and those of other people. They certainly have experiences (there is no doubt about this) which they interpret as deceased people returning to communicate in their 'astral bodies'. Sometimes they do not 'see' (clairvoyance) but they 'hear' hallucinatory voices (clairaudience), and these experiences are sometimes veridical. Occasionally they have strong feelings or impressions (clairsentience) without actually seeing or hearing much. Often these psychic impressions appear to be fantasy or the results of telepathy from a sitter who is present. (The excellent scientific evidence for all this is to be found in the psychical research literature.)

It is important to appreciate that mediums, through whom most of the evidence of this section has been obtained, are mostly, in my experience, transparently honest. They are not, however, scientists and sometimes do not appreciate that there are other 'explanations' fitting their pseudo-visual and auditory experiences, which do not always involve human survival of death. These explanations often require no more than the psychic's own conscious and unconscious guesses about possible communicators, and the contents of the memory store of the sitter. The latter would clearly involve telepathy, for which there is plenty of evidence, produced in over 100 university laboratories. All these 'communications from the departed' are 'dramatised', and appear as though they are arriving through the normal senses of the psychic, by the same unconscious mental machinery which produces our dreams at night.

The mental functioning, conscious and unconscious, of a human being is somewhat complicated and usually neither understood nor studied by psychics. There are vaster depths than the personal unconscious mind and there are the great heights of the superconscious, where is, I consider, the 'Real Self' (the Christ Within, of St Paul). Many people have an overly simple mental representational model of a human being, including only a body and soul (sometimes thought of rather like a captive balloon – and to be 'saved' by religious belief). Many people also even confuse Soul and Spirit, which might be looked upon rather like the mind and the Real Self respectively.

MENTAL MODELS

Human beings might be defined as mental-model-building creatures. We like to 'understand' things. We frequently confuse these postulated models with 'Truth' or 'Reality'. Our Western philosophy, on which our science and culture are based, is one of realism. This does no more than assert that the world is 'out there', independent of our perceptions of it. However, this philosophy of 'naïve realism' seems to me to be crumbling at the edges as a result of human experiences that do not fit the realism model – experiences gained in both particle physics (in the microstructure of our model) and psychical research (in the macrostructure).

All the religions have mental models too, in terms of which they 'explain', or rather describe, their views and experiences. The shared language with which they do this is necessarily based on the model of the physical world 'out there'. The words do not exist for an explanation of a mystical experience, and such a religious experience cannot possibly 'make sense' to someone who has not had such an experience. Scientists try to make their sets of models correlate; they try to make them congruent and consistent. Some of the less competent scientists, forgetting the basic tenets of their craft, reject real human experiences such as these because they do not fit their current set of models. And, it is important to note, their models/paradigms are so valuable to them, and they have invested so much of themselves in them, that they are surrounded by almost impregnable psychological defences.

Many stage magicians are realists and consider that because they are able sometimes to duplicate the appearance (under their own conditions) of a psychic phenomenon this shows that all such phenomena are delusory. It is self-evident how foolish this view is.

SPIRITUALIST SEANCES

On the basis of their model, spiritualists would say that during séances 'dead' people come and give evidence to the medium/ psychic, who perceives it with 'psychic senses' and passes it on to the sitter. The difficulty with this simplistic explanation is the clear presence both of telepathy and unconscious dramatisation (the creating of pseudo-sensory impressions by the unconscious mind) mentioned earlier. This is clearly shown to be the case as a result of 'communications' from fictitious charactes, made up by the sitter, of which there are a number of good examples in the scientific literature of psychical research. However, despite this and as we shall see later, some of the best evidence of human survival of bodily death has been obtained through mediums.

OUT-OF-THE BODY AND NEAR-DEATH EXPERIENCES

It has been determined that about one in ten of the population has had out-of-the body experience (OBE). They would perhaps sometimes consider it to be evidence of the existence of a 'spiritual body'. However, this may be a little too simplistic. Experiences have been described of several so-called 'subtle' bodies. In the OBE the 'physical world' apparently observed often appears to be different in subtle and sometimes symbolic ways. It is clearly not quite the same as the 'ordinary physical world'. The OBE is certainly not evidence of survival, even though it might appear to be that on first sight. It is, however, compatible with the idea.

The near-death experience goes rather further. Many millions of human beings have had this experience since the techniques of resuscitation of the clinically dead have been developed. One early stage of the near-death experience (NDE) includes an OBE in which everything that is going on concerning their clinically-dead body is accurately observed from another position in physical space by the subject, whose normal five senses would certainly appear to a realist to be inoperative in the clinical death state. There is also wide-ranging extra-sensory perception. By careful comparison in many cases of the patient's medical file account with their described near-death experiences, cardiologist Dr Michael Sabom has shown that the patient's observations are accurate. If the realism model of a physical world 'out there', independent of human beings and observed via the five senses and in no other way, is valid, then surely these facts could not possibly have been obtained. The NDEers explain that their thinking and knowing during their experience were with crystal clarity and not in any way confused, as would have been the case had their experience been the result of oxygen deprivation on the brain or the side-effects of drugs.

Many books on the NDE have made the experience quite generally well-known during the last ten years or so. NDEers who have experience of what Moody calls the 'Being of Light' see that 'spiritual entity' in various ways depending on the experiencer. Sometimes it is experienced as a ball of light (materialists, or those having no religious beliefs) sometimes as the traditional Christ (Christians) and sometimes as the traditional Buddha (Buddhists). Presumably members of other religions would see their own religious founder. Beliefs would appear to provide the structure,

Human Survival of Death 179

and something deeper and more significant would appear to provide the substance. Many NDEers describe going on, after a review of their life, into a beautiful world, like the Spiritualists' Summerland (a glorified version of the physical world) where they are met by deceased relatives, looking young and happy. Some others (seemingly less common) describe going into surroundings rather like the traditional ideas of hell. (May I remind the reader that I am describing real human experiences of normal people and not giving religious beliefs.)

REINCARNATION

As pointed out earlier, human beings have obviously survived death if they reincarnate. The best evidence for reincarnation, it seems to me, is set out, cogently and unemotionally, in the many books of Ian Stevenson. He has found young children in various parts of the world who have clear memories, and have given comprehensive descriptions, of an earlier life and surroudings. In the best cases the place of the earlier life has been discovered after the child has given the descriptions and much is found to be as described. (It should be mentioned that age regression under hypnosis usually produces information on pseudo past lives, the results of unconscious dramatisation, and rarely produces anything of very much interest to a scientific investigator.)

I am reminded of one of Stevenson's cases: the case of Jasbir, of Northern India. The boy was thought to have died of smallpox in the evening. He was left until the following morning when he stirred and was revived. He then showed a strange change of behaviour, said that he was the son of another person in another village, and wished to go there. He would not eat because he claimed to be of a higher caste than the family amongst which he found himself. He gave details of his former life as a young man.

All these details corresponded to those of a death in another village, fortunately reported to the family by a visiting lady who was recognised by 'Jasbir' as his Aunt. 'Jasbir' was later taken there and led the way round the village to his former home. Stevenson interviewed many witnesses in both villages and so produced exceedingly strong evidence that the facts were as stated. 'Jasbir' was asked what happened between his death and entering the other body. He said that he saw a holy man who advised him to go into Jasbir's body. He sometimes still saw the holy man in dreams.

THE CROSS-CORRESPONDENCES

The so-called cross-correspondences appear to have been devised towards the beginning of this century by several deceased Council members and founders of the Society for Psychical Research (SPR). They were classical scholars and appear to have contrived the puzzles, based on the Greek classical literature, parts of which they transmitted through one medium and parts through others. Further mediums produced clues which linked the separate parts. The fragments were produced by 'automatic writing', in which the medium holds a pencil on paper and it writes without conscious volition. These ostensible communications from the deceased classical scholars would end with some such phrase as 'This is F. W. H. Myers: please send this to the Society for Psychical Research in London.' When the separate fragments were examined by living classicists, present members of the SPR, it was found that they fitted together like a jigsaw, some fragments providing clues to other fragments, so that the whole produced a consistent meaningful picture. The ostensible communicators claimed in the scripts that they had devised the scheme, technically called the 'cross-correspondences', in order to eliminate cross-telepathy between the mediums. All of them (with the one exception) were not familiar with the material, and the individual fragments did not make sense anyhow. The communicators wished to show that they had devised and transmitted the puzzles, and so existed as thinking, planning entities in the present but not in this physical world.

The cross-correspondences have only three explanations, it seems to me. One is the 'super extrasensory perception hypothesis', in which we have to imagine that the unconscious minds of a number of mediums around the world who did not know each other, got together and planned the whole scheme, getting the necessary information from the minds of classical scholars; and they did all this (without the conscious knowledge of the mediums) in order to deceive us about survival. I know of no evidence for such wide-ranging ESP.

The second hypothesis would involve wide-ranging fraud by all the mediums all over the world and by the distinguished classical scholars involved. However, this appears to me to be so foolish and unlikely that it is hardly worth mentioning. The cross-correspondences continued for some thirty years and no one has produced any evidence that fraud took place.

The only other hypothesis is that the ostensible communicators really did survive death and were whom they claimed, devising and executing the scheme in the way described.

CONCLUSIONS

All this evidence cannot exactly be said to be 'proof of survival'. There is no conclusive proof of anything – accept tautologies. (For example, I could be in bed dreaming that I am writing this article.) We run our lives on the balance of probabilities. We all have sufficient confidence in our model of a stable physical world 'out there' to manage our lives adequately.

For reasons of space I have been unable to deal comprehensively with many topics in this vast subject. There is the perfectly respectable philosophy of idealism, which fits well both normal and paranormal experiences. I have not mentioned the psychological considerations suggesting that the near-death experiences of another world are just what might be expected. The important mystical experience of the one life shows, to the experiencers at least, that separation is part of a great illusion and that the One life is the source of the Good, the True and the Beautiful. This experience, if it is accepted as valid, appears to be at a much 'higher level' than any of the experiences I have described earlier. If separation is indeed part of a 'great illusion' (as the Hindu scriptures have for so long taught) and each of us partakes of the one life, death is even more of an illusion: it signifies the beginning of a return to Reality.

I suggest that the evidence I have given is probably as good as we shall get that human beings are a great deal more than electrochemical machines and really do survive death. Whether we all reincarnate or not I do not know. And as a human being is so much more than just the personality we know so well, I am not sure that reincarnation in the simple sense can be quite as it seems.

May I conclude that I am only as certain that I shall survive the death of my physical body as I am confident that I am at present writing this article. I have a feeling that I am a component of something vastly greater than I, and probably eternal – but I cannot possibly prove that to someone who wishes not to accept the evidence, or who perhaps disagrees with me on its best interpretation.

15
Life after Death: A Fate Worse than Death
A. N. WILSON

I do not believe in life after death. My belief in it was never strong, and I discarded it gradually. Life has seemed much pleasanter since I gave up subscribing to the horrible fantasy that it would go on forever.

When we look at a corpse, it is easy to see where the idea of immortality springs from. I have only looked at four of those whom I loved – two human beings, and two cats. In the human cases, in particular, we gaze at these pale masks, which only bear a grotesque and distant resemblance to the person we love, and we ask 'Where have you gone? Where is your colour, your animation, your laughter, your voice? Come back!' The contrast between the live personality whom we have loved, and the dead corpse suggests that the true self has flown away, and gone to a better place above the clouds. And yet we know, of course, that it is possible for the personality to be removed, by strokes, or accidents of surgery, long before the heart stops beating; that death of a kind can visit us ten, twenty years before the body gives up its struggle for life, that all our memories, all our sense of humour, all that animates us, could be destroyed by moving a few strands inside our brain with a scalpel.

Nor is it for reasons of frivolity that I mention the death of cats in the same sentence as the death of much-loved human friends. For in the cases of the cat deaths, the phenomenon was just the same. There was the same, terrible mysteriousness. At one moment, here was the being whom one loved. The next, there was only stillness. I can not say by what logic it would be possible to distinguish between a human death and a cat death unless you were to assert, as a matter of received doctrine, that cats do not have souls, and people do.

For my part, if there were life after death for human beings, there ought, logically, be life after death for cats. Certainly, if there were such a thing as heaven, it would be unimaginable for me unless it contained cats. I do not say this flippantly. It is a serious point. What leads us to believe in life after death is precisely the feeling that something has gone, leaving only a corpse behind; that the soul, or the life, or the anima, or the breath, the pneuma, has gone home.

Life beyond death is actually a meaningless phrase. Either we believe that death is an illusion, and that life merely continues; or we believe that death, by definition, is that beyond which there can be nothing. If death is death, then there cannot be life beyond it.

Two philosophers come to mind when we contemplate the concept of personal immortality: Plato and Spinoza. Their two, rather different, pictures of death have a sort of plausibility which is lacking in traditional Christian teaching about the matter.

I will describe both these pictures as broadly as I can. Plato believed that the soul was the immortal part of man. It is pre-existent. It was there before the somewhat unfortunate accident of material birth. It will be there still, when we have paid our debt of a cock to Asclepius, that is when we have been delivered of the sickness of life itself. Socrates goes to his death serenely, even joyfully, because he is so certain, so confident, that he is an immortal being. Bertrand Russell can grudgingly say that 'his courage in the face of death would have been more remarkable if he had not believed that he was going to enjoy eternal bliss in the company of the gods',[1] but we need not be so scornful. One definition of nobility must be the capacity, which we should all try to develop, to laugh in the face of death, not to allow death to be our master. For Plato, this capacity derived from his belief in soul, not merely in life after death but in life before life. Plato's slave boy in the *Meno*, however, had a pre-existent soul. This was demonstrated to Plato's satisfaction, if not to our own, by the fact that he had an intuitive knowledge, or as Plato would say, memory, of the laws of geometry. Wordsworth, who was a poet, not a philosopher, claimed to have had intimations of this belief in his greatest Ode. We come into this world, trailing clouds of glory from God who is our home. The Death of Socrates in the *Phaedo* is the archetypical expression of this belief.

For Spinoza, personal immortality is an impossibility precisely because God is the only reality. Anything or anyone who is real is, by Spinoza's definition of things, an attribute of God. When we die, in Spinoza's view, we can be said to return to God who is our home, but it is not our ego which survives. God, for Spinoza, is certainly God, but it could be said that he is really a word for everything which is. Spinoza is a pantheist. Spinoza's death, like that of Socrates, was also calm and untroubled: not because he imagined that he was going to wake up to a life of eternity but because he believed that 'a free man thinks of nothing less than of death; and his wisdom is a meditation not of death but of life'. Wordsworth, illogically, also made use of this concept in his 'Lucy' poem when he imagined the dead girl 'rolled round in earth's diurnal course in rocks and stones and trees'. What is divine and immortal within us – our knowledge of truth and justice, our ability to be virtuous, are attributes of God, and to God they will return.

This is very different from the picture of the afterlife which we might derive from Dante's *Commedia*, where human beings survive in all their grotesque individuality, still seething with lust, ambition and rage or still displaying those qualities of heroism and unselfishness which made them so recognisably themselves while on earth.

The Dantean picture is what most of us would suppose was the traditional Christian picture, give or take the obvious post-reformation denominational differences about the notion of purgatory. For Christians, as we discover every time the matter of research into human embryos or abortion is debated in the House of Commons, it is a fundamental tenet of belief that the human soul in not, as Plato believed, a pre-existent immortal being, but a created entity, made in the image and likeness of God at some specific moment during or shortly after conception. It had no existence before this moment, but thereafter it is indestructible. Hence the extraordinary and rather obsessive importance attached by the Roman Catholic Church, in particular, to sex – an activity which to the rest of us is sometimes serious, and sometimes trivial. But not so for a Christian, for whom the purpose of sex is to make souls. And the destiny of the soul under God is determined by the extent to which it is guided by Providence into the ways of everlasting salvation, or, if you take a more Catholic view of things, by the extent to which it exercises its free will and resists the temptation to sin. Human beings who are in possession of this soul can never hope to be rid of their existence. Whether they like it or not, they remain the children of God, with an immortal destiny and an immortal moral responsibility. At the moment when their bodies are being lowered into the municipal cemetery or gliding through the doors of the crematorium to the tune of 'Sheep May Safely Graze', they are coming face to face with a new phase of existence which some Christians may choose to say is unimaginable, but which their creeds and churches have in fact described to them in some detail.

Evelyn Waugh was a great comic genius, but he was also a seriously devout Christian man. It is necessary to remind oneself of this fact when reading his exchange of letters with Nancy Mitford on the subject of the afterlife. 'Darling Evelyn If you're not too busy (and if you are when you're not) will you explain something to me', Nancy wrote to him when she was herself dying with hideous pain of Hodgkin's disease. 'You know *death* (My brother Tom aged 3 once ran up to his father and said, you know *adultery*) Well, one dies, is buried & rises again and is judged. What happens then between death and the end of the world? One or two friends (Catholic) were quite as much puzzled as I am when I put it to them, and said they would be glad to know what I find out on the subject.' She could not, of course, have come to a better person for information than to a well-instructed and thoroughly believing Catholic convert.

'At the moment of death', he confidently assured her, 'each individual soul is judged and sent to its appropriate place – the saints straight to heaven, unrepentant sinners to Hell, most (one hopes) to Purgatory where in extreme discomfort but confident hope we shall be prepared for the presence of God'.[2] If one had pointed out to Waugh that he had merely described a version of English middle-class childhood, where Heaven was an analogue for the pleasures of grown-up life and Purgatory was a private boarding school, he would probably not have been shaken in his belief since most believing Christians have absorbed enough Platonism into their systems to think that most things on this earth are mere foreshadowings of the greater reality to come.

There we have three views of the afterlife: the Platonic idea that the soul is pre-existent and returns to its natural condition of immortality after the body dies; the Spinozan view that the soul in effect ceases to exist with death and is absorbed into God; and the traditional Christian view that the soul has been called out of nothingness for an eternal destiny which could, very conceivably, end in tears – worse than tears, in everlasting flames. The first two ideas might not be acceptable to any modern philosopher, but they have a respectable philosophical pedigree. Plato's 'proof' of the pre-existence of the slave-boy's soul does not really stand up because we can see that what he is talking about when he says that the boy has a memory of the laws of geometry is merely that the boy understands certain *a priori* truths about mathematics. In other words, although Plato wants at this moment to make it an argument about the boy's soul, the truth, if it is a truth (which many would question) is really a truth about mathematics and not about the boy. It would be more impressive if the boy had memories of empirical truth.

There are Buddhists and other believers in the transmigration of souls who will tell you stories of uneducated women in, let us say, the North of England in the twentieth century, suddenly, under hypnosis, speaking fluent eighteenth century French and describing the execution of Marie Antoinette on the guillotine. This is the kind of 'knowledge' which would make Plato's *Meno* a more convincing document if such stories could be substantiated. What tends to happen is that people who believe the theory in the first place believe such stories, whereas those who are predisposed to think otherwise about the question of personal immortality find something in the story which does not ring true. In any case, if such stories could be verified beyond reasonable doubt, they would certainly give the lie to Christian theories of the afterlife, since the soul of a French *tricoteuse* could hardly at one and the same time be suffering in Purgatory and returning to Newcastle-upon-Tyne as a highly susceptible spirit-medium.

Spinoza's theory is much more easily absorbed because it can be translated without much difficulty into slightly different thought-patterns such as Wittgenstein's. God, in Spinoza, is not so different from Wittgenstein's *That which is the case*, and we all know, whatever theories we might or might not possess about the future of our souls, that death is a reality. We are not going to escape it. Where we might differ is whether we choose to be like Spinoza and meditate only upon life, or whether, like the majority of Christians from the early fathers to Jeremy Taylor, from Ignatius Loyola to Thérèse of Lisieux, we think that virtue is to be acquired by a ceaseless and frequently ghoulish preoccupation with death itself.

Temperamentally, I am much more inclined to aspire to the wisdom and virtue of Spinoza than to that of Dante and the Christians. On the only occasion in life when I have known that I was extremely close to death – a bad case of viral pneumonia in which for three days the doctors believed that it was 'touch and go', I felt no interest in, or desire for, immortality, and absolutely no sense that I was about to pass out of one phase of existence into another. Admittedly I felt too tired to think; but in so far as I was aware of existence, I felt it as merely something which was quietly ebbing away from me, with no hope of return. The passages of the Bible which meant most to me then, and which mean most to me now, are those passages of the Psalms and the Writings which speak most categorically of our Mortality. 'In death there is no remembrance of thee: in the grave who shall give thee thanks'? (Ps. 6:5) – or, one of my mother's favourite texts, which she inscribed on my first Bible for me: 'Whatsoever thy hand findeth to do, do it with thy might; for there is no work, nor device, nor knowledge, nor wisdom, in the grave whither thou goest' (Eccles. 9:10).

Of course, it would be a bold man who stated with the categorical vigour of Evelyn Waugh, exactly what was going to happen beyond death. I would wish to say, however, that, like Hamlet, I can imagine no more depressing prospect than the possibility that the traditional Christian view of the afterlife might be true. Just because a thing is depressing does not mean that it is not true. I know that. AIDS is depressing. Cancer is depressing. Famine is depressing. They are all there. They are all facts. The prospect that the universe has been created by some insanely malicious despot who has gone to the trouble of inventing a place of torment where unimaginable horrors have been prepared for sinners – horrors beside which AIDS and famine and cancer pale into insignificance – is one which would drive me mad if I believed it, and which is incompatible with the claim that God is love. For this reason, many Christians have abandoned a belief in hell, and will tell you that they only believe in heaven. But this is to substitute an ancient and terrifying system of belief which at least has nearly two thousand years of antecedents for making it up as you go along. It is making the afterlife into a sort of Disneyland, with fun for all the family.

We could never prove these things – and even taking opinion polls at Christian funerals, for example, would probably shed no light on the matter, but I suspect that fewer and fewer people, including Christians, actually entertain any belief in an afterlife.

By the strictest standards, it is absurd to have beliefs about it anyway. How can you have a belief about something which by definition you can know nothing about? Most people, as my earlier example of Wordsworth shows, have nebulous and illogical feelings about these matters which vary and vacillate depending upon their experience of bereavement. To have seen someone that one loves wrestle with life and death, to watch the life, and with it the pain, ebb out of their body, can be an experience which leaves us with the longing for them still to survive, somehow, somewhere, over the rainbow; or it can leave us with such profound gratitude that they have been released from suffering that we would not wish to think of their survival in any form, except perhaps in the vague rolled round in earth's diurnal course variety. As we pass through these experiences, or as we think of our own impending and inevitable deaths, we are not for the most part indulging in purely cerebral processes. We are seizing upon mythologies to help us with fear. It is helpful when philosophers and others try to put into words why, precisely, from one generation to another, we might be more likely than at other times to entertain particular fancies about life after death. Don Cupitt for example, says that one of Darwin's most important contributions to the imaginative development of the nineteenth century was to destroy the possibility of believing in the immortality of the soul.[3]

These things are a matter of collective imagining, as much as they are matters of individual response. The noblest period of Hebrew literature knew little or nothing of the concept, and indeed their idea of God and his justice and mercy would be diminished if it were to be burdened with a mediaeval Catholic-style system of heaven and hell and purgatory. Certainly, by the time of Jesus, there were many Jews who had come to believe in the immortality of the soul, and in the existence of a future life, but no Biblical literature, even in the New Testament, builds up the sort of detailed picture of the afterlife that we might find in Dante; and though the stories of Jesus and his resurrection might be supposed by post-Dantean Christians to be the ultimate indication of the idea of personal survival, that is not necessarily how they would have seemed to the authors of the Gospels.

True, all of them believed in the possibility of rising from the dead. Lazarus did it. John the Baptist was believed by Herod to have done it. The son of the widow of Nain did it. Jairus's daughter probably did it. Many, if not all, the dead bodies in Jerusalem did it (according to Matthew) while Jesus was dying. And Jesus himself did it. But the point of Jesus's resurrection for the New Testament writers is less that it demonstrates the truth of personal immortality (that was something they took for granted), than it was a personal and divine vindication of Jesus's mission, purpose, person.

How human beings of a later generation respond to the claims of the New Testament about the resurrection of Jesus will be largely determined by what theories they entertain about the afterlife. I doubt whether there are many Christians, or any non-Christians, whose views about these matters have been changed or determined by reading the stories in the Gospels about Jesus's resurrection appearances. To that extent, they are an irrelevance. A modern Christian who probably has doubt about the existence of the future life, or certainly doubts the wisdom of speculating thereon too deeply, would probably be happy with the notion that there was no empty tomb. He or she would still, in some sense or another, respond to the idea of God vindicating Jesus by raising him up. Anastasis, as we have been reminded, means more than the resuscitation of a corpse. A more traditionally-minded Christian who has derived his or her picture of the afterlife from Dante or the Catholic catechism would realise that Jesus had indeed risen from the dead, and believe that when he met Mary Magdalene in the garden, he was in transit. He had just been harrowing hell, and was about to ascend to the right hand of God to judge the quick and the dead. Neither of these interpretations are in the original story, but the stories – one of their reasons for surviving for two thousand years – are deep wells. They are capable of almost any amount of interpretation.

To my way of thinking, life after death seems such a greedy idea, and such an ungrateful one, and one which is so likely to make us pass through this valley, which we are (many of us) agreed we shall only pass once, with such grudging hearts, such closed eyes. It was not only Jesus who came that we should have life and have it more abundantly. We all came for that purpose. Belief in personal immortality leads automatically to the sin of asceticism, with all its distrust of the body, and all the resultant misery which thereby inevitably ensues. Mr Brocklehurst is a character in fiction but he bestrides Western civilization like a Colossus. Freud tried to put him to sleep. So did Darwin, but he is still there.

When I was at school, we were still taught by the chaplain in our divinity classes that the concept of life after death was the only thing which could reconcile the idea of God's love with the fact of innocent suffering. He knew about innocent suffering, poor man, having been tortured for three years by the Japanese during the Second World War. At the time, it was the thought which caused one of those frequent adolescent abandonments of religious belief, and I now find it a wholly abhorrent notion. That there might be an omnipotent God, preparing for them that love him such good things as pass man's understanding, but waiting a little.... It is a horrible prospect. Imagine, if you or I were omnipotent, and we could remove the suffering of the starving, and the destitute and those wracked with the miseries of mental illness? Would we say 'Let them wait until they get to Heaven?' Would we not see that the very idea of Heaven has provided Christians with the most wonderful excuse for not being Christians. How can anyone read the Gospel and think that slavery is compatible with the teaching of Jesus, who taught his disciples that they should become the slaves of all? And yet for 1800 years Christians hardly even thought about the matter. The slaves would go to Heaven the same as everyone else – or to hell – and it would all sort itself out in the wash.

I think that we can also see that the concept of Heaven is all tied up with the anthropocentric vision of the universe which has done such untold damage to our environment. We are here as stewards, because God put us here. That means that the earth is our plaything, that animals only exist for our sustenance, that we have every right to make as much mess and dirt and squalor here as we choose because it is ours, and, besides, it's not the only life we've got, so what does it matter; we're bound for heaven, and *après nous,le deluge*. It was only after human beings lost their belief in heaven that they began to take life on earth with the seriousness which it deserves, and to treat the earth, and our fellow-occupants of this mortal planet, with the affection and respect which they deserve.

In my experience, a Blakean idea of eternity can be restored to us if we discard and forget the myths of heaven and purgatory and hell, which are diseased, ugly ideas.

> He who binds to himself a joy
> Doth the wingèd life destroy.
> But he that kisseth the joy as it flies
> Lives in eternity's sunrise.

We should learn to kiss joy as it flies. The intolerable facts of death – the deaths of those whom we love – the deaths of the young who have not been given the chance to realise the full potential of their lives – these facts are not made more bearable by pretending that we shall see them again in some pearly palace, or, more horrible still, through the conversation of a spirit medium.

Anyone who has watched animals die must have come to the conclusion that in some ways they are better at accepting death than we are. Grief should be grief. It should be absolute. Rachel weeping for her children would not be comforted because they are not. There is no consolation in that, but at least one can be certain that it is true. We are not being paid off with a trivial placebo.

As Christianity gradually dismantles itself in the West – and it is only a matter of time before the same thing happens in Africa and the East where it is allegedly flourishing – we will come to understand how possible it might be to return to a truly noble vision of life, such as Spinoza taught in his philosophy and such as obtains in Ecclesiastes and Psalms. That has not happened yet in the West. We are not truly meditating upon life as Spinoza would want us to do. We are whistling in the dark to pretend that – it – that er, ahem – you know, does not happen.

Keep eating the muesli is not a substitute for our old immortality myths. It is a pathetic and undignified transmutation of them. The old believers taught that when we die we would go on forever. The new health freaks believe that before we die we shall go on forever: if only we lay off the booze and the fags and the polyunsaturates.

Wisdom can't be learnt until the fact of death is accepted and then, in the Spinoza manner, not run away from, but put out of our minds. We should take a leaf out of the cats' book. They are wiser than we. They know when to lie in the sun. They know when to play and to hunt and to make love. They know when to turn their faces to the wall and to die. If their legendary nine lives run out faster than the allotted span, their parents or lovers grieve as inconsolably as Rachel weeping for her children. Only time heals such wounds; what some would call nature. The wounds perhaps remain forever, but other things come to take their place – new hunting grounds, new lovers, new seasons. It is so, or it could be so with us.

Philip Larkin defined religion as:

> That vast moth-eaten musical brocade
> Created to pretend we never die...

He was a man who dreaded extinction with a passion:

> no sight, no sound,
> No touch or taste or smell, nothing to think with,
> Nothing to love or link with,
> The anaesthetic from which none come round.

It is a thought with good literary antecedents. Milton's Beelzebub asks:

> For who would lose,
> Though full of pain, this intellectual being,
> Those thoughts that wander through eternity?

Even angels and archangels can dread having 'nothing to think with'. I am certainly aware that one of the reasons I write is a feeling that I wish to be immortal. I lack the Blakean ability to delight in essentially evanescent moments. I wish to write them down, to stick them in some mental photograph album.

It would be wiser to be like Jesus and Socrates, and not to write: to trust one's thoughts to conversation, to make one's stories oral stories. The written word is unquestionably one of the illusions with which Western man has, particularly in literature since Milton, disguised from himself his own mortality.

I feel reasonably certain that cats do not have such egotism.

Thoughts presumably pass through their heads as often as they pass through mine. I do not say that these thoughts are always as interesting as those which wandered through eternity or through the brain of John Milton – but then, whose are? The point is, they pass, and it is not a matter of regret to cats. This must in part be because they do not anticipate death. Dostoyevsky, who should have known, because he faced the firing squad, says that knowing the hour of one's death, the exact time of it, makes its terrors doubly worse. But surely the mere fact that we, as human beings, can define to ourselves our own mortality, can say that we know that we shall die, and that this is the event which we fear more than any other.

In the days when I knew Philip Larkin, I used to think that there was a certain paradox here. I was still holding on by my finger-tips to Christian belief, and therefore technically assented to a belief in the resurrection of the body and life everlasting. But in my inner heart I did not really believe in the resurrection of the body, not really – not a reconstitution of my flesh as resurrection flesh, not a rising up of my bones as in the Epistles of Paul or the paintings of Stanley Spencer in Cookham Churchyard. Above all, as I had gradually realised after my near-death experience, I did not WANT immortality. I had no innate dread of death, though like everyone I dread dying or the possible manner of my dying. I simply did not wish to carry on forever and ever. If I had been able to state my wishes to the Almighty I should have wished to put them in the words of the Old Testament psalmist, that the days of man were three score years and ten; I would have wanted to say that I was grateful for this; He really had no need to lay on that everlasting encore to assure me of his love or presence. For Larkin, however, who was incurably atheistic, the idea of mortality was unendurable and he would have done anything to make himself believe in some form of survival. That was why, rather to his annoyance, I used to question his lines about religion being 'Created to pretend we never die'. Surely the majority of religions, for whatever purpose they were created – if that is how they came into being – are only too ready to remind their adherents of the fact that they will die, quite often threatening them with horrible punishments thereafter if they do not, at all times and in all places, subscribe to the orthodoxies of faith and morals. And religion, whatever else it is, has been one very simple way of ritualising our knowledge of mortality. Jesus reminded his followers that not a sparrow falls to the ground unseen by its heavenly father. This is not an Animal Rights plea that sparrows should be granted the same status as human beings, or that after a major shoot of pigeon or grouse there should be state funerals or requiem masses. One of the implications of Jesus' saying, however, must be that we should conform our lives to those of other beings in the natural universe. We can spend the fortune of Solomon on fine raiment and still look no more beautiful than the flowers of the field; the earth provides us with sustenance in exactly the same way that it provides the beasts of the field with their food, even though we might be more ingenious in the cultivation, storage and preparation of food than the fowls of the air and the fishes of the sea. The fact that God sees the fall of the sparrow does not mean that the sparrow should start to wail or rail against his mortality. It is a lesson in how to die. We should learn to die like sparrows.

There can be no more childish egotism, in my view, than in supposing that the universe has a creator who is constantly on the look-out, like some sadistic headmaster, for the way in which we behave or misbehave. At the end of term, the good children will be rewarded. The remainder will see him afterwards in his study. However sophisticated Christian theology becomes, its theories of the afterlife always boil down to this absurdist picture: of the First Cause, the source of all Life and Goodness, being perpetually engaged, sometimes with the assistance of a spy network of guardian angels, in assessing the condition of our souls. Those who have done sins, without repenting of them in time, will suffer eternally. The origins of this Dantean horror-story are to be found in the pages of the New Testament – with Jesus's stories of the division of the sheep and the goats, and his mentioning of the last judgment, when those who visited the sick and the imprisoned will be rewarded and those who neglected such works of charity will be punished. But he could not have supposed when he said such things, that a whole elaborate system of celestial rewards and infernal punishments would be concocted on the basis of these parables. It would be as literalist as to suppose that he genuinely thought true repentance was impossible until we had all undertaken a spell as swineherds; or that he was genuinely and literally a door, and Peter, James and John were in fact not human beings at all but sheep (like some of the holier desert fathers, at least one of whom developed the nether half of the sheep).

But to die as a sparrow dies, or as a cat dies, is to realise that we can leave our body behind, and our lives behind, like bathers hanging up their clothes in the locker before going into the swimming bath. It need not be horrific. In fact, it is something to rejoice over.

Larkin was a very popular poet. He was always complaining in his curmudgeonly way that he was popular, but it pleased him, and at the same time baffled him. Surely a man who expressed such strong views, who hated anywhere except Hull, (and wasn't very fond of that) who lived a life of such seclusion, and who hated women, blacks, most art – ought not to have been so popular. It worried him.

He was popular because he spoke to our condition. It is not of course religion which pretends we never die, it is the strange amalgam of superstitions and aspirations which possess the collective consciousness at this juncture of the late twentieth century. The health fads, the dread of nuclear war, the obsession with the wickedness of drink and cigarettes, are all part of the same weird view. My doctor, who has been looking after me for two or three years, is a conscientious man. All new patients in his practice undergo a test – blood-pressure, kidneys, and so forth. It would appear that when last heard of all my bodily functions were operative to the doctor's satisfaction. He then asked me how much I drank. I told him, roughly speaking truthfully, and he expressed a pained astonishment. He said that anyone who drank more than two glasses of wine PER WEEK was endangering their liver. He then gave me a lecture about smoking cigarettes. Doubtless if he knew that I sometimes like to eat a fried breakfast he could have given me a lecture about that.

It was only a vivid and extreme example of an attitude of mind which emanated I suspect from the USA and which is now all but universal in the West. I happen to dread old age much more than I dread death, so that it does not particularly worry me that an indulgence in fried eggs, cigarettes or whisky might make my spell in the geriatric ward rather shorter than that of a more abstemious patient. But even in the geriatric ward you come across doctors and nurses who seem to have such a horror of the most obvious fact about human beings – that they are mortal – that they will do anything to preserve the life of their patients even though the kindest thing that could happen to them would be death. It is the kindest thing, in fact, which could happen to any of us, and without being morbid or suicidal in any way, I think we should all, if not positively looking forward to death, rejoice in the fact that life has perimeters. It does not go on forever, and nor should we wish it to go on forever. It would be a hell if it did.

We are physical beings and we inhabit a physical universe. If we discard the myths of self and soul and spirit, and recognise that all our life and sensation, all our capacity to think and to feel, are inextricably tied up with our bodies – if, in short, we see that we do not have bodies, we are bodies – then we might begin to realise what an extraordinary place we inhabit and what a mystery, in the true sense, life is. To be born, to grow up, to fall in love, to realise that by our actions, we can bring more human beings to life, and in watching them grow and develop, see the whole mystery re-enacted: is not all this wonderful? And to watch the changing seasons, and to find out more about the strange world of plants and fishes and beasts and birds with whom we share life on this planet – is that not wonderful too? And to realise the ingenuity of the human mind – which can produce the symphonies of Mozart, and the novels of Dostoyevsky and the canvases of Rembrandt and all the ingenious scientific discoveries of the twentieth century – is not that a humbling thought, when we realise that all human beings are made up of ingredients which could be bought for a pound or so at a chemist's shop – even Mozart, even Shakespeare. Is not that enough mystery, without your wishing to invent new mysteries of heaven and of hell? And is this life not rich, and varied and beautiful enough for you: or do you, like a greedy child, having stuffed its face with food, do you demand yet more? I don't. Are you so obsessed with being you that you can't accept the fact of your own nonexistence? Can't you realise that the most deliriously happy moments in life have come when we have forgotten ourselves; and that, not only is it inconceivably unlikely that we should survive bodily death, it would be horrible if we did – a fate far worse than death itself.

Notes

1. B. Russell, *History of Western Philosophy* (London, 1961) p. 156.
2. S. Hastings, *Nancy Mitford* (London, 1986) p. 233.
3. D. Cupitt, *Only Human* (London, 1985).

16
Beyond the Crematorium – Popular Belief
CHRISTOPHER LEWIS

EXPECTATION OF LIFE

It has been estimated that prehistoric people had an expectation of life of about 18 years. Life was short. In ancient Rome, the life-span was only slightly greater. In the middle ages in England, it was about 33. By 1841, the expectation of life in Britain for a man was 40, for a woman 42. Now, for Westerners, it is somewhat more than the biblical target of threescore years and ten.[1]

So it might be said that we enjoy something of everlasting life, for it goes on and on. For the 18-year-old, living in the West and outside one of the notorious trouble-spots, life stretches into what is an almost infinite future giving a sense of immortality without recourse to cryonics. Add to this the fact that he or she will, for all kinds of well-rehearsed reasons, be less aware of the death of others than those of previous generations and it is perhaps not surprising that consideration of the fact of death and speculation as to what comes next are not high priorities. Life is longer and materially much more luxurious; we are less familiar with the ending of it and have often not reflected very deeply on what, if anything, is to follow.

Few would not wish to welcome greater prosperity and longevity or, for example, better hospital provision. The consequence of these desirable developments is that death and life beyond it are of less consequence to people now. So there is no mysterious taboo preventing people from addressing these subjects. Wringing of hands at people's ignorance of death and programmes to educate them about it, will not change their everyday experience. It may only be when contemporaries start to die that death and what comes next are brought home to people. What then appears as an abnormal experience may be treated as significant and traumatic: the sudden breaking in of something which had not previously been seriously considered. Perhaps this comparatively new sense of death as an aberrant intrusion into what should be a trouble-free existence explains the flurry of courses and books on death and bereavement which have recently been promoted by members of the caring professions. What had been part of everyday experience has become a crisis to be analysed and managed by professionals.

Consistent with decreased familiarity with death and a sense of near-immortality *within* life, is a decline in interest in what comes after death. Far from being 'caused' by some mysterious force of secularisation, a change in belief would be the natural accompaniment of altered social circumstances.

Survey figures are notoriously difficult to interpret and there is added complexity when they relate to such an uncertain area as the afterlife. If you approach people in the street or at their door, bent on their shopping or on watching television, and ask them whether they believe in life after death, then you may not receive coherent or indeed accurate answers. What, after all, counts as belief? If someone believes that her soul will continue in the memories of her children, should she be answering 'yes'? If she has rejected what she sees as orthodox Christian teaching, but replaced it with some other belief, will she answer 'no'? Is a belief in reincarnation seen to be the subject of a separate question or is that covered by an enquiry about afterlife?

Interpretation is complex, but less so if the same question has been asked at different times, producing what are called longitudinal data. Even if the total figure may be open to all kinds of dispute, the comparison between figures may provide insights into trends in belief.

In Britain, the figures for those who believe in life after death show a decline, both in the population at large and also among churchgoers. During the First World War, the enquiry *The Army and Religion* found that although few men went to church, the majority 'though vaguely, believe in the life to come'. In 1955 a BBC survey found that about 43 per cent of its listeners believed in life after death and Gallup research in 1964 reported the figures for Roman Catholics as 74 per cent, for Free Church members as 56 per cent and for Anglicans as 49 per cent, rising to 88, 86 and 85 per cent respectively for regular attenders. The *Values and Social Change in Britain* surveys of 1981 and 1990 give fairly stable figures for belief in the afterlife (45 and 44 per cent) while tracing a decline in belief in heaven (57–53 per cent) and – contrary to what is often imagined – in belief in reincarnation (27–24 per cent). In the 18–24 age group, the figures for life after death for the same period are 44 and 35 per cent (with those who do *not* believe in it increasing from 39 to 52 per cent); belief in reincarnation was also in decline in this group (29–19 per cent).[2]

These figures appear in the context of a greater decline in specifically Christian beliefs, for example that 'People who believe in Jesus as the Son of God can expect salvation'. The incidence of belief needs to be distinguished from the nature of it and, while there seems to have been some overall reduction in belief in life after death especially among the young, this has been accompanied by a shift from 'Christian' to more generalised or 'implicit' expressions of belief. With fewer children in Sunday school and fewer adults in church, people are not being taught Christian beliefs.

BELIEVING AND NOT BELIEVING

To discern what people actually do believe is more difficult. We try to make sense of reality with the tools which we have available, and in this particular area the tools are few and the language is of the most approximate kind. So, when the child asks about death, the adult, faced with a difficult question, reaches for a suitable belief. The Christian believer, no doubt, struggles to convey something of what is understood as Christian teaching. For others it is easier: 'You go to heaven' or 'You go to be with God – if you're good.' Heaven is a place of enjoyment with entry to it often linked with good conduct. The purpose of the parent may be disciplinary and he, or more usually she, may have no other mythology to reach for than 'pie in the sky' for the good and punishment (if not actual damnation) for the bad. The information conveyed may be used by the child to piece together a world view, at least for a time.[3]

The sense that death is not all is by no means always connected with religious belief. Thornton Wilder expresses an apparently secular version in his book *Our Town*: 'I don't care what they say with their mouths – everybody knows that *something* is eternal.

And it ain't houses and it ain't names, and it ain't earth and it ain't even stars – everybody knows in their bones that *something* is eternal, and *that* something has to do with human beings.'[4]

The very facts of consciousness, of imagination, of relationships with others, may be seen to imply 'something more', as may the need to compensate for present suffering. There is the psychological difficulty of conceiving of oneself as non-existent and this is extended in an unwillingness to imagine others as cut off by death. It may not be easy to conjure up a vision of other worlds, outside time and space. But this difficulty is matched by that of imagining life as we experience it, cut off, with only void beyond.

Lacking other information, people who believe in an afterlife tend to think of it as an extension of life as it is now, but with the desirable aspects pronounced and the undesirable traits removed. The most important feature of life now is usually relationships with people. Therefore the key to life in the future is a continuation of chosen relationships. The continuation may take a number of forms. It may be an extension of personal life made possible by a heaven, whether sustained by a loving God or just 'there'. Or it may be that an individual sees himself as continuing in his children; they not only continue his life in a genetic sense but they also remember him. Perhaps the increase of interest in genealogy, far from being a symptom of social insecurity, is part of a revised concept of immortality with the researcher granting life beyond death to his ancestors!

An alternative or supplement to such beliefs about relationships is a more collective continuity: in the life of the community or the nation to which contributions have been made and, indeed, for the sake of which life may have been sacrificed. The individual dies, but the group continues, having benefited from the contributions of all its children. War is not the only occasion for such beliefs, for the individual may be seen as continuing in lasting creative achievements – immortality through books written, pictures painted or factories founded.

A third possibility is to believe in the continuity of nature. The individual is part of nature and although he fades, the world and its cycle of life goes on. Indeed, with the prominence of nuclear and ecological threats, the individual may see his own efforts as contributing to a life which, without those efforts, might not be eternal.

Fourthly, there are traditional Christian beliefs about the afterlife, expressed most frequently either in Jewish terms of resurrection of the body (i.e. the whole personality) but also in Greek terms of immortality of the soul. At least for the more orthodox, death is seen as decisive. After it, for those in a right relationship with God there is, at some stage, heaven; for those alienated from God there is another state. In such states relationships to people are subsumed in relationship to God, as in Jesus' reported reply to a question about the resurrection: 'For when they rise from the dead, they neither marry nor are given in marriage, but are like angels in heaven' (Mark 12:25).

Representatives of the churches are not, of course, immune to the context in which they think and write, whether or not they make an explicit attempt to relate to that context. It is hard to generalise, but there have certainly been adjustments of belief from that of resurrection and judgement followed by eternal heaven or everlasting hell. In 1864, perhaps in part to protect the authority of the bible, 11,000 Church of England clergymen signed a public declaration of belief in eternal hell.[5] Very few would sign such a declaration today. Except in certain very Protestant circles where there is a closely quarded 'reference group' for mutual support, damnation is now rarely mentioned. Belief in it may have been consistent with a medieval world-view, or indeed with a Victorian sense of justice, but it is not seen as appropriate to believe it now. If hell is referred to, then it has been altered to a kind of purgatory for the therapeutic treatment of persistent offenders. Keith Ward's words represent the view of many in the churches: 'What one does, as a modern theologian, is to disentangle false cultural beliefs from the core of universal truth – which is that Jesus shows the love of God to be self-sacrificial and unrestricted'; he sees this theological process as excluding beliefs in, for example, demonic possession or the existence of an everlasting hell.[6]

By concentrating on those parts of the Bible and of the Christian tradition which emphasise love and relationship, a picture is built up which is confident in life with God beyond death – for all, or at least for all who do not choose actively to reject God. As for the other details, they remain a mystery: 'Beloved, we are God's children now; what we will be has not yet been revealed' (1 John 3:2).

Then lastly, there are those both within the Christian church and outside it, who have either been horrified by the idea of life beyond death or at least have not believed in it. They have preferred the present with its disciplines and pleasures. The Revd Homes Dudden, Master of Pembroke College and Vice-Chancellor of Oxford University in the 1920s, expressed his unusual view in a donnish manner: 'As an ordained clergyman of the Church of England I am constrained to believe in a future life, but I don't mind admitting, my dear fellow, that personally I should much prefer extinction.'[7] The playwright and author John Mortimer is more direct: 'I think paradise would be unbelievably tedious. That's why I don't want to have immortality. My father said what a terrible idea it would be, like living in a huge transcendental hotel with nothing to do in the evening.'[8] Every minute now is precious and must be kept so.

Thus there is variety – a marked pluriformity of belief and unbelief. With the departure from specifically Christian beliefs, that is hardly surprising. It may be said that near-death experiences give hard evidence or that religious faith gives the assurance of things hoped for, the conviction of things not seen, but most people find nothing to build on, save parts of their own experience. For some believers, biblical passages can be taken more or less literally, or Jesus' resurrection may be experienced as giving assurance of the fate of the Christian at least, but what is known of people's beliefs appears to show that such conclusions are only drawn by a minority.

ALL WILL BE WELL

Belief in an afterlife within the churches has been modified; outside the church, belief has declined and changed. It is risky to generalise, but it is probably accurate to say that for most of those who believe in an afterlife, the shape is indefinite; there is just *something* beyond. Belief is built up from experience, while borrowing from what seems right and comforting in traditional religion – elements of heaven, for example, with hell kept only for jokes about Peter and the pearly gates. Churches may be perceived as having a 'selective education model' of death, proclaiming the finality of consignment to one or the other place. Popular mythology appears, however, to be more on the lines of a 'comprehensive system'; the view is very rarely expressed that a person who has died is now in undesirable circumstances. He or she is seldom even in the 'higher education' of purgatory. Rather, he or she is now free and in the company of loved people and animals. Indeed, the educational illustration may be inappropriate, for he is not institutionalised or subject to assessment and appraisal.

Such a belief may be demonstrated as much in actions as in words. Visits to cemeteries, special treatment of photographs and furniture and particular observance of anniversaries are known parts of the process of mourning, but they may also be ways of expressing the hope or belief that the dead person lives on. Rituals and symbols are probably no less prevalent in the modern, supposedly rational, world. Indeed they may take on greater importance now that there is less wider-family and communal support surrounding death. They imply a continuing relationship with the one who has died, while enabling the survivors to adjust to the fact that he or she is no longer present in an obvious manner.

Ironically, one of the best summaries of popular belief is part of a sermon preached by Henry Scott Holland and quoted without its context at many funerals. In the sermon, Scott Holland contrasts the first (and positive) experience on seeing a dead person with the 'blind, dismal, unutterable darkness' of death and he works towards a view which is both conscious of the decisiveness of death and also confident in the resurrection of Jesus. What is quoted, however, is only what the dead loved-one seems at first to be saying:

> Death is nothing at all. It does not count. I have only slipped away into the next room. Nothing has happened. Everything remains exactly as it was. I am I, and you are you, and the old life that we lived so fondly together is untouched, unchanged. Whatever we were to each other, that we are still. Call me by the old familiar name. Speak of me in the easy way which you always used. Put no difference into your tone. Wear no forced air of solemnity or sorrow. Laugh as we always laughed at the little jokes that we enjoyed together. Play, smile, think of me, pray for me. Let my name be ever the household word that it always was. Let it be spoken without effort, without the ghost of a shadow upon it. Life means all that it ever meant. It is the same as it ever was. There is absolute and unbroken continuity. What is this death but a negligible accident? Why should I

be out of mind because I am out of sight? I am but waiting for you, for an interval, somewhere very near, just round the corner. All is well. Nothing is hurt; nothing is lost. One brief moment and all will be as it was before. How we shall laugh at the trouble of parting when we meet again![9]

Attempts to avoid death or to reduce its seriousness have always been opposed by the major religious, but that is the direction in which (at least some Western) popular belief seems to be going. Purists may view crematorium music with disdain, but it is nevertheless not an inappropriate symbol for what is believed to come after this life: background music for the Elysian fields in which a happy retirement will be enjoyed. This is the kind of life which the dead are imagined to live. Even if life is fraught with problems now, it is believed that all will be well.

Notes

1. J. Hick, *Death and Eternal Life* (London: Fount, 1979) p. 81.
2. The figures are given in J. Hick, ibid., Ch. 4; D. S. Cairns, *The Army and Religion* (London: Macmillan, 1919) p. 16; R. Gill, *The Myth of the Empty Church* (London: SPCK, 1993) pp. 201–6.
3. See S. Anthony, *Discovery of Death in Childhood and After* (London: Allen Lane, 1971) pp. 121–2.
4. Quoted in R. E. Neale, *The Art of Dying* (New York: Harper and Row, 1973) p. 95.
5. O. Chadwick, *The Secularization of the European Mind in the 19th Century* (Cambridge: Cambridge University Press, 1975) p. 105.
6. K. Ward, *A Vision to Pursue* (London: SCM, 1991) p. 120.
7. Quoted in O. Lancaster, *With an Eye to the Future* (London: Murray, 1967) p. 62.
8. R. Hartill, *Writers Revealed* (London: BBC, 1989) p. 58.
9. H. S. Holland, *Facts of the Faith* (London: Longmans, 1919) p. 126.

Suggestions for Further Reading
PAUL BADHAM

Ainsworth-Smith, I. and Speck, P., *Letting Go: Caring for the Dying and Bereaved* (London: SPCK, 1982).
Alger, W. R., *The Destiny of the Soul* (New York: Greenwood Press, 1966).
Anderson, R., *Theology, Death and Dying* (Oxford: Blackwell, 1986).
Badham, P., *Christian Beliefs about Life after Death* (Basingstoke: Macmillan, 1976) revised edn 1994.
Badham, P. and Badham, L., *Immortality or Extinction?* (Basingstoke: Macmillan, 1982; revised edn 1994).
Badham, P. and Badham, L. (eds), *Death and Immortality in the Religions of the World* (New York: Paragon House, 1987).
Barr, J., *The Garden of Eden and the Hope of Immortality* (London: SCM, 1992).
Berger, A., *Aristocracy of the Dead: New Findings in Postmortem Survival* (Jefferson: McFarland, 1987).
Berger, A., Berger, J., Badham, P., Kutscher, A., Perry, M. and Beloff, J. (eds), *Perspectives on Death and Dying: Cross Cultural and Multi-Disciplinary Views* (Philadelphia: The Charles Press, 1989).
Blackmore, S., *Beyond the Body* (London: Heinemann, 1982).
Bowker, J., *The Meanings of Death* (Cambridge: Cambridge University Press, 1991).
Bowlby, J., *Attachment and Loss* (New York: Basic Books, 1964, 1973, 1980) vols I–III.
Carnley, P., *The Structure of Resurrection Belief* (Oxford: Clarendon Press, 1987).
Charles, R. H., *Eschatology* (New York: Schocken Books, 1963).
Dahl, M. E., *The Resurrection of the Body* (London: SCM, 1962).
Daley, B. E., *The Hope of the Early Church* (Cambridge: Cambridge University Press, 1991).
Davis, S. T. (ed.), *Death and Afterlife* (Basingstoke: Macmillan, 1989).
Dearmer, P., *The Legend of Hell* (London: Cassells, 1929).
Duthie, C., *Resurrection and Immortality* (London: Bagster, 1979).
Edwards, D., *The Last Things Now* (London: SCM, 1969).
Edwards, P. (ed.), *Immortality* (New York: Macmillan, 1992).
Evans-Wentz, W. Y., *The Tibetan Book of the Dead* (Oxford: Oxford University Press, 1957).
Flew, A., *The Logic of Mortality* (Oxford: Blackwell, 1987).
Gauld, A., *Mediumship and Survival* (London: Paladin, 1983).
Gill, R., *The Myth of the Empty Church* (London: SPCK, 1993).

Grey, M., *Return from Death: An Exploration of the Near-death Experience* (London: Arkana, 1985).
Harris, M. J., *Raised Immortal* (Basingstoke: Marshalls, 1983).
Hay, D., *Religious Experience Today* (London: Mowbrays, 1990).
Hebblethwaite, B., *The Christian Hope* (Basingstoke: Marshall, Morgan & Scott, 1984).
Hick, J., *Death and Eternal Life* (Basingstoke: Macmillan, 1976).
Kung, H., *Eternal Life?* (London: Collins, 1984).
Lang, B. and McDannell, C., *Heaven: A History* (New York: Random House, 1990).
Le Goff, J., *The Birth of Purgatory* (London: Scolar Press, 1984).
Lewis, H. D., *The Self and Immortality* (Basingstoke: Macmillan, 1973).
Lorimer, D., *Survival? Body, Mind and Death in the Light of Psychic Experience* (London: Routledge & Kegan Paul, 1984).
Lorimer, D., *Whole in One: The Near-death Experience and the Ethic of Interconnectedness* (London: Arkana, 1990).
Macquarrie, J., *The Christian Hope* (London: Mowbrays, 1978).
Neuberger, J. and White, J. (eds), *A Necessary End* (Basingstoke: Macmillan, 1991).
Parkes, C. M., *Bereavement: Studies in Grief in Adult Life* (London: Tavistock, 1972).
Parrinder, G., *The Indestructible Soul* (London: Allen & Unwin, 1973).
Penelhum, T., *Survival and Disembodied Existence* (London: Routledge & Kegan Paul, 1970).
Penelhum, T. (ed.), *Immortality* (Belmont, California: Wadsworth, 1973).
Perrett, R., *Death and Immortality* (Dortrecht: Nijhoff, 1987).
Rahner, K., *On the Theology of Death* (New York: Herder & Herder, 1971).
Reichenbach, B., *Is Man the Phoenix?* (Washington: University Press of America, 1983).
Sabom, M., *Recollections of Death* (London: Corgi, 1982).
Smith, J. and Haddad, Y., *The Islamic Understanding of Death and Resurrection* (Albany, New York: University of New York Press, 1981).
Stendahl, K. (ed.), *Immortality and Resurrection* (New York: Macmillan, 1965).
Stevenson, I., *Twenty Cases Suggestive of Reincarnation* (New York: ASPR, 1966).
Sullivan, L. E. (ed.), *Death, Afterlife and the Soul* (New York: Macmillan, 1989).
Sutherland, S. R. and Clarke, P. (eds), *The Study of Religions: Traditional and New Religions* (London: Routledge, 1991).

Index

absolution, 13–14
acceptance: of death, 98–9, 110–11
the Afterlife *see* the Hereafter
Aga Khan, 93
agnostics, 7
AIDS, 9
Albo, Joseph, 63
alcoholism, 3, 9
Al-Ghazali, 121
All Saints Day *see* Days of the Dead
All Souls Day *see* Days of the Dead
Allah, 66–7
see also the Qur'an
Alternative Service Book (ASB), 13–14, 51
America *see* United States
American Metaphysical Movement, 129
angels, 49–50, 52, 56, 58
angels of destruction, 59–60
anger:
  in bereavement, 106
  in near-death experiences, 168
Anglican Church, 53
  Church of England, 13–14, 51
  see also Christianity
animals, 5–6, 183–4, 192, 193–4
anointing, 96, 97
  see also rituals
Anthony of Sourozh, Metropolitan, 28
apocalyptic tradition, 165–6
  see also Last Day
Aquinas, Saint Thomas, 15, 18–22, 49, 50, 121
  Beatific Vision of God, 19–23
  De Malo, 22–3, 25
  levels of knowledge, 19–20
  Summa Contra Gentiles, 18–20
Aramai, Isaac, 63

Aristotle, 15, 18, 22
  Ethics, 18
Arnold, Sir Edwin, *Light of Asia*, 94
Asian beliefs, 92
  see also Indian beliefs
astral world, 175
atheists, 7
ātman see the soul
Augustine, Saint, 17, 47, 49
autoscopy, 147–8, 161
  see also near-death experiences

Bailey, Alice, 127
baptism, 96–7
  see also rituals
bardo, 121
  see also Hinduism
barzakh (Islam), 72, 121
  see also the Qur'an
Baxter, Richard, 46
Beatific Vision of God, 15, 18, 19–26
  Aquinas's concept of, 19–23
  human concept of, 22, 23
beauty, 17
Being of Light, 167–8, 178–9
  see also light
belief systems, 173–4
Benedict, Saint, 99
Benedict XII, Pope, *Benedictus Deus* (1336), 47
bereavement, 3, 31, 35, 38, 99, 104–5
  see also mourning
Bergson, Henri, 167
beyond-life concept, 1–10
  see also the Hereafter
Bhagavad Gita, 85, 87, 88, 89
the Bible:
  teaching on heaven, 22, 44–5, 47, 49, 50
  see also Christianity

birth, 8, 71, 96
  baptism, 96–7
bitterness: in bereavement, 106–7
Blackmore, Susan, 147
Blake, William, 192, 193
bodily form:
  after death, 21, 38–40, 72–3
  spiritual, 178
  subtle, 178
the body:
  physical, 40
  and the soul, 15, 32–3, 39–40, 44–5
  spiritual, 40
body separation, 147
  see also near-death experiences
Boethius, 18, 20
Book of Common Prayer, 13, 51, 99
Bowker, John, 101
  The Meanings of Death, 100
Brahma Kumaris, 130
Brahman see the soul
the brain, 156–7, 159–60, 161–2, 164, 167, 170, 175, 183
brainwashing, 131
Brookes, Reuben S., *A Guide to Jewish Knowledge*, 54
Buddhism, 83, 90–2, 120–1, 125
B-values, 169

Calvin, John, 46
Catholicism see Roman Catholicism
Chaitanya Mahaprahbu, 128
Chandogya Upanishad, 85, 86–7
  see also the Upanishads
Charles, R. H., 55
children:
  experience of reincarnation, 179–80
  near-death experiences, 170
choice: freedom of, 23, 26
Christian death, 27–41, 48
Christian life, 13–16, 27–8
Christianity:
  Anglicanism, 53, 122
  the Bible, 22, 44–5, 47, 49, 50
  Church of England, 13–14, 51

  concept of heaven, 42–53
  concept of the soul, 121
  definition of personhood, 14–16
  doctrines, 44–5
  and the Hereafter, 13–26, 123, 125, 185–6
  and resurrection, 122
  Roman Catholicism, 18, 19, 21, 24, 45, 51, 121, 185–6
  Russian Orthodox, 27, 28, 33, 34, 35–8, 51
  the saints, 101
Church of England, 13–14, 51, 122
  see also Christianity
Church Universal and Triumphant, 130
Cistercians, 99
clairaudience, 175
clairsentience, 175
clairvoyance, 175
Classical Judaism, 54
  see also Judaism
·clinical death, 143, 155, 163, 164, 167, 178
  see also death
Coleridge, Samuel Taylor, 143
Commedia (Dante), 185
Commentary to the Prayer Book (Hertz), 54
communications: from the dead, 176, 177, 180–1
community, 22, 202
consciousness, 161–2, 164, 167
contemplation, 18
Conze, Edward, 91
counselling, 107, 109, 111
Cranmer, Thomas, 51, 53
creation, 32
  in the Qur'an, 69–70
Crescas, Hasdai, 63
cross-correspondence, 180–1
  see also communications
Crowley, Aleister, 127
Cupitt, Don, 189
Cyril of Jerusalem, Saint, 97

Daishonin, Nichiren, 128
Dalrymple, Father John, 41

Dante Alighieri, 166, 189
  Commedia, 185
darkness:
  in near-death experiences, 168
  as a symbol, 166
Darwin, Charles, 189
Day of Atonement, 61–2
  see also Judaism
Days of the Dead, 95, 98
de Beausobre, Iulia, 35
De Malo (Aquinas), 22–3, 25
de Sola Pool, Rabbi David, 54
the dead:
  children, 95
  communion with, 35–6, 101–2
  direct contact with, 110
  prayer for, 36–8
  return from, 153–4
death:
  acceptance of, 98–9, 110–11
  blessing of, 33
  Buddhist approach to, 83, 90–2, 120–1, 125
  Christian approach to, 27–41, 48, 120
  clinical, 143, 155, 163, 164, 167, 178
  closeness of, 29–32
  creative, 31–2
  fear of, 170
  good dying, 98
  Hindu approach to, 81–2, 86–7, 120, 121–2, 125
  human survival of, 13, 24, 137–44, 173–82
  Indian approach to, 81–2, 86–7, 120
  Muslim approach to, 120, 125
  mystery of, 28–9
  near-death experiences, 8, 145–72
  and new religions, 131–3
  perception of, 8–9, 27–8
  preparedness for, 98
  process of, 9, 81–2, 186
  reactions to, 183–4
  and resurrection, 31–2, 96
  and separation, 29, 35–8
  and the soul, 120–2

tragedy of, 32–3
unnaturalness of, 29, 32–4
  see also bereavement; the Hereafter; mourning; soul
Death and Eternal Life (Hick), 137
Decartes, René, 14
deliverance:
  from hell, 61–2
  the Demons, 23
  the departed *see* the dead
Dialogues (Hume), 21
Dianetics, 128
Dostoevsky, Fyodor, 51, 194
dualist theory:
  of personhood, 14–15, 26, 44–5, 88, 121
  see also monist theory
Dudden, Homes, 204
Durkheim, E., 128
dvaita see dualist theory
dynamic meditation, 133–5

Eccles, Sir John, 44
the ego *see* personhood
Elchaninov, Father Alexander, 35
Eliot, T. S., 29, 41, 48
emotional reactions *see* mourning
Ephrem the Syrian, Saint, 40
eternal life *see* the Hereafter
Ethics (Aristotle), 18
Eucharist, 27, 51, 97, 98
  see also worship
Euthyphro dilemma (Plato), 21
evidence:
  for the Hereafter, 174–82
evolutionary theories, 44
explicate order, 162

faith, 110, 112–14, 173–4
  loss of, 31, 113, 132
fallen angels *see* the Demons
fantasy:
  and reality, 155
fear:
  of death, 98
  in near-death experiences, 168
  fires of hell, 57–9, 166
folk rituals, 99–100
  see also rituals

Francis of Assisi, Saint, 34
Franklin, Benjamin, 33–4
fraud, 181
Frazer, J. G., 119, 165
freedom of choice, 23, 26
frequency domain, 162
Freud, Sigmund, 106
Friends of the Western Buddhist Order, 132
Fromm, Erich, 108
funeral services, 33, 34, 98, 99

The Gates Ajar (Phelps), 46
Gehinnom see hell
general judgement, 47
  see also judgement
Gestalt therapy, 111
Glukharev, Makary, 35
God:
  Beatific Vision of, 15, 18, 19–25
  concept of, 17–22, 55
  insight into, 23–4
  Jesus Christ, 15, 16, 19, 21, 24, 26, 31–2, 34, 46–7, 114, 190, 194–5
  love of, 23, 24–5, 49, 114, 191
  and the soul, 88–9
  Summum Bonnum, 17–18
  timelessness of, 19–20, 21
  see also the Trinity
good dying, 98
good living, 13–16, 27–8, 66, 77–8, 80–1, 89–90, 98, 100–2, 166
goodness:
  measure of, 20, 21
gradualists, 130
  see also new religions
Greek theology, 17–18, 44–5
  see also theology
Gregory of Nyssa, Saint, 39–40, 49, 123
grief work, 106, 108, 110–11
grieving, 3, 104–5, 106–9, 192–3
  physical reactions, 109, 110–11
  see also mourning
A Guide to Jewish Knowledge (Pearl and Brookes), 54

guilt:
  in bereavement, 107

Hades *see* hell
hallucinations, 111–12
happiness *see* human happiness
Hare Krishna, 128, 135
heaven:
  belief in, 42–4
  biblical concept of, 22, 44–5, 47, 49, 50
  Christian concept of, 42–53, 165–7, 170
  Christian teaching on, 46–51, 52–3
  as a symbol, 50–1
  see also hell; the Hereafter; purgatory
Heaven and Hell (Swedenborg), 166
Heelas, P., 131
hell:
  Christian teaching on, 55–6, 170, 203
  creation of, 56
  deliverance from, 61–2
  fires of, 57–9, 166
  Jewish teaching on, 54–65
  midrashic literature of, 55, 58
  modern attitudes to, 63–5, 188
  morality of, 64
  names for, 55–6
  nature of, 57–9, 165–7
  non-belief in, 6, 43–5, 188, 203
  purpose of, 56–7
  souls in, 15, 47, 124–5
  and the Talmud, 55, 57
  and the Torah, 56, 58
  tortures of, 59–61
  see also heaven; purgatory
the Hereafter:
  Aquinas on, 18–23
  Beatific Vision of God, 15, 18, 19–26
  beyond-life concept, 1–10
  bodily form in, 21, 38–40, 72–3
  Buddhist belief in, 83, 90–2, 120–1
  Christian belief in, 13–26, 123,

125, 185–6
  definition of, 139–40, 202
  Hindu belief in, 80–9
  identity problems in, 15–16
  Indian belief in, 80–94, 124
  Jain belief in, 89–90
  Jewish belief in, 54
  in life, 13–14, 23–4, 47–8, 55, 76–8, 101–2, 120–2, 199–200
  location of, 16
  Muslim belief in, 66–79, 122
  nature of, 17–22, 184–98
  near-death experiences, 8, 145–72
  and new religions, 132, 135
  non-belief in, 183–4, 188–9, 190–7, 203
  religious belief in, 199–26, 189–90, 194–5, 200–6
  scientific evidence for, 174–82
  scientific research into, 138–44
  Sikh belief in, 93
  in the Upanishads, 80–94
  see also death; heaven
Hertz, Rabbi Doctor J. H.:
  Commentary to the Prayer Book, 54
Herzl, Theodor, 64
Hess, Moses, 64
Hick, John, 121, 123, 139
  Death and Eternal Life, 137
Hildegaard of Bingen, 46
Hillel, 62
Hinduism:
  approach to death, 81–2, 86–7, 120, 121–2, 125
  see also the Upanishads
Hodgson, Richard, 138
Holland, Henry Scott, 205–6
holographic states, 161–2
home:
  sense of, 1–2
hope:
  after bereavement, 109
hospitals, 4
the Hour (Islam), 72
  see also Last Day
Hubbard, L. Ron, 128

human beings:
  and the Beatific Vision, 20, 22
  bodily form, 21, 38–40
  knowledge of God, 19, 22
  place of, 20
  timelessness of, 21
human development, 30
human happiness, 17–19, 20
human spirit see the soul
humanism, 28
Hume, David, 147, 149–50, 151–2
  Dialogues, 21
Hyslop, James H., 138

Ibn 'Abbas, 73
Ibn Abi Zimra, David ben Solomon, 63
Ibn Rushd, 73
identity problems, 15–16
immortality see the Hereafter
implicate order, 162
India, 129
Indian beliefs:
  Buddhism, 83, 90–2, 120, 125
  in the Hereafter, 80–94, 122, 124, 135
  Hinduism, 80–9, 120–2, 125
  Jainism, 89–90
  Sikhism, 93
  see also the Upanishads
insight:
  into God, 23–4
intercession see prayer
International Society for Krishna Consciousness see Hare Krishna
Isaac of Nineveh, Saint, 29
Islam, 67, 76, 93
  fundamental beliefs, 69, 120, 122, 123, 125
  see also the Qur'an
Israel, 64
  see also Judaism; Zionism

Jacobs, Rabbi Louis, 64
Jainism, 89–90
James, William, 138, 167
Japan, 129

Jesus Christ:
  concept of, 19
  incarnation, 15
  resurrection, 16, 21, 24, 26, 31–2, 34, 46–7, 114, 190
  teaching, 49, 194–5
  see also God
Jewish emancipation, 63–4
Jewish Theology (Kohler), 64
Jinas, 89
  see also Jainism
jivas see the soul
Job, 113, 165
John of the Cross, Saint, 7
Joseph, Morris:
  Judaism as Creed and Life, 65
Judaism, 32, 114
  Classical, 54
  Day of Atonement, 61–2
  ethics in, 62–3
  Kaddish, 114
  midrashic literature, 55, 58, 62
  Misnah, 57, 63
  principles of, 63
  rabbinic, 54–5, 56–65
  rites of, 61–2
  Talmud, 55, 57, 58, 62
  teaching on hell, 54–65
  teaching on the Hereafter, 54
  Torah, 56, 58, 62–3
  Zionism, 64
Judaism as Creed and Life (Joseph), 65
Judaism: Religion and Ethics (Waxman), 65
judgement, 165
  general, 47
  importance of, 67–8
  particular, 47
  in the Qur'an, 67–8, 73–4
judgement day see Last Day
Jung, C. G., 32, 162
justice see judgement

Kaddish, 114
  see also Judaism
Kant, Immanuel, 162
Karma, 80–1, 82, 83, 120, 135
  see also the Upanishads

Katha Upanishad, 84–5
  see also the Upanishads
Khayyam, Omar, 170
Kierkegaard, Søren, 23
King, Henry, 100–1
Kingsley, Charles, 46
knowledge:
  Aquinas's levels of, 19–20
Kohler, K., 55
  Jewish Theology, 64
the Koran see the Qur'an
Kuhn, Thomas, 174

Langland, William:
  Piers Plowman, 46
Larkin, Philip, 193, 194, 196
Last Day, 15, 33, 39, 42–3, 47, 165–6
  the Hour (Islam), 72
Lawrence, D. H., 28
Lazarus, 153, 161, 166, 190
leisure pursuits, 129
ben Levi, Rabbi Joshua, 58, 59
Lewis, Cecil Day, 30, 39
Lewis, H. D., 44
Liberation theology, 43
  see also theology
life after death see the Hereafter
life expectancy, 199
life review see panoramic recall
life-threatening events, 146–7
  see also near-death experiences
light:
  in near-death experiences, 147, 159, 161, 164–5, 167–8, 170, 171, 178–9
  as a symbol, 166
Light of Asia (Arnold), 94
liturgy, 51–2
  see also worship
living, 196–7
  Christian approach to, 13–16, 27–8
  good lives, 13–16, 27–8, 66, 77–8, 80–1, 89–90, 98, 100–2, 166
  and the Hereafter, 13–14, 23–4, 47–8, 55, 76–8, 101–2, 120–2, 199–200

loneliness, 108
longevity, 196–7, 199–200
loss:
  of faith, 31, 113, 132
  see also death
love:
  of God, 23, 24–5, 49, 114
  God's love, 191
  of human beings, 23, 46, 113–14
  sense of, 168, 169
Luther, Martin, 46, 49

MacDonald, George, 30
Madhva, 88
Maimonides, 63
Makary, Father, 37
Man see human beings
Marcus Aurelius, 7
the material world, 7, 9, 13
materialists, 74–5
Maurice, F. D., 42
Meanings of Death (Bowker), 100, 101
meditation:
  dynamic, 133–5
mediums see spiritualism
memento mori, 98–9, 101
  see also death
memory, 26, 162, 187
Meno (Plato), 184, 187
mental models, 174–5, 176–7
Mesmer, Franz, 127
Mexico, 95, 98
midrashic literature, 55, 58, 62
  see also Judaism
the Mishnah, 57, 63
  see also Judaism
missionary religions, 92, 127–8
Mitford, Nancy, 186
Moltmann, Jurgen, 43
monastic life, 51, 99
monist theory:
  of personhood, 86, 87–8, 89–90, 121
Moonies see Unification Church
Morse, Doctor Melvin, 170
Mortimer, John, 204
Moses, 59–60
mourning, 34, 35, 38, 104–15, 205

grieving, 3, 104–5, 106–9
  see also bereavement
mourning period, 109–10
Muhammad, 67, 69
  see also the Qur'an
Muslims see Islam

natural world, 202
NDEs see near-death experiences
near-death experiences, 8, 145–72, 178
  of children, 170
  content of, 147, 151, 158
  context of, 146–7, 151
  and death, 154–7, 158–9
  definition of, 146–8, 164–5
  emotions during, 167–70
  empirical approach to, 149–52
  evidential value of, 149–54
  experience of light during, 147, 159, 161, 164–5
  negative, 167, 168–9, 171
  panoramic recall, 147–8, 167, 169
  positive, 167–8
  stages of, 147–8, 149–50
  test for, 156–7, 159–60, 163
necromancy, 35–6
negative near-death experiences, 167, 168–9, 171
networking, 111
new religions, 127–33
  appeal of, 129–30
  approach to death, 131–3
  and the Hereafter, 132, 135
  politically biased, 130
  types of, 127–9
New Thought Movement, 129
Newman, Cardinal John Henry, 52
Nichiren Shoshu, 128
Nirvana see the Hereafter
normal science, 174
  see also scientific evidence

OBEs see out-of-body experiences
occult revival, 127
  see also new religions
old age, 196–7

see also longevity
Otherworld Journeys (Zaleski), 166
Our Town (Wilder), 201–2
out-of-body experiences, 1, 142–3, 170, 178–9

panoramic recall, 147–8, 167, 169
  see also near-death experiences
paradigms see mental models
Paradise see the Hereafter
paranormal phenomena, 139–44, 162, 175–6
parapsychology, 146
pareschatology, 139
Parsis, 93
particular judgement, 47
  see also judgement
Paul, Saint, 25, 40, 45, 48, 96–7
peace, 114, 147
Pearl, Chaim:
  A Guide to Jewish Knowledge, 54
perfection, 49
permissive theory: of consciousness, 167
personal relationships: ending of, 4–5
personhood:
  Christian definition, 14–16
  dualist theory, 14–15, 26, 44–5, 88, 121
  Indian definition, 86–7, 120
  monist theory, 86, 87–8, 89–90, 121
  nature of, 14–16, 43
  and new religions, 132–3
  psycho-physical theory, 15–16, 44–5
  and the soul, 15
Phelps, E. S.:
  The Gates Ajar, 46
philosophy, 174–5
Piers Plowman (Langland), 46
Pinsker, Leon, 64
place:
  sense of, 1–2
Plato, 14, 18–19, 50, 162, 184, 186
  Euthyphro, 21
  Meno, 184, 187
  Republic, 82

  Symposium, 17
pleasure, 18
Plotinus, 17–18
plurality of souls, 89–90
  see also the soul
politically biased movements, 130
  see also new religions
positive near-death experiences, 167–8
prayer:
  for the dead, 36–8, 61–2, 114
  see also worship
preaching:
  on purgatory, 166
Pribram, Karl, 161, 162
Price, H. H., 121, 171
productive theory:
  of consciousness, 167
psychic experiences, 174, 175–6, 177
psycho-physical theory:
  of personhood, 15–16, 44–5
punishment:
  in hell, 57–9
  morality of, 64
  in the Qur'an, 74–6
purgatory:
  concept of, 170
  souls in, 15, 47, 48, 166
  see also heaven; hell
Pusey, Doctor Edward, 37

Questions of Milinda, 91–2
  see also Buddhism
the Qur'an:
  barzakh, 72, 121
  and the creation, 69–70
  and the Hereafter, 66–79, 122
  the Hour, 72
  and judgement, 67–8
  and resurrection, 68, 69–71, 72–3

rabbinic Judaism, 54–5, 56–65
  see also Judaism
Rahner, Karl, 45, 48
Rajneesh, Shree Bhagwan, 132–3
Rajneesh movement, 129, 131, 132–3
Ramanuja, 88

Rawlings, Dr Maurice, 167
realism, 176-7
Recollections of Death (Sabom), 162-3
recompense *see* punishment *and* reward
regret:
  in bereavement, 107-8
reincarnation, 179-80
  Indian belief in, 82-3, 122, 124, 135
  in Jesus Christ, 15
  and memory, 83, 187
  see also resurrection
rejection, 31
renouncers, 130
  see also new religions
repentence:
  of sins, 57
Republic (Plato), 82
resurrection:
  belief in, 44-5, 122, 123-5
  bodily form after, 21, 38-40
  and death, 31-2, 96
  of Jesus Christ, 16, 21, 24, 26, 31-2, 34, 46-7, 114, 190
  Muslim teaching on, 68, 69-71, 72-3, 123
  see also reincarnation
reward:
  Muslim teaching on, 74-6
  see also punishment
Righteous Remnant, 165
  see also Last Day
Ring, Kenneth, 147, 161-2, 168
rites of passage, 96, 104
  see also rituals
rituals:
  anointing, 96, 97
  of birth, 96-7
  of death, 95-103, 205
  folk rituals, 99-100
  and social experience, 99-100
  wakes, 98
Roman Catholicism, 18, 19, 21, 24, 45, 51, 121, 185-6
  see also Christianity
Rumi, 93
Ruskin, John, 50

Russell, Bertrand, 184
Russian Orthodox Church, 27, 28, 33, 34, 35-8, 51
  see also Christianity

Sabom, M. B., 178
  Recollections of Death, 162-3
sacrifice:
  concept of, 100
  the saints, 101
  see also Christianity
Samsara, 135
Satanism, 23
Schechter, Rabbi Dr Soloman, 63
Schiller, F. C. S., 167
Schmemann, Alexander, 51
scientific evidence:
  for the Hereafter, 174-82
scientific research, 166-7
  into the Hereafter, 138-44
Scientology, 128, 129, 130, 135
seances *see* spiritualism
second judgement, 21
  see also Last Day
self *see* personhood
self-giving, 13
Self-Religions, 131, 132, 135
  see also new religions
separation, 30-1
  in death, 29, 35-8
shalom see peace
shame:
  in bereavement, 108
Shankara, 87
Sheol *see* hell
Shi'ite Ismailis, 93-4
Shi'ites, 93
  see also Islam
Shvetashvatara Upanishad, 88-9
  see also the Upanishads
Siddhartha Buddha, 90
  see also Buddhism
Sidgwick, Eleanor, 138
Sikhism, 93
silent brain test, 156-7, 159-60
  see also near-death experiences
Silver, Rabbi Abba Hillel, 54
sins:
  punishable in hell, 57, 59-61

sleep, 30, 81, 143
Society for Psychical Research, 180
Socrates, 17, 21, 184, 185
Soka Gakkai, 128, 130, 135
the soul:
  Beatific Vision of God, 15, 18, 19–26
  and the body, 15, 32–3, 39–40, 44–5
  Buddhist belief in, 90, 92, 120
  Christian belief in, 121
  at death, 120–2
  and God, 88–9
  in hell, 15, 47, 124–5
  Indian belief in, 81–2, 86–7, 120–2
  Jain belief in, 89–90
  Muslim belief in, 72
  nature of, 15, 83, 84–5, 183–4
  plurality of souls, 89–90
  in purgatory, 15, 47, 48, 166
  transmigration of, 90, 92, 93–4
Spinoza, Baruch, 184–5, 186, 187–8, 192
the spirit *see* the soul
spiritual awareness *see* faith
spiritual bodies, 178
  see also bodily form
spiritualism, 35–6, 112, 174, 176, 177, 180
Spurgeon, C. H., 46
Stevenson, Ian, 138, 170–1, 179
subtle bodies, 178
  see also bodily form
Sufis, 72, 93
  see also Islam
Summa Contra Gentiles (Aquinas), 18–19, 20
Summerland, 179
Summum Bonnum, 17–18
supernatural experiences, 127
Survival Research Foundation, 137–44
Swedenborg, Emmanuel, 127, 171
  Heaven and Hell, 166
Swift, Jonathan, 95
Swinburne, Richard, 44
symbolism, 50–1, 96, 166

Symposium (Plato), 17
synchronicity, 162

the Talmud, 55, 57, 58, 62
  see also Judaism
telepathy, 175–6
Temple, Archbishop William, 37, 123
Ten Open Questions, 91
  see also Buddhism
Teresa of Avila, Saint, 7
theology, 37
  Catholic, 19, 21, 24
  contemporary, 42–3
  Greek, 17–18, 44–5
  Jewish, 62–6
  Liberation, 43
  traditional, 52
Theravada tradition:
  of Buddhism, 120
Theroux, Paul, 101
This is My God (Wouk), 54
Thoulness, Robert H., 138
Tibet, 120
Tibetan Book of the Dead, 121, 131, 168, 171
timelessness:
  of God, 19–20, 21
  of human beings, 21
the Torah, 56, 58, 62–3
  see also Judaism
tortures:
  of hell, 59–61
Traherne, Thomas, 101–2
transcendent stages:
  of near-death experiences, 147, 148, 149–50
transcendental experiences, 142–3
transmigration:
  of the soul, 90, 92, 93–4
transmissive theory *see* permissive theory
the Trinity, 15, 20
  see also God
Trubetskoy, Prince Evgeny, 27
truth, 20
Tug, Dr Salih, 123, 124

Unification Church, 130, 131

United States:
  new religions, 127–8
the universe, 191
unresolved grief, 107
the Upanishads, 80
  Chandogya, 85, 86–7
  and death, 81–2, 86–7, 120
  and the Hereafter, 80–9
  Katha, 84–5
  and reincarnation, 82–3
  Schvetashvatara, 88–9
  see also Indian beliefs

Value Creation Society see Soka Gakkai
Vasileios, Archimandrite, 51–2
Vaughan, Henry, 95
Vedanta school, 87
Ver, Fabian, 119
veridical experiences, 167
  see also out-of-body experiences
Vishnu, 88, 128
  see also Indian beliefs

wakes, 98
  see also rituals
Ward, Keith, 203
Waugh, Evelyn, 186, 188
Waxman, M.:
  Judaism: Religion and Ethics, 65

weeping, 110
  see also grieving
Wilder, Thornton:
  Our Town, 201–2
Williams, Bernard, 45, 49
Williams, Ralph Vaughan, 41
wills, 98
Wittgenstein, Ludwig, 187
Woman see human beings
Wordsworth, William, 184, 185
Worldwide Church of God, 131
worship, 36
  Eucharist, 27, 51, 97, 98
  prayer for the dead, 36–8, 61–2, 114
Wouk, H.:
  This is My God, 54

Yahweh see God
Yajnya-valkya, 80–1
Yoga, 85
Yoshinori, Takeuchi, 125
Young Life, 127
Youth for Christ International, 127
Youth with a Mission, 127

Zaehner, R. C., 88
Zaleski, Carol:
  Otherworld Journeys, 166
ben Zemah Duran, Simon, 63
Zionism, 64
  see also Judaism
Zoroastrians see Parsis